Creativity and Education Futures
Learning in a Digital Age

Creativity and Education Futures

Learning in a Digital Age

Anna Craft

Trentham Books

Stoke on Trent, UK and Sterling, USA

Winner of the IPG DIVERSITY Award 2010

MT

Trentham Books Limited
Westview House   22883 Quicksilver Drive
734 London Road   Sterling
Oakhill   VA 20166-2012
Stoke on Trent   USA
Staffordshire
England ST4 5NP

First published 2011

British Library Cataloguing-in-Publication Data
A catalogue record for this book is available from the British Library

ISBN: 978 1 85856 462 3

Scribed cartoon illustrations provided by Andrew park, Cognitive Media http://www.cognitivemedia.co.uk/ created alongside Anna Craft's keynote to the June 2010 CELT symposium on creativity in higher education, held at National University of Ireland, Galway

Designed and typeset by Trentham Books Ltd and printed in Great Britain by Page Bros (Norwich) Ltd, Norfolk

2/03/12

For those who dare to co-author the story...

Contents

Acknowledgements   xiii

About the author   xvi

Preface   xvii

Foreword
Professor Erica McWilliam   xxi

Chapter 1
Childhood and youth in flux   1

   The family, childhood and youth in flux   3
      The cocooning of children and young people
      Television: the birth of children as empowered consumers
      Social change reflected in childhood and youth
      The digital revolution: further empowerment

   Childhood and youth: two discourses   8
      Childhood at risk
      Childhood empowered

   Reach and role of technology changing childhood and youth   9
      The digital revolution: enabling or endangering?
      New ways of being, knowing and playing
      Children and young people empowered at home

   How does education respond to childhood and youth in flux?   15

Chapter 2
Creativity and education futures   19

   Shifting conceptions of creativity?   19
   The rise of creativity in education   20
      Driver 1: economic
      Driver 2: social
      Driver 3: technological

   The response of education   24
      The rise of creativity as universalised

   The challenge of performativity   25
   Emergent rhetorics for creativity in education   27
   Education futures?   29
      Probable education futures
      Preferred education futures
      Possible education futures

   Creativity and education futures integrated   32
   The four Ps of changing childhood and youth   33

Chapter 3
Pluralities   35

   Childhood and youth pluralised   35
      Plurality of place
      Plurality of people
      Plurality of personae
      Plurality of activity
      Plurality of literacy

   Plural implications?   50

CONTENTS

Chapter 4
Possibilities   51

'Possibility thinking': from *what is to what might be*   51
    Possibilities with young children
    Possibilities with older children

Possibility Spaces   58
Multiple possibilities in childhood and youth   58
    1. Breadth and nature of choices
    2. Possibility thinking with others
    3. Learning by doing and doing by learning
    4. Making ideas happen

Multiple possibilities and the classroom   66

Paradoxes for educators   67
    Privacy and openness
    Authority and agency

Chapter 5
Playfulness   71

Exploration and Playfulness   73
    Play at risk in education...
    A problem revisited by educators

Expansion of play online   75
Extended make-believe in possible worlds   76
    Virtual make-believe
    Self-creating online

Playing with feeling   77
    Play as enabling learning
    Feeling our way with difficulty
    Fragmentation and reconstruction?

Complexity, connectedness and networked individualism   81
    Playful networking for learning

The long reach of playful consumerism   82
    Children as active players

Challenges for educators   84
    Principles
    Practicalities

Play on   86

Chapter 6
Participation   87

Participation as pervasive   87
High participation online   88
The irresistibility of online participation   88
    Participation through enacted imagination
    Playful co-participation
    Gender differences in participation

Participation and children's voices   93
Participation in playful, plural possibilities?   94
    Marketised participation
    Being heard

Tensions and dilemmas in participation   97
    Freedom or control?
    Privacy or participation?
    Children and young people as objects or agents of change?
    Clashing perspectives on responsibility and risk

Participation and the classroom   102

Chapter 7
Extending Literacy and Medium?   105

Two quests, a landscape and a compass   105
A landscape of playfulness and plurality   106
Participation and possibilities as a navigational tool   107
Extending literacy and medium   108
    New literacies
    Visual primacy
    Integrated multi-modality

Enabling high participation and possibility   111
The demands for educators of extended literacy and medium   113
    Transitioning from low to high participation and possibilities
    From indifference to aspiration

Dilemmas in extending literacy and medium   116
    Spanning the gap
    'Myspace is My Space – when I say so'. Is personal private?
    Critique and creativity?
    Living with uncertainty
    Text: where less is more?

Implications for educators and education   124
   Curriculum
   Pedagogy
   Assessment

From past to future   127

Chapter 8
Co-creating Educational Futures   129

Participation and Possibilities: grappling with engagement   129
   Creative, emotional, empowered learners
   From risk to resilience to reconstruction

Pluralities and playfulness: changing social capital   132
Possible education futures: the social responsibility of all   133
Trust, certainty, reality and innovation   134
   Trust
   Certainty
   Reality
   Innovation

From fire to ice   141
Seismic shifts   143
Creative education futures: triggering seismic shifts   144
   Goals of education
   What's the story?
   Whose story is it?
   How are these stories developed?

Co-authoring creative education futures   152

References   153

Index   171

Acknowledgements

This book is the product of many conversations over a number of years, focused around creativity and how education can harness creativity to transform provision for children and young people in the 21st century. These have involved researchers, practitioners and policy makers from England and in many countries beyond. Many have taken place in the two research groups I lead at the University of Exeter: CREATE and Educational Futures, and with colleagues at The Open University, much of this work stemming from early thinking developed with Jana Dugal (now Rowland) and Christine Kimberly during a collaborative project we ran between the Institute for Creativity and The Open University in the mid-1990s.

I owe a particular debt of gratitude to the many students, teachers, parents, governors, advisers and policy makers with whom I have worked to effect transformation in the Aspire programme[1] currently based at the University of Exeter. Some of my most inspirational conversations I have had have been with students and their teachers, brave enough to look closely at their current practice and daring to conceive of education in new ways. I am also grateful to teachers and students involved in the Possibility Thinking Study[2] co-ordinated through The Open University and University of Exeter. Also invaluable has been co-participative research with dance practitioners, teachers, students and University researchers involved in Dance Partners for Creativity (DPC)[3,] based at the University of Exeter, informing theoretical insights developed with in particular Dr Kerry Chappell. Undergraduates, masters and doctoral students at the University of Exeter and The Open University have contributed to all three projects and their insights have been invaluable. Vital to both projects have been colleagues and co-researchers, in particular Dr Kerry Chappell and Linda Rolfe at the University of Exeter, Professor Teresa Cremin at The Open University, Dr Pamela Burnard at the University of Cambridge, Veronica Jobbins at Trinity Laban, MSc student Debbie Watson and doctoral students Dawn Alderson, Jim Clack, Margo Greenwood, Rupert Higham and Melanie Ting together with recently qualified Dr Joy Lin. The contributions of others along the journey have also been appreciated.

Consideration of how creativity is conceived of across disciplines and how shared understandings of progress in skilfulness and depth in creative work is developed, has been vastly enriched by the work I have had the honour of being involved in with a US-based team led by Dr Russell Quaglia and part of the EdSteps programme, funded by the Bill and Melinda Gates Foundation. Russ Quaglia's Aspirations Research Center (generously supported by the Pearson Foundation) with which I have the further honour of being involved, has afforded opportunities for joint conceptualisation of creativity, leadership and aspiration. My thanks are due to all those involved in both EdSteps and the Aspirations Research Center for their stimulating engagement in the nature and nurturing of creativity in learning.

Invaluable in considering relationships between creativity and educational futures have been discussions with Pat Cochrane, Chief Executive of CapeUK, and Jane Creasy, with whom I worked, until March 2010, to advise government in England. In the last year I have been privileged to develop with colleagues a seminar series on educational futures funded by the Economic and Social Research Council (ESRC) in England. My thanks are due to Professor Keri Facer of Manchester Metropolitan University, Professor Carey Jewitt of the Institute of Education, London University, Simon Mauger of NIACE, Richard Sandford of Futurelab and Professor Mike Sharples of Nottingham University together with the many speakers and participants in our seminar series, for stimulating discussions on educational futures.

As I completed the book, many colleagues, working in universities, schools, community, arts and education projects commented on its final draft stages, too many to mention by name. To each and every one I am grateful. I hope they will see in the final product, responses to the valuable points they raised.

Thanks are due to Gillian Klein of Trentham who saw the book's potential, and for her patience as each deadline for completion came and went. Thanks, too, to the Trentham team for their care in its production, and to support teams at both Exeter and The Open University who responded to last-minute technical glitches.

As the book went into production, I began to speak about the ideas in it, beginning with an international symposium on creativity in higher education, held at the National University of Ireland, Galway. As I spoke about changing childhood and youth in a digital age and the consequences for creativity and education futures, my words were scribed into an extraordinary visual map, by Andrew Park of Cognitive Media (http://www.cognitivemedia.co.uk). I am delighted to be able to include this material in the book, with Andrew's permission.

Closer to home I owe a huge debt of gratitude to friends and family for whom the gestation of this book has been longer than most I have written. Simon, Hugo and Ella have again endured the laptop's pervasive presence and my frequent absence during evenings, weekends and family holidays. Naomi, Maurice and Alma have again offered moral support and, in the case of Ella and Alma, first one laptop and then another, as mine gave up the ghost more than once.

I hope the ideas which this book now brings together adequately represent the contributions made by all these people and more, that they are worth the wait, and more than anything else, that they make a difference to educational provision.

Professor Anna Craft
University of Exeter and The Open University
September 2010

Notes

1 Aspire is a learner-led school transformation approach originated at The Open University and currently based at the University of Exeter. http://education.exeter.ac.uk/aspire

2 Possibility thinking is a long-term qualitative study investigating possibility thinking – the heart of creativity – with learners aged 3-18, together with pedagogical strategies which foster it.

3 DPC is a two-year study funded by the Arts and Humanities Research Council (AH/F010168/1) exploring creativity in dance with 11-14 year students, fostered through creative partnership. http://education.exeter.ac.uk/dpc/

About the Author

Anna Craft is Professor of Education at the University of Exeter and at The Open University. She works with learners, teachers, researchers and policy-makers in England and abroad to develop imagination, creativity and educational futures. She has written many books on these topics and is committed to supporting adults and children alike in the transformation of learning opportunities.

A qualitative researcher, committed research leader and teacher, Anna leads studies on possibility thinking, learner voice and student aspiration, as well as creative partnership. At Exeter she teaches undergraduates, masters and doctoral students and leads the CREATE research group and she co-leads the Educational Futures research group. At The Open University she teaches doctoral students and most recently co-chaired in production *The Early Years: Developing Practice* (E100). Supporting 2,000 early years practitioners during its first year of presentation, this course forms part of The Open University's Foundation Degree in Early Years.

She is Founding Co-Editor of the peer review journal *Thinking Skills and Creativity* and co-convenes the British Educational Research Association Special Interest Group, *Creativity in Education*, which she co-founded almost a decade ago.

Preface

The early years of the 21st century have been characterised by rapid and often unpredictable change in the local and global economy, social structures and environment. Permeating our experiences is the rapidly extending reach of digital technology which engages increasing numbers of children, young people and adults as consumers and producers. Our lives have been transformed by virtually ubiquitous access to the internet through mobile phones, laptop computers, gaming devices, and other technology, much of it pocket-sized. And with this shifting technological landscape, childhood and youth is changing. Children and young people are increasingly connected around the clock, and have a parallel existence in virtual space, seamlessly integrated with their actual lives. They are skilful collaborators, capable of knowledge-making as well as information-seeking. They navigate digital gaming and social networking with ease, capably generating and manipulating content, experimenting with forms of their social face.

How can we characterise these changes in childhood? As children and young people increasingly access space alongside adults, what are the implications for how we view children in society? And as children gain increasing control in their lives beyond school, how can those providing education do so in ways that feel relevant and interesting for them?

This book introduces two dominant and competing discourses currently evident in approaches to childhood and youth. One sees children and young people as vulnerable and at risk and in need of protection by adults. The other, in contrast, views children and young people as capable and potent, seeing the role of adults as being to enable and empower them. The former perspective brings anxiety about the digital revolution and the latter embraces it as exciting and enabling.

How can and should educators respond to these discourses? This book argues that neither perspective alone is sufficient. The local and global challenges and changes that we face mean we have perhaps never before in our history needed to draw on our creative potential as urgently and with as much insight as we do today. Education needs to foster lifewide creativity in all of us, and educational provision in itself needs to act creatively in doing so.

This book argues for seeing childhood as empowered as a dominant although not exclusive framework for action. Doing so brings out the key characteristics of changing childhood and youth. Four Ps: pluralities, playfulness, possibilities and participation, offer means by which appropriate educational provision may be developed, highlighting creativity in its means and its ends.

Pluralities: the virtual dimension to children's lives brings opportunities to engage and experiment with multiple pluralities. The places where children and young people can play, socialise and create are multiple, as are the people they can engage with and the activities they can engage in. The literacies open to children and young people in a digital medium also offer opportunities for exploration of other and multiple personal identities.

Playfulness: online, children and young people experience expansion of playworlds into both extended make-believe and opportunities to self-create through gaming, social networking and generating content of their own. Active players, the virtual worlds they inhabit alongside the actual, are emotionally rich spaces which offer complexity, connectedness and a networked playful world extending on into adulthood. A key aspect of this emergent and extensive playfulness is its umbilical link with consumerism; through their digital engagement, children and young people are actively engaged as discerning consumers.

Possibilities: virtual, multiple spaces for play, connecting and constructing content, bring multiple opportunities for possibility thinking – making the transition from what is to what might be. Possibility spaces open up the breadth and nature of choice facing children and young people, together with ways of co-constructing with others.

Participation: virtual connectivity through mobile as well as fixed devices including phones, gaming consoles, laptop and fixed computers, offers children and young people enticing opportunities for high participation. Characterised by its playfulness, digital media seem to offer children and young people opportunities to take action, and to have their voices heard with relative ease. Whilst in a marketised context, digital media offer children and young people opportunities to be highly visible on their own terms, and to act as agents of change in their own lives and beyond.

What the emergence of these four Ps means for what we privilege, how we go about structuring learning systems, and how we support learning and develop pedagogy, all come under scrutiny in this book.

Doing so brings into focus and challenges values. Educational provision is at a crossroads. We choose to reproduce and improve the Victorian legacy of universal education through cohort-based face to face local schools, with an assessment system which rewards individuals and a performative framework seeking constantly to drive up standards, or we allow technology to open up new possible ways of learning. Learning beyond boundaries, across age phases, harnessing motivation, enabling high participation and nurturing creative possibility thinking, are all possible if we are brave enough to acknowledge the potency of childhood and youth and to co-create the future. This book argues for co-creating possible education futures through dialogue and collaboration – both enhanced through digital media.

My hope is that through discussion of the four Ps of childhood and youth, educators will not only seek to reflect changing childhood and youth but to take an active and co-participative role alongside young people in continuing to change it through dialogic interaction.

Foreword

Professor Erica McWilliam

No-one who cares for or about children would willingly de-limit their future. Among the panoply of adults who impact the lives of children – parents, teachers, caregivers, employers, policymakers – only the perverse or the malevolent would choose to obstruct the path to the best living, learning and earning a child may be capable of.

And yet, and yet....

We live in a time when 'doing the right thing' by our children is becoming more contested and problematic. We have moved on historically from unenlightened times when children were seen as the property of adults, or as needing the devil beaten out of them, or as miniature adults capable of performing work every bit as hard as that done by the fittest adult, or as slaves to adult whims. We pride ourselves that children in most parts of the globe now have unalienable rights as human beings, and that these rights should not be diminished by age, class, gender or ethnicity.

Yet consensus around 'what is best' is becoming more elusive. We want all children to fulfill their potential, but somehow the clarity of this intent gets blurred in the context of heightened anxieties around the risks to children that come with living in this century. Propelled towards the exciting affordances of the new, we are fearful of losing touch with the sureties of the old. We want children to access every opportunity that this new decade affords, while at the same time we worry about the dangers of everything from body simulation to bad spelling.

Public expressions of anxiety about 'what's best' continue to remind us that the current generation of children experience living, learning and earning quite differently from former generations. What adults call 'using technology', children may experience simply as living. Today's children are likely to have a different relationship with the electronic world from that of previous generations; technological tools are not mysterious or magic but are integrated into their lives, more like prostheses than gadgets. Young people are less likely to be printcentric than their predecessors – their social engagement is very much focused on the Screen rather than the Book. Truth is often assembled and dis-assembled in images and sounds. It comes in the form of endless bites, half baked ideas, gossipy tidbits, all in constant flux. In the digital world, their cut-and-paste can be serious play. Young people like to wear their mobile 'connectors' 24/7 – they don't leave them at home or at school. And they also expect them to *work* 24/7, because that is how they form and maintain so many of their social relationships.

All this points to the power of the internet to connect every individual to global data-bases of information, events and people, and this has, in turn, thrown a grenade into the knowledge base that has until now been stock in trade for building social, emotional and intellectual capacity in children. Correct spelling, neat hand-writing, the memorising of times-tables – the skills that were once the bedrock of literacy and numeracy and thus the keys to future social success – are no longer easily rationalised as 'core' or basics. Yet neither are they easily relinquished in a political climate in which nostalgia for tradition maintains its often fierce resistance to a future-oriented educational agenda, and where performance on standardised tests is taken as *the* marker of real learning.

As educators, we are committed to assisting young people in making sense of their social world with all its complexity. This has its risks and its opportunities. A key premise in this book is that young people are more likely to be successful sense-makers now and in the future if they develop robust capacities to negotiate within and across shifting pathways and options. This disposition to negotiation does not proceed from fixed notions about what the future holds and what it means. The four Ps that are fleshed out in the pages that follow – pluralities, playfulness, possibilities and participation – are presented as strategies or tactics for enabling young people to engage more fully with the future and its relationship with the present. The four Ps are *not*, it follows, pieces of a template for getting a quick fix on the correct answers. Of course, efficiency, precision and accuracy will continue to matter in the completion of certain kinds of tasks. However, the more compelling challenge – and therefore the more important pedagogical work – is to support and direct (not control and command) children in imagining the numerous ways and means of framing up an idea or a question. If the answer is '27', what is the question? And what is a better one? And better still? And how is this useful for engaging with other thorny problems, and not just numerical ones?

Digital technologies can be useful tools when pursuing better questions. Yet, as becomes evident in the pages of this book, educating for optimal futures is not a simple matter of handing education over to technology. The main game, as it unfolds here, is not about *going digital*; it is about *going pedagogical*, and that includes making optimal use of digital affordances for pedagogical purposes.

There is no doubting that the current generation of digital tools and technologies are unprecedented in what they can offer learning. Indeed, computer-centred network technologies have impacted so powerfully on social systems and social relationships that we can no longer speak of *the social* without implicating *the technological*. Yet digital technologies cannot be relied on in themselves to deliver a new or improved set of social dynamics. When cut adrift from ethical and informed pedagogical reasoning, they may have as little potential to challenge social reproduction as any fixed and hierarchical school classroom.

The emphasis placed in this book on *co-creation* is an acknowledgement that young people need more from education than advanced skilling in the use of new technologies. Digital technologies and related modes of production make it possible for everyone – indeed they *require* everyone – to be active co-creators of value for themselves and others, not just passive consumers at the end of a supply-and-demand chain. Alongside this cultural shift in modes of production, there is growing acknowledgement that creativity is not simply a matter of individual artistry; it is powerfully enabled by an educational environment in which learners closely engage with, and are acutely attentive to, the needs and aspirations of those around them. They look to support pro-actively the contributions of others, not just for the purposes of social harmony but in the interests of enabling innovation through higher quality learning outcomes. The products of such learning become authentic productions of the synergies that exist between individuals and the team. Co-creation, then, is not about turning away from competition, but it places the focus on achieving outcomes that are more than the sum of individual talents.

Processes of production and distribution have accelerated the pace of change and disrupted traditional industrial processes. This makes it unlikely that children will be spending long periods in any one place doing only one thing. With so much technological innovation driving new ways of engaging in social activity, young people are much more likely to be engaged in fast-moving, complex problem-solving than we have been. If our young people can learn to cross borders of all types – disciplinary borders, geographical borders, relational borders – they are more likely to be successful in the world of 21st century work. They will have acquired the mental and cultural agility to needed to live, learn and earn creatively.

The challenge faced by educators, then, is to provide children with an experience of learning that is *both important and relevant* to their differently lived social futures. In this century, schooling has become *more important* and *less relevant* than ever. We know it is more important because of the weight of evidence that the more highly educated our young people are, the better their lifestyle, their community infrastructure, their levels of civic participation, their financial security, their life chances. Yet we also know that more of the same education is increasingly irrelevant to our super-complex economic and social order. Glossy brochures and syllabus preambles keep promising to help young people reach their full potential; meanwhile, schools and universities continue to deliver much that has little to do with their futures, or indeed the future of learning.

A better education cannot mean *more of the same* education. The last century was one in which the core business of education was preparation for the routine accessing of information to solve routine problems. The capacity to learn and reproduce appropriate social behaviours is no longer the key to success that it once was. Instead of opening up possibilities, much formal learning is actually unhelpful because it assumes a fixed or predictable social world that no longer exits. Meanwhile, the focus of learning is moving beyond the individual and the cognitive to incorporate the moral and the aesthetic, and the interplay among these various social elements.

The future will continue to surprise us. Surprise occurs when we find that what happens tomorrow is neither more of the same nor a gradual process of improvement or decline, but the sort of transformational change that cuts across our thoroughly reasonable plans and expectations. Many of our predictions from the past turned out to be wrong – the millennium bug, the paperless office, more leisure time, and so on. Yet there are crucial changes we did not predict – how email would reshape our work, how the internet would make for a very different social and commercial world, how much time young people would spend texting each other, how a Stanley knife could become a weapon of mass destruction. It is this surprising world that presents so many challenges for contemporary educators. And it is this same world of surprises for which this important book has been written.

Professor Erica McWilliam
Education Futurist
Brisbane Girls Grammar School, Australia.
www.bggs.qld.edu.au

ARC Centre of Excellence for Creative Industries and Innovation
Queensland University of Technology, Australia.

1
Childhood and youth in flux

In mid-2009, I had a conversation with a fourteen year old boy attending a secondary school in England which prided itself on close preparation of all students for rapid change in 21st century life. Jake told me with some irritation that all the students' mobile phones are collected in by staff at registration each morning, and returned when the last bell signals the end of the school day. Students are discouraged from bringing their mobiles to school except where they are necessary for the journey to and from this significant place of learning. Jake had heard about a different scene at a school just down the road. Here, a group of student leaders, working through a programme of school transformation, succeeded in having homework suspended as an experiment. Shortly afterward, they requested its re-introduction, this time using their mobile phones. The Modern Foreign Languages department took up the challenge and students used mobiles to consolidate language learning through podcasts. Public exam results in that department soared. By the time it came to choosing options for the two-year preparation course for public examinations, Modern Foreign Languages had gone from being an under-subscribed option to having a waiting list.

Jake wondered, with evident frustration, why his own school had such a different attitude to mobile phones and their potential for social networking, generating content and information-searching. For Jake, being separated from his phone signified an infringement of freedom, it meant shutting down aspects of his life during a part of the day in which he was supposed to be preparing for adulthood. Inherent in this rule for Jake, however, was an incoherence; the lack of access forced by the school in this way prevented him from acting with mature independence of judgement in relation to information and to people; it prevented him from building knowledge in relationships with others, for him precisely what school should be preparing him to be able to handle.

Yet, this infringement of freedom was exactly what school intended. For the school, use of mobiles signified uncontrolled and unfiltered access and inter-action, with the possibility of inappropriate use, and potential for students to multi-task beyond the requirements of the curriculum in unregulated space. Whilst Jake's phone allowed him not only to talk with friends but to parti-cipate in accessible, motivating, open and often playful digital conversations, where he could marshall and manipulate information to a significant degree, the school's view was that this held distractions (for example, texting other students) and also dangers and difficulties (including problems of possible cyber-bullying) and the inevitable comparison of handset between students, perceived to be more insidious than the comparison of make up or trainers. Despite regular student attempts to bring this up for discussion through the School Council, a representative forum of students and staff, the school re-mained of the view that the best course of action was simply to ban mobile phones from school entirely.

The conversation with Jake highlights a number of questions in relation to the nature of Western childhood and youth in the early 21st century, the nature of

technology appropriate to education at this time and the role of the school in both. The actions of Jake's school suggest a com-partmentalised view of mobile communi-cations technology and education, where the connectedness and agency promised by mobile phones was seen as likely to dis-rupt the core activity of school. Although the school sees itself as a school of the future, it appears to Jake to do this through providing opportunities within school and not at the interface between school and other existences, both actual and digital. The actions of the school down the road

This image plus the images on pages 5, 11, 94, 103, 128 and 141 are part of a larger piece scribed by Andrew Park, Cognitive Media http://www.cognitivemedia.co.uk/ created alongside Anna Craft's Keynote to the June 2010 CELT Symposium on creativity in higher education, held at National University of Ireland, Galway. Full image can be found on page 150-151.

from Jake's, however, suggest a view of learning in the 21st century as enhanced by what students could do in that digital interface between the actual space of school and beyond it.

But perhaps most significantly, contrasting courses of action in each school in relation to mobile phones, symbolise and reflect distinctive views of Western childhood and youth which reflect lines of commitment and activity stretching back into the late 20th century, which this chapter now goes on to examine.

The family, childhood and youth in flux

It has been argued that the 1990s saw the emergence of childhood as worthy of study in itself (Lee, 1998). This, according to Lee (2001), represented a distinct shift from seeing children as appendages of the family, recipients of care and the raw material of education. This former tendency to view childhood through the 'layer of adults' (*ibid*, 2001:155) was, Lee suggested, both representative of and responsible for the 'institutional cocooning' of children (*ibid*, 2001:155).

The cocooning of children and young people

According to Lee, the high point of cocooning in the West came after World War Two, an era in which the home began to take precedence as the cradle of childhood, as children moved away from taking on an economic role in society and the family (Cunningham, 1995, 2006). The home began to acquire a number of protective characteristics in relation to childhood and youth which underpinned its function as a cocoon (Lee, 2001).

First, the home was seen as safe in the aftermath of evacuation in which city children were sent to the country to escape bombing of cities during the war. Health and social welfare was safeguarded more extensively as the post-war period brought with it the introduction of the Welfare State, a product of the Beveridge Report (1942) which sought to wipe out problems related to the five giant challenges facing society at the time (want, disease, ignorance, squalor and idleness) by providing a minimal level of support. The Welfare State brought non means-dependent free health, education and social welfare, together with heavily subsidised housing for those most in need, paid for on a national scale through compulsory weekly flat-rate insurance contributions. A comprehensive scheme, it was universal (open to all) thus guaranteed families a minimum standard of living and reduced insecurity by protecting against sickness, unemployment, bereavement and old age. The improved security thus experienced by families was further enhanced by State provision of the highest standard possible in a range of social services.

Economic boom led initially to distinction between gender roles, with men earning a living outside the home and women on the whole taking the nurturing roles of making the home itself and raising the children. Analysis of longitudinal cohort data from two generations beginning in 1946 showed that by the 1990s increasing numbers of women were returning to work after having children, with class and regional differences diminishing over time (Joshi and Hinde, 1993). There is evidence that the home, and childhood, continued into the late 20th century to be predominantly presided over by mothers (eg Voydanoff, 1988) even where gender roles are shared (Thompson and Walker, 1989). Although, moving into the twenty-first century, the boundaries of the home are increasingly permeable both in terms of women's constructions (eg Yantzi and Rosenberg, 2008) and in the myriad ways the external world can form part of lived experience in the home (a phenomenon discussed throughout this book), the home is frequently idealised as a place of safety, particularly by children (Harden, 2000).

Along with being seen as a safe place, post World War Two domestic life acquired a *mystique*. Home, and childhood, were seen as innocent, as separate from but also mysterious in relation to the rest of life. The home, according to Lee (2001) represented patriarchal reproduction where women's power and sexuality was repressed by the superordinate responsibilities involved in domestic care and the reproduction of the line took precedence.

Finally, in relation to childhood itself, the home, post World War Two, was *secret*. Children were cocooned, distinct from adults, and safe in this domestic space in turn fashioned and protected by women (Lee, 2001).

The post-war home of the 1940s and early 1950s had increasingly featured technology (labour-saving devices, such as washing machines, vacuum cleaners, food blenders) gradually making the work of the isolated woman carer and home-maker easier with less need for children to help. As a result, the lives of children were increasingly characterised as distinctive from adulthood. Childhood thus emerged as a construct distinct from the responsibilities, pressures and dangers of adulthood. During the post-war period of the 1950s and 1960s, however, Postman (1983) argues, alongside this 'cocooning', consumer society gradually invaded the home – and childhood – through television. For, he notes, the protected world of childhood and youth nurtured in this safe-home context, was changed completely by the advent of television as a means of mass communication. Television, as the seminal study by Himmelweit *et al* confirms (1958), had begun to empower children as consumers.

Television: the birth of children as empowered consumers

Television offered children and young people opportunities to engage with the wider world in new ways, through the changing economy. Since the 1950s the increasingly globalised economy and a wide range of new media within it have significantly framed childhood and youth, linked of course to environmental and ecological change. Children and young people are both recipients of the benefits of this 'marketisation' of childhood (Livingstone, 2003) and, as a consequence of the very dynamic of the market, their actions contribute to its development in specific directions. For Lash and Urry (1994) this reach of market dynamics deep into the life and identity of the family, is symbolic of the era of 'high modernity' characterised by a powerful and uncritical belief in grand narratives of 'progress' which include the global capitalist marketplace.

Image part of a larger piece scribed by Andrew Park alongside Anna Craft's Keynote to 2010 CELT symposium, Galway. Full acknowledgement p2, full image p150-151.

The family, childhood and youth in the early 21st century are harnessed deeply to the globalised economy. Globalisation means economies are interdependent as never before; the start of a global recession in 2008 brought increased complexity as relationships between state and private enterprise interwove to re-stabilise the banking system and to seek to restore market confidence. Changes in employment together with speed of economic development and re-development, mean that innovation, creativity, enterprise are all seen as primary to success, alongside traditional skills and knowledge. The consequent shifts of gear in education (toward striving both for excellence and also for creativity) reflect and interact with views of childhood and youth as actively engaged in both constructing and consuming. The possible relationships between creativity and educational futures are explored in Chapter 2.

Social change reflected in childhood and youth

The reach of the globalised economy into the home, then, is a significant influence on changing childhood and youth. But there are others, too. The last fifty years has been characterised by significant social change. Ever decreasing certitudes in social engagement, social, emotional and geographical mobility, together with demographic and intergenerational change can all be seen as tied to economic aspiration. And this social change brings with it increased pressure on young people and indeed on adults, to make sense of and choices about how best to navigate complex possibilities.

Some sociologists of childhood emphasise the individuality involved in such decision making. For example, Beck (1992) argues that the fragmentation and customisation of life worlds and life styles in a marketised world means not only a shift away from the collective, community worldview but also an emphasis toward individuation in choosing courses of action. Buchner (1990) called this the 'biographisation of the lifecourse' (p78). Others, for example Hakim (2000), emphasise that decisions made by women in relation to entering the workplace are made possible through the improvement of contraception, the revolution in equal opportunities, the expansion of white-collar work and increasing availability of jobs which are not seen as the be-all and end-all of identity, together with increasing emphasis on life-design choice in wider society. Hakim suggests that with a majority of women choosing to combine work with parenthood, there exists an increasingly variegated environment of social choice with regard to relationships made with family, work and wider economy. But whether the analysis focuses on employment-related, intellectual, geographic, socio-economic, cultural, political, identity-related or family-structure oriented change, it seems that unprecedented social upheaval and increased personal choice imbued with an assumption of capacity for 'self-actualisation' (Maslow, 1987) or mobility, is a characteristic of Western 21st century living.

This self-actualisation was, it could be argued, both triggered and supported by the growth of the media. The reach of television and film media into the lives of even very young children continues to be remarkable, with an increasing number of children having universal access. A relatively recent comprehensive study of media access and use among North American children aged 0-6 reported recently that three quarters watch TV, and a third watch videos/DVDs for an average of an hour and twenty minutes per day. A fifth of 0-2 year olds and more than a third of 3 to 6 year olds had a television in their bedroom, the most common reason given being that it then enabled other family members to watch their own choice of show (Vandewater et al, 2007). The study called for further research on media use by very young children, and the exploration of possible interaction between media use and children's developmental health.

The digital revolution: further empowerment

Whilst the big breakthrough may be seen as television in beginning the process of the global marketisation of childhood, the *digital revolution* has brought something even more powerful into the mix, as Ziehe (1994) foresaw. It developed from fertile ground, given the impact of television on how people saw their capacity to make choices.

With access to digital media in and beyond the home from a young age (Vandewater *et al*, 2007, report nearly a third of 5 and 6 year olds using a computer for 50 minutes on a typical day, for example) and with increasing access to hand-held devices, children and young people are now able to develop a sense of identity, meaning, direction, and even lifecourse progress, through local and global, actual and virtual engagement with others. Children and young people are, with the tools of a digital environment (which often facilitate a more developed sense of agency than in a face to face context), greatly empowered compared with their counterparts fifty years ago.

The phenomenon of instant access that is afforded by technology, enabling two or more people thousands of miles apart to have access to the same information, has been described by the provocative US journalist, Thomas Friedman, as 'flattening' the world (Friedman, 2005). Friedman argues that the flattening that allows such ease of access by so many to so much information, is the result of the convergence of at least three factors: widespread access to personal (and increasingly, mobile) computers, the development of software allowing computers to talk to each other without humans facilitating this, and the infrastructure of the web. These, he notes, have occurred against the post-cold war backdrop in which the dominant global economic model is capitalist, and globalisation therefore links economies with each other, integrating state with economy in newly complex ways. The result is a flattened world with high access and empowerment within a global marketplace.

What this book, focusing on creativity and education futures, explores, is how this flattened context manifests in the lives of children and young people. For it could be argued that children and young people are actively involved and empowered in this flattening world, through ease of access and participation – and that they expect to be.

But *are* they empowered? To what extent does this extended agency of children and young people, characterised, as Livingstone puts it, as 'staying younger longer, yet getting older sooner' (2009:5), pose a risk to children, to young people and to others?

Childhood and youth: two discourses

Analysts exploring the nature of Western childhood and youth from the late 20th century into the 21st represent cluster around at least two contrasting worldviews, which can be viewed as a continuum. At one extreme is a view of the child as being at risk (Frechette, 2006) where the role of the adult is primarily to protect. At the other end of the continuum, by contrast, the analyst sees the child as empowered and the role of the adult as far more marginal, with the child seen as effectively moving beyond adult control (Newburn, 1996).

Childhood at risk

Perspectives acknowledging the danger of risk emphasise the vulnerability inherent in childhood and youth (Cordes and Miller, 2000). They also emphasise the importance of preparation for future work (Buckingham, 2007) and the danger and implications of disenchantment (Facer *et al*, 2001a). Such perspectives can be seen, as Frechette (2006) notes, as exploiting the fears of parents, which seem to guide parents to centring play on the home rather than in public spaces (Valentine and McKendrick, 1998). These perspectives are perhaps reinforced by a situation where, in Western societies, formal education has been extended to late teens, so that some of the traditional milestones of adulthood, such as financial and domestic independence, are delayed (France, 2007).

Childhood empowered

Perspectives that by contrast acknowledge the empowerment inherent in youth, emphasise the liberation of the child, the significance of preparing young people to be future workers (Buckingham, 2007), and the 'techno-savvy' dimension of childhood and youth (Buckingham, 2007:84). As indicated above, such perspectives can be seen, Newburn (1996) argues, as recognition and celebration of children moving beyond adult control.

Such perspectives on childhood and youth as empowered, are frequently tied to marketisation. The marketised view of childhood followed Postman's (1993) analysis which suggested that the introduction of a consumer society in the 1950s and 1960s, and in particular the reach of television and mass communications, led to the empowerment of children as consumers. Postman (*ibid*) argued that technology, in the form of television, was responsible for introducing the possibility of independent action for children and young people, by linking them to the increasingly global marketplace – effectively a marketisation of childhood. Applying Postman's argument to the current day,

8

harnessing imagination and social engagement in play to the global market-place means that experience of and identity with childhood is not only framed but also defined by fashion and the consumer marketplace. Else-where (Craft *et al*, 2008), I and others have challenged this as problematic, a position developed further in Chapter 2 and Chapter 8.

Extending the reach of technology from television in the mid 1950s through to digital technologies nearly fifty years later, a pan-European study led by Livingstone (2003) recognised that the characteristics of youth, transitioning into independence, self-identity, individuality and engagement with con-sumer culture are now emerging in younger children. She argued that media-tion by new media including digital technologies, is largely responsible.

Reach and role of technology changing childhood and youth

When we consider the evidence, we see a rapidly changing technological landscape for children and young people. For as Palfrey and Gasser (2008) note, no aspect of our lives is untouched by the digital era which is transform-ing how we live and relate. By 2005, in England we saw 89 per cent of children aged 10-16 with a computer at home, 84 per cent of Y2 parents reporting that children used a computer at home, 90 per cent had games consoles, 70 per cent had handheld games machines and 93 per cent of teenagers had mobile phone for their own use (Valentine, Marsh and Pattie, 2005; Interactive Edu-cation, 2001; European Research Into Consumer Affairs Survey, 2004; Future-lab, 2007).

By 2007, in the USA we saw more than half of 12-17 year olds using social net-working sites (Lenhart and Madden, 2007) and by the end of that year, 93 per cent of teens were using the internet with 64 per cent of those generating their own content, and 55 per cent having created a social networking site profile (Lenhart *et al*, 2007).

Mobile and fixed digital technology, then, is reaching into the lives and pockets of children and young people, offering opportunities for digital identity and play. Web 2.0 technology allows children and young people to play with and engage with others either directly or indirectly. It enables

■ *social networking* – through Facebook, MySpace and other social net-working sites

■ *gaming* – through online multiplayer games, including from those with a real-time mission where children play with each other here-and-now (such as World of Warcraft, Toontown, Runescape), those which allow children to play with ideas made by others but not directly with each other (such as Spore) and those without any such mission (such as Second Life); most of these games can support enormous numbers of simultaneous, geographically diverse players, hence are often known as 'massively multiplayer online games' or MMOGs

■ *means of generating and uploading content* which can occur within games and also social networking sites (including forums associated with specific interest groups, or general-access sites such as U-tube)

What lifts this form of play far beyond what was available in childhood previously is its availability online, 24 hours a day, seven days a week, from anywhere in the world with internet access and, often although not always, for a small fee. Children as young as 6 may therefore be playing imaginative games with others their own age (or older), who live on their own street, or on the other side of the world. Children and adults can in theory play together in these spaces, which are characterised by their playful democracy. Everyone can contribute, all are welcome. And, of course, the games being played online may be reproduced face to face. Social networking often occurs between children and young people who already know each other (for example, from school) and games played on the internet may be reproduced in real life. During a recent family holiday, the younger of my own two children, at that point aged 11 and 9, developed an embellished actual version of a cartoon-based online multiplayer game they had been playing for at least five years. The actual game, which was played out in the swimming pool of the holiday house, was, like the virtual game, logged in and out of across the whole week. On return from holiday, my son ran straight to his laptop to log in to the online version, having not played that particular game online for at least a year. This sort of activity is documented by others, including Livingstone (2003) who describes two 8 year old boys 'playing the internet' (p207), in other words reproducing an internet-based game in their own home, immediately after playing with it online together around the same computer terminal.

Although less extensive, versions of each of these forms of digital play are also possible within material available only offline (and thus available through CD-Rom). What they all have in common, however, as Livingstone (2003) notes, is that they are forms of media which invite activity, participation, engagement and interpretation. They assume agency and interaction in and between users rather than a passive audience positioning.

Driven by the extensive and appealing long reach of digital technology, then, childhood and youth are in a new kind of flux, perhaps comparable to but

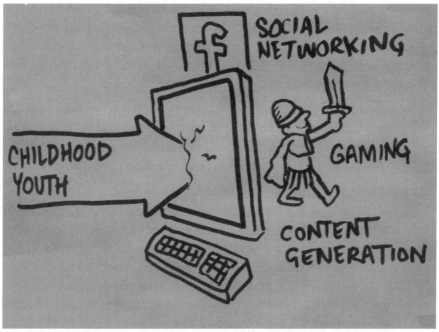

Image part of a larger piece scribed by Andrew Park alongside Anna Craft's Keynote to 2010 CELT symposium, Galway. Full acknowledgement p2, full image p150-151.

possibly more significant than the shift into the cocooning post-war childhood documented by Postman (1983) and explored by Lee (2001), as discussed earlier. For the digital dimension is becoming a significant and growing element in children's lives.

The digital revolution: enabling or endangering?

In the context of such change, arguments rage about the extent to which such digital technologies are enabling or endangering for children and young people – the extent to which adults should be concerned with protection or empowerment (Devine, 2000). Which should adults be most concerned about? The empowerment of children and young people, or their protection? On the continuum extreme which interprets digital technologies as empowering, an important question is the extent to which their use of digital technology is simply an extension of children's play-space, in which play is redefined and cyberspace offers a new bodymind balance. Facer *et al* (2001b) suggest that this is one way of understanding the nature, reach and experience of digital technology by children and young people, although they also point out a loss of privacy inherent in play through the public location of fixed computers. Clearly, increased portability – for example through hand-held devices, including mobile phones – brings the potential for mobile privacy. And given the potential offered for creativity, imagination and independence in new virtual spaces for gaming, social networking and content generation (Buckingham, 2001), digital technologies can be seen as significantly empowering for children and young people.

No wonder digital technologies as engaged in by children and young people can be seen as threatening for those seeking to protect them. They can be regarded as challenging adult identities and symbolising a loss of control over children (Marshall, 1997; Valentine and Holloway, 2001).

Among those arguing that digital technologies pose dangers to childhood are Singer and Singer (2005), who make a special argument for early childhood in particular, suggesting that the years up to the age of 5 are characterised by the emergence of imagination, the development of a sense of personal autonomy and of self-conscious thought, together with the blooming of narrative thought. These, they claim, are nourished by direct physical and social experience in the here-and-now which cannot be replaced by cyberspace. This line of argument denies the multiplication of possible worlds that children engage in, from concrete to fantasy to abstract/digital.

Following a similar line of argument, are Cordes and Miller (2000), working for the Alliance for Childhood, an international action-oriented network initiated in England to encourage reflection on traditional ethics in the healthy care and education of children. Referring to computers and digital devices/media as 'fool's gold' to emphasise their dual attraction and uselessness, Cordes and Miller argue that they bring with them a range of hazards. These include physical, emotional and social, intellectual and moral dangers to children and young people.

And then there are the dangers which come from spending too much time online and not enough on the basics, for example, traditional literacy. In November 2007, PIRLS (Progress in International Reading Literacy Study), an American-led survey undertaken in 2001 and 2006 in 45 countries, was reported in *The Guardian* newspaper (Curtis, 2007). It showed England as having dropped from third to nineteenth in the literacy league table and English children as less confident in reading and writing than they were in 2001. Yet 37 per cent of English children were shown to be spending more than three hours a day playing computer games. This latter was the highest level in the survey. The implication would appear to be that the more time spent on computer games, the less confidence in literacy children may exhibit – suggesting the potential of computer games to undermine children's basic skills. Although another interpretation might be that the Literacy Hour in English schools has undermined rather than boosted literacy among children.

Others, however (for example Armstrong and Warlick, 2004 and Miners and Pascopella, 2007), would argue that children growing up with technology develop distinctive new literacies for internet engagement, with what Downes (2002) calls 'polyfocal attention', being capable of multiple channels of communication and developing new forms of hyper-grammar rules. Supporting this perspective, Marsh and Bearne (2008) on behalf of Sheffield University and the UK Literacy Association acknowledged as part of their evaluation of a British Film Institute initiative to extend literacies, that children and young people are reading and writing more on screens than ever, and that moving image media including films, TV and computer games, are now fundamental to what it means to be literate in the 21st century. Their clear message is that literacy is changing. These questions are returned to in Chapter 3 on pluralities and Chapter 7 on extending literacy and medium.

New ways of being, knowing and playing

Whether we see technology (as it pervades our lives, reaches into our homes and even our pockets) as either enabling or as dangerous, there is no doubt that it brings different ways of being, knowing and playing, first suggested by Prensky (2001a) who proposed that Generation Y – children born since 1980 – experience very different ways of knowing and playing compared with Generation X – those born before 1980. Referring to Generation Y as 'digital natives', he recognised that growing up with technology leads digital natives to be able to work with information very fast (and to expect to do this), with a capacity to 'read' a range of kinds of data not necessarily in the linear fashion expected in conventional literacy. Digital natives, he suggested, are capable of drawing on parallel sources and kinds of information, with an expectation of digital connectedness with others, playfulness and speed and an assumption of active engagement with it.

The differences between digital natives and conventional (ie the previous generation's) ways of accessing and working with information, is summarised by Facer (2007) who suggests that digital natives work at twitch-speed rather than conventional speed, are used to parallel processing rather than linear processing, access material randomly rather than in a linear fashion, tend to read graphics first rather than text, see themselves as connected rather than stand-alone, expect to be active rather than passive, to engage playfully rather than seeing digital environments as work, are looking for payoff rather than patience, are drawn by fantasy rather than reality and overall see technology as friend rather than as foe. Some of these aspects of literacy in the digital environment are discussed in Chapter 7.

Whilst recognising that not everyone born after 1980 is a digital native, the argument, is that those (an increasing majority) who are digital natives stay connected, are creators and consumers, and love to learn and work with others through emergent kinds of exploratory play. For the digital technology demands creativity through social networking, gaming and content generation, not to mention how we work out what to let in and what to leave out – not only for Generation Y, but also for 'Millenials' (as written about by many, for example Greenberg and Weber, 2008), born since 1995. As this book spans the learning of Prensky's 'Generation Y' and Greenberg and Weber's 'Millenials' and given the increasing pervasiveness of the digital in all our lives, I refer simply to children and young people throughout this text.

Children and young people empowered at home?

Against the backdrop of digitised engagement and wider individualisation and individuation in childhood and youth (Corsaro, 1997), Giddens (2003) argues that we are seeing democratisation in the home, in that children's voices are more and more widely valued. Children see themselves as having a right to make their views heard, and to argue for what they think is fair or their due. There is an increasing culture of participation in the home and in decision-making, he suggests, than hitherto. Children's voices are increasingly valued – and not only through the marketised digital play described so far.

Whilst this participation of young voices and desires may be expanding in the family, and active in the marketplace, there is a strong sense in which children and young people are seen as a public responsibility. This perspective has its roots back into the twentieth century (Hendrick, 1997), if not earlier. So whilst there is an individualised story to tell, there is also a collective one. The perspectives of children and young people have become increasingly valued by providers and particularly by policy makers, as acknowledged by Christensen and James (2000). Policy provision is increasingly alert to how their mental health and well-being may be nurtured and how it may have been undermined by State policies (such as evacuation) in the past (Rose, 1990). It is perhaps ironic that alongside the impetus to involve young people in participation is much greater regulation and much greater alertness to risk and possible danger; this is driven by a concern to safeguard, which may have the effect of decreasing participation.

How does education respond to childhood and youth in flux?

Thinking back to the opening story of this chapter, which aspect of Jake's story do you have experience of, as a parent, student, teacher or friend? Mobile technology banned or integrated into learning? And which seems the most appropriate response for childhood and youth in the 21st century? It is tempting to look for either/or answers in these binary divisions and commentators on the state of flux which seems to characterise early 21st century childhood seem to divide into binary oppositions in understanding distinctions. Buckingham (2007) summarises the extreme stereotypical values implied in the contrasting perspectives on childhood in relation to ICT, shown in Figure 1 below.

Each of these positions opens a whole spectrum of possible perspectives on the nature and experience of the digital element of childhood and youth. Buckingham's summary reflects overall distinctions between the contrasting views of childhood discussed in this chapter. His 'childhood as natural' perspective can be seen as driving the view which understands children as being at risk; by contrast, the 'childhood as computerised' perspective can be seen as driving the view which understands children as empowered, as outlined in Figure 2 (overleaf).

Natural	Computerised
Human beings	Machines
Emotion	Abstract intellect
Interaction	Programming
Bodily/kinaesthetic experience	Cognition
Natural growth	Accelerated growth
Arts and crafts	Computation
Real, hands-on experience	Simulation
Intuition	Logic
Imagination	Information programming
Play	Instruction
Inner life	Impersonality
Creative	Destructive
Moral commitment	Emotional detachment

Figure 1: Extreme views of childhood (from Buckingham, 2007)

Childhood/youth as at risk	Childhood/youth as empowered
Vulnerability of the child	Liberation of the child
Children as consumers only through layer of adults	Children as producers and consumers
Play as 'private'	Play as 'public'
Children as passive/needing support	Children as active/seeking support
Technology signifying danger	Technology signifying opportunity
Children protected from knowledge of technology	Recognition of children as techno-savvy
Children as in danger of feeling disenchanted	Engagement driven by children
Need to prepare children for future work roles	Children routefinding into multiple work roles
Fears of parents and educators exploited	Children moving beyond adults

Figure 2: Contrasting perspectives on childhood and youth

A further binary tension we might highlight is that between individual and collective experience, emphasising the greater degree of collaboration/co-participation possible through the digital medium. This tension throws up a problem, highlighting the extreme connectedness that is possible, at the same time as being the individuated experience of operating a keyboard or console. This last example may offer a clue to alternative ways of thinking about such tensions, in considering that the dichotomies are less about polar opposites, about adopting either one position or the other, than a recognition that one of the characteristics of early 21st century childhood and youth is occupation of more than one position at the same time. When engaged in a multiplayer online game, the individual player is potentially both collaborating and connected as well as individuated and isolated at their keyboard or console. Generating content for a social networking site calls on imagination and intuition, often represents emotions and may involve crafting and honing material which frequently represents embodied experience (such as social events). For example, in making short movie clips, or stop-frame animation, or in recording music-making.

One of the challenges that education faces is recognising the integration of possibilities which are in tension with one another within the same experience. This is challenging for educators given their legal responsibilities to safeguard as well as to enable. So, whilst the experience of empowerment, and an action-oriented voice and hand in the shaping of their world, is both an expectation and an experience of many young people, the responsibility to protect remains a responsibility of adults including those working in schools (Devine, 2000). For the rights and the needs of children and young people need to be respected within an empowering and caring framework in a world characterised by rapid and complex change: economic, social, technological as discussed already – as well as environmental and even spiritual.

The challenge is toward what Hargreaves has called system redesign (Hargreaves, 2007). How do learning communities, and citizens concerned with education, respond with an eye on both discourses, child at risk and child empowered? And how do we step out with children and young people on a transformational journey that harnesses engagement of all in it, yielding education futures that are relevant, exciting and inclusive?

There is no doubt that educational provision, whether at the level of group, class, year group, school or wider system, is in need of creative engagement to produce futures appropriate to those learning within it. Chapter 2 begins to explore how creativity and educational futures connect.

2

Creativity and education futures

Shifting conceptions of creativity?

Chapter 1 concluded with the suggestion that the significant changes in childhood and youth demand system re-design in education. This requires both creativity in concept and a focus on enabling the creativity of children and young people. This chapter offers a democratic, everyday version of creativity to co-designing educational futures.

This democratic view is a characteristically 21st century one, contrasting with earlier perspectives. Historically, creativity has been understood rather distinctively over the ages. In ancient times, in the Greek, Judaic, Christian and Islamic traditions, creativity was seen as divine inspiration (Sternberg and Lubart, 1999).

It was not until much later, during the Romantic Era in Europe in the mid 19th century, that creativity was seen as involving human beings' own capabilities and the beginning of the discipline of psychology, and therefore of studies of creativity within this discipline, heralded a recognition of the subjectivity of feeling, and depth of insight, often made manifest in creative products, for example in art (Craft, 2001a).

By the middle of the 20th century, multiple psychological traditions of study had been spawned and so creativity was explored through many psychological lenses, for example: cognitive, psychoanalytic, psychometric, humanistic, social-personality, each with its own focus (Craft, 2001a; Rhyammer and Brolin, 1999) and with an increasing emphasis on empirical rather than philosophical investigation (Baer and Kaufman, 2006; Craft, 2001a; Sternberg, 2003). By the mid 20th century, creativity was being recognised as involving science as well as art. Pragmatic approaches to fostering creativity were increasingly popular (Baer and Kaufman, 2006; Sternberg, 2003) – and it was understood that as well as the expert mastery of experienced practitioners or high creators such as Gandhi, Mozart, the Dalai Lama, Freud, Einstein and so on (Csikszentmihalyi, 1994, 1996, 1999; Gardner, 1993; Gruber and Wallace, 1999; Wallace and Gruber, 1989), creativity ALSO encompasses everyday exploration by young children (Craft, 2001b, 2002).

By the early 21st century, there was increasing recognition that creativity had to be understood within its cultural context. Empirical studies exploring creativity in Afro-American, Afro-Arab Islamic, Chinese and Korean cultures began to report the incoherence of any claim to a universal concept of creativity (Forrester and Hui, 2006; Lau et al, 2004; Ng and Smith, 2004; Rudowicz, 2004). The dominant perspectives on creativity within both psychology and education were gradually being recognised as being problematic, in being over-representative of a Western view of the person, of social engagement, of generativity (Craft, 2005, 2008). And yet, whilst scholars were beginning to acknowledge the limitations of a universalised conception of creativity in education, there was increasing effort at policy level in many parts of the world to highlight and develop exactly that: a rather universalised, or one-size-fits-all concept of creativity within education. An aspect of this was the role of the social; whilst increasingly following in particular the work of John-Steiner (2000), creativity was seen as involving collaboration and not as a solo process or event. The Western influence on individualism nevertheless continued to contrast greatly with Eastern perspectives, which give greater recognition to collaborative and communal creativity.

By the end of the 20th century we saw creativity recognised as lifewide, relevant in multiple contexts and areas of knowledge and achievement spanning science, technology and the arts, together with everyday life (Craft, 2006). Creativity, then, was seen increasingly as socially and culturally situated – with implications for how it is measured. In the Western world, creativity is seen as a vital and highly valued aspect of our lives (Craft, 2006; Jeffrey and Craft, 2008).

The rise of creativity in education

As acknowledged elsewhere (Jeffrey and Craft, 2001; Craft, 2002, 2005, 2006; Jeffrey and Craft, 2008 and Claxton, 2006), creativity has been seen as increasingly significant in relation to education since the end of the 20th century, despite a powerful set of drivers toward ever-higher achievement on narrower measures (ie core curriculum areas such as English, mathematics, science and technology). The push to higher achievement involves integral links between student performance and school rewards – a set of relationships which Ball (2003) called 'performative'. A number of drivers can be seen as responsible for the rise of creativity as a priority despite the performative backdrop, of which three are discussed here: the economic, social and technological. These are in turn linked with others, including environmental/ecological and spiritual drivers.

Driver 1: economic

Perhaps the most significant of the drivers in raising the value of creativity in education is the economic one. Increasing numbers of people over the age of 30 in the Western world are now engaging in forms of work and employment which did not exist when they were at school. The economic futures of those entering school today are even less predictable, requiring of them (and of their teachers) a capacity to innovate and to respond flexibly to uncertainty. Globalisation means economies are interdependent as never before, and the economic downturn of late 2008 brought increased complexity as relationships between state and private enterprise began to interweave with opportunities as well as challenges. Increased marketisation means powerful awareness of, and action toward, choices and a Western mind-set which is oriented toward the individuated desire to possess, and to access, derived from market-defined fashion. Creativity is required to keep the economy changing fast enough to keep up this consumerism (Craft, 2005).

Changes in employment, together with speed of economic development and re-development, mean that both knowledge AND creativity are key to success where creative practices are seen as a feature of business success (Buckingham and Jones, 2001) and tied to education. This is not to say, of course, that critical thinking, and analysis of information, are unimportant, indeed creativity itself involves critical scrutiny as well as boundary-busting. And, as McWilliam (2008) argues, creativity in the classroom is increasingly characterised by shifts in the role of teacher from what she calls sage on the stage to guide on the side, to being a meddler in the middle. This latter role involves a sensitive, actively provocative scaffolding, combined with standing back, enabling students to realise ideas and to nurture possibility thinking – the transition from what is to what might be (Craft, 2000, 2001b, 2002, 2005), as discussed later.

In England a strong neo-liberal perspective focuses on the economic benefits of education which both stimulates and expects creativity (Leadbeater, 2000; Seltzer and Bentley, 1999). Close links are made between creativity and the economy at policy level (for example, reflected in the 2008 Creative Economy strategy document (DCMS, BERR, DIUS, 2008). One challenge posed to the economy in an environment where ease, reach, breadth and integration of communication technology means it is possible to work remotely, is that some functions may be outsourced to inexpensive but appropriately skilled labour markets. In England, a significant aspect of Government's support for creativity, as well as the auditing of it, in the early years of the 21st century, was the development of capacity in what is referred to as the creative indus- tries (music, advertising, film, web design etc), growing the 'creative Britain' brand.

Driver 2: social

A second driver toward creativity in education is the social one. Geographical, social and emotional mobility are increasing. Patterns of social engagement are driven increasingly by individuated preference rather than obligation or tradition, with choice at the heart of change. Family structures and locations mean increasingly complex home lives for many Western adults, children and young people. Such changes in social engagement both demand and offer increased opportunities for children and young people, and choices about how best to navigate complex possibilities.

Demographic change with a growing older population is particularly intrigu- ing when the bulge-group in that ageing population were the baby-boomer generation, many of whom experienced the forefront of change in terms of personal choice and who thus expect choice to be inherent in their own lives. For at the heart of social engagement and interaction for young and older members of Western societies, is the high value placed on personal choice which, it could be argued, is a version of possibility thinking, at the heart of creativity. The idea of possibility thinking is explored further in this chapter and Chapter 4.

Education, then, it might be argued, needs increasingly to be geared toward helping children and young people make sense of the array of choices which face them, exercise creativity in imagining potential, and follow through possi- bilities. In this sense, the social joins the economic in shaping the need for education to provide opportunities for children and young people to develop creativity.

Driver 3: technological

A third major driver toward creativity in education is technological change, particularly with regard to digital technology. The interfaces between humans and machines through, in particular, step-changes in what digital technologies can do and the ease with which these are available, both offer and demand opportunities for creativity. Already a vast amount of what we do every day in the developed world involves digital technology. From food production, storage and preparation, to how we regulate the homes we work in, the buildings and spaces we work and socialise in, and the cars and other forms of transport we use to get from one place to another; to how we purchase and sell goods and services, to how we communicate with others and with ourselves at work and in play – the list is endless. Equally, digital technology facilitates and enables control on the large governmental scale of health, security, defence, justice, education, etc.

User-generated content is active in our lives on a vast scale, from viewing and engaging with other people's uploads to making and uploading our own records of events and ideas. In these and many more ways, digital technology is integrated with our lives as never before, providing tools and also a form of raw material to be shaped. And, as tangible interfaces develop, embodied digital interaction becomes increasingly commonplace, enabling physical play/exploration with digital devices. Children, young people and adults can play tennis or golf, for example, with a Nintendo Wii game console, using the controller handset as a tennis raquet or golf club, swinging it just as they would on the tennis court or golf course.

The creativity offered and demanded by technology is indisputable, not only at the level of human-technology interaction known to us today but potentially where the relationships between humans and machines may begin to challenge what we consider it is to be human. In 2008, Harper *et al*, a team looking specifically forward to the future, asked 'what will it mean to be human when everything we do is supported or augmented by technology?' (*ibid*:10). Developments in robotics now mean that autonomous machines are emerging to help in the home and beyond (for example, the Roomba vacuum cleaner which is able to sense its way automatically around a room, and robots being designed to cook, pick up objects and even to act as companions to the infirm and the elderly). In medicine, surgery can already occur remotely.

The question of what it means to be human is raised in a different way through our potential to take on multiple online identities, literally to change our appearance and characteristics by building an online presence or Avatar, within gaming spaces in particular, an idea played with rather dramatically by the creators of the successful movie, *Avatar* of 2009.

Whether talking about support, augmentation or integration, what it means to be human is inextricably interdependent with the technology itself. Harper *et al* (*ibid*) also point out ways in which our 'digital footprints' (*ibid*:21) and 'digital shadows' (*ibid*:22) are rapidly growing, as we each leave a visible and, in many cases, permanent, digital trail of our interactions and activities. Some of this we are aware of, but much is recorded without our knowledge or permission by, for example, CCTV cameras, phone logging, ATMs, GPS devices embedded in cars, phones and even clothes. One of the defining features of being human, our creativity, is both demanded and enabled through such developments in technology; chapters 3, 4, 5 and 6 each explore the kinds of creativity that digital technologies enable especially among children and young people today.

The response of education

The response of education around the world to these three major drivers of economic, social and technological change has been to raise the profile of creativity in the curriculum since the end of the 20th century. Governments in Europe, Canada, the Middle East, Far East/Pacific Rim together with Australasia began to recognise in the last part of the 20th century and early part of the 21st, the role and significance of creativity in education. 2009 was an important year, being designated the European Year of Creativity and Innovation, the Queensland Year of Creativity, and seeing the launch of a national programme funded by the Bill and Melinda Gates Foundation in the USA to bring curiosity and imagination into all American schools, to name only three initiatives. Across the world from Europe to the Middle East, Pacific Rim, the Americas and Australasia, governments have been considering what it means to respond creatively to educational need, and what it means to foster creativity in education.

The rise of creativity as universalised

The three major drivers of economic, social and technological change are of course connected with others, including what some commentators regard as increasingly shaky foundations for the relationship between humans and the environment, as the ecological balance becomes eroded further and awareness and action in response to this lags further and further behind the changes (Milojevic, 2008; Orr, 1999). Spiritual and religious change provide a further dimension of shifting perspectives on values. The rise of fundamentalism, linked with global terrorism and anti-capitalism, in some parts of the world, challenges the 'developed' or 'Westernised' world-view, which rests on the high modernity platform of globalised capitalism and acquisition, raising intriguing tensions for educational provision. Creative responses are needed to both the environmental and spiritual challenges facing humanity – in terms of how educational systems, and the people learning and teaching within them, respond with wisdom (Claxton *et al*, 2008).

The global environmental challenges are more and more keenly felt. These are rapidly becoming yet another powerful driver for creativity in education. Similarly, the quest for spiritual meaning and expression seems increasingly urgent across the developed world and so adds to the possible drivers for creativity in education.

As the drivers for creativity fan out to include so many pervasive dimensions of life on earth, creativity is cast as potentially enabling wise and far-reaching responses, both personally and collectively. Creativity has accordingly been harnessed to a discourse which sees it as universalised and therefore tends towards a view of creativity that encompasses, but goes beyond, the arts (Jeffrey and Craft, 2001). This is despite the close links policy makers have forged consistently over time between creative and cultural development in England and elsewhere. As explored later in this chapter, the universalisation perspective is problematic, and elides a range of agendas which in practice drive creativity policies and practices, but perhaps the most visible challenge for creativity in education is the disconnect with performativity.

The challenge of performativity

In England, and elsewhere, the last ten years of the 20th century brought particular challenges in the fields of creativity and education. With an increasingly performative agenda in operation globally (Ball, 2003) where students' efforts in their studies were measured through formal test and examination results and seen as reflecting on their teachers and schools, and as a (and perhaps 'the') key arbiter of educational quality, the relevance of creativity in education was increasingly problematic. And yet, as commentators point out, creativity policies co-existed alongside the performative ones, the former highlighting flexibility, ingenuity, generativity, and the latter emphasising lack of trust in professional judgement in favour of technicist curricula, pedagogy and targets, in a context of market competition and league tables of achievements (Boyd, 2005; Jeffrey, 2003; Jeffrey and Woods, 1998, 2003). This tension was highlighted in a series of studies set in England and Australia and published in a Special Issue of the *British Educational Research Journal* in 2008 (Nicholl and McLellan, 2008; Simmons and Thomson, 2008; Troman, 2008; Clouder *et al*, 2008; McWilliam and Haukka, 2008; Burnard and White, 2008).

This challenging context was perhaps summarised by a conversation I had with a senior university colleague in the early 1990s. I had recently joined the university and was undertaking research with artists working in education, co-exploring how aspects of creativity in the arts might nourish the creativity of teachers – later published (Craft, 1996, 1997, 1998a, 1998b). With two of the lead artists I had designed a masters level course for educators focusing on these issues and with one, and a group of others, I had begun to write a book raising these questions among others which, like the articles, would be published (Craft *et al*, 1997). The senior colleague called me into his office and offered me some advice, as I was a relative newcomer to research. As Head of Department, at a time of increasing performativity in England, he was concerned to let me know of his misgivings about my choice of research topic. For him, he explained, creativity was a bit 'at the edge', a bit 'odd' for a promising young researcher to be looking at, in particular my work with artists and artistic processes in the arts. He thought that I might perhaps like to take his advice and refocus on something sensible, like science.

It was a critical moment for me, when time stood still for a moment within the melée and I understood the danger of the performative push. It resulted in my resolve to champion, research and develop the role of creativity in education, across the curriculum and across provision. For it struck me that whilst creativity does occur at the 'edge' of understandings, habits and traditions, shifting, developing and transforming these, it is also at the heart of what it means to be human – to imagine the possible. And the contrast of 'science' as 'sensible' and as competing with 'the arts' which were 'edgy' seemed misplaced, for creativity is inherent to humanity, as it is inherent in everything we engage with, science included.

This experience helped me re-examine how creativity might be understood in education. And it highlighted for me the tendency among educators and policy makers, even then, to reduce creativity to the arts, a tendency which has become more pervasive since the mid 1990s when that conversation occurred. In the United Kingdom, creative and cultural development have been seen as occupying very similar terrain since the publication of a government-commissioned report on creative and cultural education in 1999 (NACCCE, 1999). From its recommendations, and those of a second paper, *Culture and Creativity: The Next Ten Years* (DCMS, 2001), followed 'Creative Partnerships', a large national programme of curriculum development investing in projects involving community artists of all types, focused on developing creative learners along with cultural cohesion. In 2008, this was extended in England to a five hour a week 'Cultural Offer' overseen by the Youth Culture

Trust, encouraging young people to participate as both producers of, participants in and spectators of culture and enabling them, through partnership, to find their own talent. It led to the re-framing of the Creative Partnerships programme as emphasising 'cultural learning' (McMaster, 2008), thus perpetuating the conflation of creativity with culture seen in other Government statements, for example the report: *Nurturing Creativity in Young People* (DCMS, 2006a) and the Government's response to this (DCMS, 2006b). The mixed creative and cultural programme recommended by these two papers was reflected in the findings of a subsequent Parliamentary Select Committee (House of Commons Education and Skills Committee, 2007) and taken forward by Government (House of Commons Children, Schools and Families Committee, 2008).

Emergent rhetorics for creativity in education

And yet, despite this expanding policy agenda conflating creativity with culture, as in Banaji, Burn and Buckingham's (2006) document, and as developed further elsewhere (Craft, in press), at least eight clearly distinctive rhetorics of creativity in education can be seen as emerging over this late 20th century period in England:

> *Creative genius rhetoric* – roots in European Enlightenment, this post-Romantic perspective emphasises fostering extraordinary creativity in a range of domains

> *Democratic and political rhetoric* – roots in Romantic era, creativity as empowerment

> *Creativity as ubiquitous* – ie as pervasive

> *Creativity as a social good* – creativity necessary for good life

> *Rhetoric which emphasises the economic imperative* – drawing on neo-liberal discourse around economic programme

> *Approaches emphasising play* – roots in Romantic era, childhood play origin of adult creative thought

> *Approaches focusing on creativity and cognition* – from 20th century Piagetian and Vygotskian work, emphasis on cognitive processing

> *A discourse around creativity and new technologies* – affordances of these in relation to creativity

> *The creative classroom* – connects spirituality, knowledge, skills and pedagogy

These multiple discourses represent vehicles for a wide range of values evident in England, despite the universalised discourse.

By the end of the 20th century, countries all over the globe were recognising the necessity of creativity in a rapidly changing world. School curricula were being re-written to incorporate creativity, and such changes encompassed two significant assumptions (Lin, 2009); the first that creativity is accessible to all – a 'democratic' view of creativity (Craft, 2001b; Feldman and Benjamin, 2006) and the second that it can actually be developed (eg Fryer, 1996) – and both assumptions fed the desire to nurture creativity as necessary to both surviving and thriving (Craft, 2005).

Whilst educational provision at all levels and across the world has become much more sensitive to the need for creativity than it was at the time when my colleague sought, in good faith, to steer me away from creativity, creativity in education has nevertheless battled to co-exist alongside the drive toward performativity. So, whilst it is certainly true that achievement in education involves both excellence and creativity, it is also the case that the excellence agenda, geared to market-driven and measurable standards, has been very powerfully prevalent. Particularly striking are recent findings suggesting that the market-driven performativity agenda may be becoming the encompass-ing one for teachers, children and parents, rather than sitting in tension with creativity (Jeffrey *et al*, 2008). This team's work, undertaken with a grant from the Economic and Social Research Council in a number of primary schools in England in the early 2000s, suggested that teachers saw creativity increasingly as a means of addressing the performative agenda and not in conflict with it. This bears out other recent studies which suggest that partnership work with the creative and cultural sector can enable schools to maintain and even join the two tracks of creativity and performativity (Arts Council and Creative Partnerships, 2005; Jeffrey and Woods, 2003; Jeffrey, 2006).

On one level this may be reassuring, in that teachers may not be experiencing the dissonance in the tension between creativity and performativity in a way that confuses. On another level, however, this may signal a possible superficia-lity in how the potential for creativity may be realised in some primary schools. For whilst creativity can challenge the *status quo*, a marketised rationale for creativity may result in a narrowly marketised response in schools with a limited range of acceptable possible outcomes to creative engagement. In addition, some commentators express concern that the performative context stifles risk-taking in both teaching and learning (Cochrane and Cockett, 2007; Cochrane *et al*, 2008).

More recent findings reported in Jeffrey and Woods (2008) suggest that for these schools, the economic driver at least is operating loud and clear, even if the social and technological, environmental and spiritual ones are less evident. Linking this finding with the documentation by many commentators of the marketisation of childhood and youth, as discussed in Chapter 1, raises questions about what creativity is actually demanded. For marketisation demands creativity in a narrow sense, born of artificial perceptions of need and reifying individualised choice. As already indicated, the universalised perspective on creativity as tied naturally to a global marketplace can be seen as problematic, in being culture-blind, narrow in values and ethically, environmentally and ecologically insensitive (Craft, 2005, 2006, 2008; Craft *et al*, 2009).

Education futures?

At any point in time there is always a past, present and future to our educational and other activity; what makes this particular moment especially potent, however, is the urgency of the need to consider the intersection of probable, possible and preferable futures. Work developed by the Educational Futures Research group at the University of Exeter adopts a set of distinctions between the three broad approaches of probable, possible and preferable futures, distinctions originally made by Bell (2003).

Probable education futures

Considering the *probable futures* facing education takes us into a focus on analysis of trends, at a global level, with an emphasis on prediction and forecasting. Detectable trends include increases in uncertainty, change, cultural diversity, environmental challenge, digital engagement, population growth, economic challenge, with perhaps the most significant aspects of these being uncertainty, digital engagement, environmental and economic challenge. In his work on the mapping of educational futures, Inayatulla (2008) refers to this broader situating as 'the disruptive context' (2008:13) in which climate change, terrorism, new technologies, and so on are markers of multiple levels of seismic change.

Such probable futures facing education suggest probable areas of response by education, including a need for greater enterprise, community cohesion, focus on health, sensitivity to identity, and participation at a number of levels. The need is unquestioned but commentators seem in agreement that our capacity to respond is dulled by the initially religious and then industrial habituation on which 20th century educational provision was based – what Claxton (2008), writing from England, calls 'dead metaphors' of education as monastery and factory.

According to Egan, writing from Canada, the legacy of educational continuity and the difficulty in initiating change, reaches far back into ancient Europe, to 'three big ideas... socialisation, Plato's academic idea, and Rousseau's developmental idea' (Egan, 2008:9). For Egan, it is these three ideas which prevent a capacity to change. The first is the belief that schools in particular should convey and expect certain approaches to behaviour and values consonant with society, a process usually referred to as 'socialisation' but which he suggests might be more accurately referred to as 'indoctrination' in the high value placed on binary distinctions, known as 'rationality' – knowing us from them, right from wrong, good from bad, etc.

The second is the belief, from Plato, that literacy allows the transmission of knowledge which in turn, and in Egan's words, 'transforms the minds of learners and enables them to understand the world more accurately and truly' (Egan, 2008:18). Yet Egan, in the footsteps of philosophers such as Montaigne and Rousseau, suggests that the transmission of knowledge through symbolic language (ie in its written form) actually disrupts the orality and embodied primacy of learning. He suggests that, far from bringing 'justice, objectivity and truth' (Egan, 2008:22), Plato's idea does not necessarily deliver this promise, being inaccessible to most and unrepresentative of the realities of living.

The third big idea that Egan refers to is the principle of 'development' proposed by Rousseau in the eighteenth century, of intellectual and personal growth, which comes, as Egan puts it, from 'discovering our individual nature and focusing our attention on creating the conditions for its fullest growth, not from learning some approved body of external knowledge' (Egan, 2008: 23).

Whether or not we accept the Eurocentric analysis offered by Egan as an explanation of our current framing of educational futures, it seems undisputable, as Inayatullah, writing from Australia and Taiwan, argues, that we struggle to work with more era-appropriate metaphors. He sums it up: 'we know we need to change but we seem unable to. The image of a new future, while emergent, is pulled down by the weight of the industrial era' (Inayatulla, 2008:14). He argues that we need to be wary of 'used futures' (*ibid*:15) which were fuelled by 'unbridled growth... leading to a global crisis of fresh water depletion, climate change, not to mention human dignity' (*ibid*:15).

Thus, probable futures of education include a range of predictable unpredictabilities; what Gosling (1994) called *the knight's move*. Discourse about probable educational futures, accordingly, focuses on higher achievement, turning out confident, successful learners, enterprising economic contributors, responsible citizens, a recognition of the global and culturally diverse dimensions to our engagement, a focus on health and, perhaps most significantly, the need to develop creative and critical thinkers. Yet at the same time, such probable futures are accompanied by what seems to be a global human struggle to find ways of responding to these in ways that have inherent within them these agile, responsive and anticipatory new patterns of value and engagement, and appropriate respect and recognition for global resources which such action depends on.

Preferred education futures

A focus on preferred education futures takes us into a less predictive and more emancipatory place of critical values which, together with informed critique-oriented ethical and political debate, leads to proposals for alternative educational futures. Clearly preferred futures are determined by patterns of values; given the difficulties we seem collectively to have with imagining possibilities at this point in the early 21st century, together with the time-lag we experience in moving from policy to practice – thus it may be more useful to explore possible futures.

Possible education futures

In contrast with the forecasting stance of probable futures and the more decisive position of preferred futures, a focus on the possible futures facing education takes us into the realm of imagination, considering flexible, creative possibilities. It thus begins to connect creativity with education futures.

I have argued for some years that at the heart of creativity is the shift from what is to what might be – from recognition to transformation: a process that I have called 'possibility thinking' (Craft, 2000, 2001b, 2002, 2005) and which has been researched over a number of years by a team based at Cambridge, The Open University and Exeter University (Burnard *et al*, 2006; Chappell *et al*, 2008; Cremin *et al*, 2006). In recent work, the research team exploring this concept in practice has focused on the process of questioning at the heart of possibility thinking. From empirical investigation the team has, amongst other things, distinguished between 'possibility broad' (vista-opening) questions and 'possibility narrow' ('functional' or practical) questions.

Considering possible futures for education can be seen as a form of possibility-broad questioning and may conjure a range of potential dimensions in relation to what is valued and seen to be needed in the context of probable continued and increasingly rapid change, as discussed earlier in this chapter. Possible educational futures, therefore, are likely to be congruent in the identification of need, with visions of probable educational futures. For what possible and probable educational futures share in common is recognition of the need for higher achievement, turning out confident, successful learners, enterprising economic contributors, responsible citizens, a recognition of the global and culturally diverse dimensions to our engagement, a focus on health and encouraging creative and critical thinkers.

Possible educational futures are also mediated by the potential offered by digital and bio-technological futures discussed briefly earlier in this chapter and the demand for self-motivated learners and citizens to an increasingly powerful degree. Possibility-broad questions around educational futures concern themselves with a range of issues, including what is to be learned and how (the curriculum and pedagogy), what is to be the outcome in terms of learner capabilities, and systemic issues in relation to how such curriculum, pedagogy and capabilities can be adequately developed.

Creativity and education futures integrated

Educational futures, then, demand creativity, both in terms of what education is concerned with, and also in how futures in education are conceived of, born and nurtured. Thus, imagination, ingenuity and flexibility are required both in the process of considering possibilities and also in the nature of what the educational process is set up to produce as outcomes in learners. But what kind of creativity is appropriate to the processes and outcomes of educational futures? The three major drivers of creativity in education pose live challenges as far as education futures are concerned.

To what extent is it wise to accept uncritically the economic argument that 'since a successful economy is a creative one, the role of education is to nurture creativity'? The premises on which this argument rests include the assumption that wealth-creation, acquisition and novelty are without question of high value. Yet these assumptions also imply that growth can be indefinitely sustained – which is clearly not the case as environmental problems rooted in unchecked growth are recognised. As Inayatullah reminds us, we must attend not only to the 'used futures' implicit in our current learning systems but also to the 'disowned' futures which may be present in them (*ibid*,2008:15).

To what extent is it appropriate simply to accept the social and demographic changes which demand such skilful route-finding among children, young people and adults? What role does, could or should education play in mediating or even challenging the reification of individual choice (Craft, 2005), perhaps born of the mantra of market supremacy?

And how far should educators accept the widespread use of digital technologies discussed in Chapter 1 that offer enormous affordances in how people relate, learn, work and play, which are altering the nature of childhood and which seem to promise to blur the line between humans and machines? To what extent does the argument 'because it is possible, we embrace it' win out and what sorts of caveats might educational processes and outcomes appropriately harness in doing so?

These are all questions which this book sets out to explore. It is written from the perspective that acknowledges and problematises tensions and dilemmas inherent in the marketisation of education. It argues for the development of wise creativity drawing on other commentaries (Craft, Gardner and Claxton, 2008a; Gardner, 2008), which argue that educators, wherever they are located, have to shoulder a responsibility to nurture individual and collective generative potential in ways that are both wise and rewarding. And it explores possible educational futures with a close acknowledgement of what might be seen as the four Ps characterising childhood and youth in the 21st century.

The four Ps of changing childhood and youth

Whilst views of what constitutes creativity in education are changing, so is childhood itself. The digital landscape, which co-exists in children's lives alongside the actual, is profoundly changing childhood and youth. And in turn, these changes interface with the development of creative approaches to learning and teaching, and the enablement of young people's creativity.

I characterise the four key features of changing childhood and youth triggered by the digital revolution as *the plurality of identities* (people, places, activities, literacies), *possibility-awareness* (of what might be invented, of access options, of learning by doing and of active engagement), *playfulness of engagement* (the exploratory drive) and *participation* (all welcome through democratic, dialogic voice). The next four chapters look at each of these in turn. The book then explores how education can become inherently more creative, while also nurturing creativity more effectively.

3

Pluralities

Chapter 1 laid out some significant changes in the landscape of childhood and youth. Chapter 2 argued that creativity is inherent in education and I introduced four characteristics of changing childhood and youth. The four Ps of childhood and youth inherent in the digital dimension of children's lives are:

- Pluralities
- Possibilities
- Playfulness
- Participation.

This is the first of four chapters which explore these characteristics in turn.

Childhood and youth pluralised

In chapter 1, I pointed to a tension between views of childhood as fragile and thus needing protection and those conceptions of childhood which emphasise *empowerment* and therefore need enablement. These perspectives, whilst in tension with one another, proponents of each volubly contributing to debate, frequently co-exist, reflecting perhaps the complexity of this issue. This complexity is evident in attitudes and behaviours in both practice and policy.

For example, it is hard for an adult to imagine wanting to challenge the safeguarding of children and young people, and yet there is plenty of evidence of capability among children and young people as active agents in a world of choice. Government policies in England acknowledge and reinforce the safeguarding role of 21st century schools for example, as stated in an education White Paper, published by the DCSF in 2009. The White Paper encourages creativity, flexibility and adaptability in the face of huge environmental and economic challenge. But despite this commitment to creativity, the safeguarding perspective is the inexorable path which frames practitioners' work in schools. This involves, in effect, being averse to risk: the very opposite of what creativity demands, which thus would seem in tension with the propensity to nurture and encourage the creativity of children and young people. Yet the phenomenon of 'child panic' (Wallace, 1995) is a loudly-heard influence on policy-making and educational provision. The management of risk can be seen as a dominant imperative of life in the 21st century developed world (Giddens, 2003).

Alongside the fears accompanying risk-averse perspectives are behaviours designed to protect and cocoon rather than to enable and to empower. Increasing evidence suggests this is an extending pattern in English schools (Hope, 1999; McWilliam and Jones, 2005), where staff working in and with schools are concerned to ensure that children and young people are sufficiently controlled to keep all members of the community safe. Hope's study documented, in particular, CCTV and other school surveillance processes in English schools – a scene which may have been exacerbated by the protective walls (actual and virtual) created as part of the Every Child Matters agenda in England since the early 2000s – McWilliam and Jones explored the discourse of child protection in Australia and New Zealand, and the 'tyrannies' (McWilliam and Jones, 2005:209) this imposes on teachers.

There is an illuminating parallel in adult education; Ecclestone (1999) reports evidence that non-participation in lifelong learning by many of the most 'vulnerable' members of the adult learning community may signal the low expectations and sense of pessimism about their agency in the future that may be felt by such adults. It leads Ecclestone to suggest that participation in lifelong learning might be made compulsory for the most 'at risk' groups; an intriguingly authoritarian conclusion for a group potentially characterised by their expression of agency.

Against the context of controlling responses to educational provision, which are driven by a desire for equity and openness of opportunity, is a somewhat contrasting picture of evolving childhood and youth. For the pervasive nature of ICT and therefore of digital connectedness in their lives, means that childhood and youth in the 21st century are characterised by a much greater sense of personal agency than in previous times (Livingstone, 2009). At the least, forms of educational provision need to acknowledge this and, in an ideal world, work with it.

Along with the greater sense of agency among children and young people is the *pluralising* of childhood and youth. This chapter explores pluralities in the lives of children and young people, in terms of the places they learn and play in, the people they engage with, the personae they can adopt, the activities they get involved in, the widening literacies they are increasingly expert in and the opportunities for play, learning and socialising they may experience. Each of these aspects of the pluralising of childhood and youth is enabled and enhanced by, but not necessarily restricted to, digital play, networking and content generation.

Plurality of place

ICT enables children and young people to play and learn with others in a wide variety of actual and virtual spaces, ranging far beyond the front doorstep, street, garden and playground. In common with actual spaces, online multiplayer games, social networking spaces, tools and forums offer a range of degrees of pre-existing spatiality in which to play and to communicate. Yet in contrast to actual spaces such as the front room or playground, most can be manipulated by users to a greater degree. Whilst in the actual spaces of the home and playground, parents and carers may be willing to have sofa cushions, tins of beans, pieces of string and soft toys rearranged to represent variously a zoo, a hospital ward, trips to the seaside or to the moon, in online space the user may be able to build, deconstruct, decorate, acquire and develop properties of space with a vast amount of freedom. In the case of online multiplayer games, children and young people in particular may be able to enhance characteristics of their avatars (online selves) and other beings too.

In such virtual spaces, children and young people can engage with others whose geographic location is actually congruent with or close to their own, as well as those who are physically located many thousands of miles away, in different cultural contexts and time zones. Personal spaces for playing in within online multiplayer games can be manipulated by individuals or by project teams. Although designing a home space often carries certain restrictions (for example in terms of the components that can be combined), due to the pre-programmed nature of the environment, choosing where to locate one's personal space is often fairly open. And for older players, it is possible to play in online spaces such as Second Life, in which building personal spaces requires use of simple computer programming skills. The manipulation of space may be driven by individual impetus, but is often manipulated with the feedback from or collaboration of others, characterised frequently by generosity in the sharing of knowledge and skill between players to help in the realising of ideas.

Moving from one place, or space, to another is not usually dependent upon adult mediation in the same way as leaving the home to go to a local public play-space might be (when an adult might need to accompany a child) but, by contrast, is a mouse-click away and restricted only by any parental controls in operation on the handset or machine. And because of this, the range of virtual spaces that a child or young person might choose to spend time in may well be wider than the actual spaces available to them. The connection between spaces and activities may also be more blurred. Using a laptop computer, a teenager can do their homework, download and listen to music, browse through a social networking site, edit video material taken on their phone and upload it to their own or another website, find out news or sports results, send e-mails to friends, play in a multiplayer online game – all in parallel with the homework task in hand. We no longer maintain simple and distinct spaces for distinct activities. Instead, our spaces are crowded with plural applications, media, activities, people, communication and even levels of reality.

With the enactment of play, socialising and learning in a plurality of spaces comes the development of a range of assumptions about the speed and range of testing out what spaces feel like, at least visually and through the visual, emotionally, with the implied agency behind the point-and-click which enables this in a blink. The plurality of spaces carries assumptions about their parallel nature; it is possible – indeed normal – to play or exist in more than one at a time, for example to have a social networking space open on screen whilst playing in a multiplayer online game and listening to music (an auditory space). And using handheld gaming devices such as the Nintendo DS, two or more children can play on a multiplayer game in the same room, garden, park or beach, interrupting the digital game for lunch, to go for a swim, to swap collectible cards, to do face painting or dressing-up.

Perhaps most significantly, the physical and digital spaces are interwoven, both in real-time as in the DS example above, and in connecting the actual space here and now with virtual and parallel spaces, many of which are linked to other actual physical spaces which may be thousands of miles away and in different time zones. This brings a new, flexible, hybridisation and experience of space and time, with embedded assumptions about how we can mani-pulate both. Along with the multiplicity of values and perspectives to which digital spaces offer access is the potential to assume that all content is of equal status. One consequence is that we may well confuse information with knowledge. Another is that we treat conflicting values-positions uncritically (Livingstone and Bober, 2004; Weigel, James and Gardner, 2009; Kiili et al, 2008).

If children and young people experience such multiplicity of place and space in their lives beyond education, we have to wonder whether educational experiences need to adapt in order to engage with emergent ways of learning in parallel space. Whether motivated from the perspective of encouraging an empowered childhood and youth, or from the cocooning perspective, working with young learners to bring thoughtful, informed critique and an ethical dimension to information, social interaction and engagement and to content generation is surely a significant and growing role for education in terms of social responsibility as well as the integration of physical and digital space.

Space itself, whether digital or actual, can be understood as socially defined or, as Massey (1999) puts it, 'a product of interrelations... constituted through a process of interaction' (p279) and thus characterised by plurality and multiplicity of possible configurations of interactions and potential. For children and young people, the co-existence of parallel digital spaces alongside actual ones adds both complexity and challenge to the co-existing multiplicity of perspective negotiated by users in each. Conflict and difference, traditionally negotiated in the playground, is now embedded for children and young people in new and virtual contexts. This raises interesting issues for parents, carers and educators keen to encourage *social responsibility*. For whilst these negotiations between children are now more visible to those who are within the digital space, and perhaps more personal in their reach, they are also more private in a sense, as they are less visible to and accessible to parents, carers or educators. No longer can a parent, carer or teacher necessarily become involved in the ethics and resolution of conflict where this occurs in a digital rather than actual space. Given the potency of digital interaction to reach far into the lives of others, this raises questions about the role of educators in the ethics of interaction in digital space.

Intriguingly, as Turkle (1994) notes when writing about multiplayer online games (though her comments are just as relevant to other digital spaces in which people can converse, navigate and construct ideas together), these potent, private and powerful contexts for engaging with others exist in computer programmes sustained in networks between computers accessed by individuals through an individual machine. So in one sense, these spaces do not actually exist at all. Yet in a virtual sense they do exist – and the integration between actual and virtual is, as the 21st century rolls on, an increasing feature of our lives whether through the insertion of a satellite navigation system in the car, the ubiquitous use of mobile phones or the relationship between fixed and mobile computers and people in buildings and other spaces. Early in 2010, as this book was being completed, the 3-D feature film,

'Avatar', was a runaway box office success across the world. It seemed to have captured the zeitgeist on human/computer interaction, taking the collective imagination of cinema-goers to a new level, using animated fiction integrated with film to explore the potential for actual and virtual space to merge. It explored how the embodiment and identity of actual and avatar existence might co-exist in new ways. Although it was a work of fiction, the huge success of the film perhaps signals the compelling potential that is offered by the merging of actual and virtual space, opening new dimensions of plurality.

Considering the integration of physical and digital space at a more prosaic level, as Horan (2000) notes, there are challenges for architecture and design in how physical spaces including buildings are conceived of and enacted, such that this multi-layered participation is not only easy (with sufficient power and worktop space for personal computers as well as other material, for example) but actually enhanced by their dual spatiality. Horan coined the term 'digital places' to denote the impact on physical spatiality of digital communication and the consequent evolution of 'hybrid places' with characteristics of both. He recognises a continuum of digital place from what he called 'unplugged' designs at one end, which show little or no digital adaptation in construction or design, to 'adaptive' designs which include modest adaptions to incorporate digital space into physical space to, at the far end of the spectrum, 'transformative' designs of rooms, buildings or whole communities which are composed of truly integrated physical and digital space.

An example of Horan's *unplugged* design in the classroom might be one where there is no digital technology in use at all. In such a classroom, the opportunities for plurality of place or space are limited. A feature of an unplugged design is the virtual celebration of the absence of digital technology and an emphasis on what can be done without it. What is particularly interesting about this is that for children and young people, an unplugged classroom environment offers a disconnect with what most are experiencing beyond it. Whilst few, if any, classrooms in England except perhaps those in some independent schools are likely to manifest the unplugged design, the question arises as to whether a disconnect is good or bad for learning – something we return to in chapter 8.

An example of an adaptive design might be a modest change in an existing classroom to allow for an interactive whiteboard and some computer terminals for students. A defining feature of *adaptive* design is the lack of any attempt to fully integrate the actual and digital by attending to social engagement in both, and the need for supportive physical design or re-design.

Whilst many classrooms currently exhibit adaptive design, the experience of learning is often focused more on the actual than the digital spaces, which are seen as an add-on or a way to replicate or document what has been done without the technology.

By contrast, a *transformative* design in education is one where physical spatiality is carefully integrated with the hardware and software use, and with learning activities undertaken both with and without the technology. If education is to engage with any commitment with the multiplicity of places that characterise childhood and youth, it is difficult to see how transformative design of digital place could not form a part of possible education futures, particularly, as Horan (2001) puts it, the speed of change in digital technologies which promise 'an era of digital ubiquity' (Horan, 2001:13). And given emergent ways in which digital and physical worlds collide, particularly in gaming, the transformative possibilities are intriguing.

Murphy (2004) describes how console video games provide players with simulated activity in a digital space which is contiguous with the physical space of their own bodies. What this expanded learning space offers, as Wegerif (2007) points out, is a *dialogic* medium for thinking, learning and playing, where individuals engage with others in negotiating explicitly their differences in perspective, which may equally result in both agreed and shared action and also irreconcilable difference. A characteristic of interactive online spaces, Frasca (2003) demonstrates, is the production of complex and, frequently, reflective understandings developed in a community, not usually found in non-interactive media.

The dynamics exhibited in digital virtual spaces in particular, as Molesworth and Denegri-Knott (2005) suggest, contribute to their 'liminality' – their openness, interminancy and ambiguity, being in transition or on the threshold between two different existential planes or states. There is, they suggest, a built-in liminality to participation in digital spaces, which means such spaces may provide arenas in which culture shift can occur. Inherent to such liminality is the extension of possible interactions with people offered in digital engagement; another dimension of the pluralities experienced by children and young people today.

Plurality of people

Through plurality of place and space, children and young people can – and often do – interact with people well beyond those they know personally, although an interesting feature of social networking is that most choose to connect digitally with people they have actual face to face relationships with (through school, for example), as documented by Livingstone and Bober (2004). Whilst this may be true of social networking, it is not so much the case with other kinds of online engagement such as playing in massively multi-player online games. Here, although children and young people do occasionally meet actual friends in the game, the majority of people they play with are unlikely to be known face to face. And for those who have difficulty in meeting and making friends, the virtual environment can provide a powerful means to identify with others with whom they may share interests or perspectives (Wallace, 1999).

So, which is real? There is a concrete sense in which both actual and virtual lives are 'real'. Writing some time ago about the potential offered by computers for leisure, Turkle (1984, 1994) notes that, although playing online – and especially in virtual reality multiplayer online games – is not 'real', it nevertheless has a relationship with the real, in terms of representations (ie representing and extending the actual) and ethics (in terms of impact of actions on others). The ethical dimension of digital play space is explored a little further in the section of this chapter on plurality of activity, and is returned to in Chapters 7 and 8 which consider the ethics of digital engagement.

There is some evidence, perhaps unsurprisingly, that whilst online spaces offer opportunities for invention and reinvention of persona, offline identity does influence online behaviour (eg Boyd, 2001). It is undoubtedly the case that a feature of childhood and youth in the early 21st century is the opportunity provided by digital spaces for initiating and engaging in dialogue with multiple others. This may be harnessed to a goal (such as that inherent in an online game, or to a thread in a discussion forum or wiki) or it may be a more meandering or less outcome-focused interaction (such as that inherent in social networking). But whether goal orientated or not, the Internet provides what Wegerif calls an 'unbounded space of dialogue' (Wegerif, 2007:9) offering children and young people unprecedented opportunities for devising how interactions actually occur and play out in practice.

The unbounded space also raises issues of trust for adults regarding those with whom children and young people are playing and networking, and the extent to which their contacts (and even their own children or charges) are truthful online about their actual identities. Children may be tempted to say they are older than they are, so as to gain access to a social networking tool or a game normally restricted for their age range. Adults may pretend to be children for a variety of motives. Clearly this aspect of plurality of people inherent in the digital dimension to childhood and youth brings with it ethical challenges as well as potential dangers. But perhaps more interesting is the concept of self-identity, or personae, that online engagement extends.

Plurality of personae

Many games expect players to assume a digital persona, or identity, to make a representation of their embodied self or their alter-ego, usually in the form of a three-dimensional model, using components offered within the particular game. And whether browsing, social networking, generating content or playing, there are always choices about how to engage.

Studies of this phenomenon appear to draw contrasting conclusions. Some research shows that identities developed in digital games may be quite distinct from (and even in contrast with) the player's normal identity (Gee, 2003). Although Gee is writing about digital games, experimenting with personal identity may happen in social networking and other contexts online too. Thus, following Gee, it would seem that digital spaces not only bring children and young people into contact with multiple others but they also allow them to experiment with being multiple selves within what Turner (1992), drawing on theatre, calls liminoid spaces, which he defines as places of opposition and resistance.

By contrast, others suggest that 'digital natives' actually see little distinction between online and offline identity and do not separate versions of identity adopted, rather perceiving their identity as unified but expressed in distinctively different representations (Palfrey and Gasser, 2008). By adopting a distinctive identity in a particular space, players can explore and even reflect on contrasting perspectives to the ones they usually hold.

The debate between Gee's position and that of Palfrey and Gasser is, however, united by recognition of the potential for identity development offered by digital spaces and the people playing, learning or socialising in them. The freedom afforded by the digital space together with power and connectedness with others seems to add up, according to youth accounts documented by Macszewski (2002), to experiences of expanding notions of self and identities through online interactions.

Digital spaces, then, can be seen as offering opportunities not only for children and young people to develop a changing and yet shared and ordered space, but space also of inversion and disorder. Digital space may thus enable the manifesting of largely make-believe possibilities where 'as if' has a strong sense of meaning and reality through the immersive adoption of role; where it is possible to make and, often, reverse, decisions which have an immediate visual and auditory manifestation and where others are immediately impacted by the decisionmaking. And the liminal space of online gaming appears potent in the facilitation of powerful and far-reaching social relationships (Cole and Griffiths, 2007).

Just as corresponding with a long-distance penpal in the days before the microcomputer, webcams and affordable global travel might offer correspondents (who may never actually meet one another face to face) opportunities to try to present reconfigurations of their normal identity and thus to experiment with a sense of self, so today's digital environment offers many opportunities for stretching identity. Whether this is playing in an online game as someone of the opposite gender (Turkle, 1994), or with different interests from oneself, or registering in a social network such as a forum with a false birthdate, the digital space and especially virtual reality games provide easy means for such experimentation. Inherent to this experimentation are ethical dilemmas, explored in the next section. These are both ubiquitous and pervasive because of the convergence of function in digital environments that enables *plurality of activity*.

Plurality of activity

A characteristic of digital media is its convergence of functions now possible using digital means. Audio-visual entertainment, gaming and communications can all be integrated within digital media where previously television, telephone, film, radio, games and so on were all separate media forms. Mobile phones alone can act as text exchange, play music, record conversations, act as calculators, cameras, alarm clocks, timers, video cameras and game players, access the internet and send e-mail. The social and cultural dimension of technological convergence is remarkable, as Jenkins (2006a) points out, enabling the integration of play, work, genres and markets. And through technological and cultural integration or convergence, expanding plurality of activity is made possible, be it documenting, editing and publishing audio, visual and other material or gaming within virtual reality, or social networking through a forum or social networking space.

Especially remarkable is the experimental and exploratory dimension of this plurality of activity – and expanding possibilities for participatory democracy. Shirky (2008) gives an example from the United States of a personal website set up to retrieve a lost mobile phone which a teenager had appropriated; through the mobilisation of citizens' interest, this led ultimately to an arrest.

Examples of such mobilising power using digital media are increasingly commonplace.

In England, during the late Spring of 2009, Ian Tomlinson, a 47 year old newspaper seller, walked across a line of police officers in the City of London who were patrolling the final stages of an organised and legal G20 demonstration. As he walked, hands in his pockets, he was attacked from behind by a police officer for no apparent reason and fell awkwardly to the ground. He was immediately helped to his feet by members of the public and, after remonstrating briefly with the officer, moved away. A visiting American who had joined the protest out of interest captured the entire event on his mobile phone. Shortly afterwards, that footage was sent to *The Guardian* newspaper and was shown on its front page. *The Guardian* also uploaded it to video website, *You Tube*, and this, together with other footage, much of it from mobile phones or personal cameras, began to appear in numerous other digital spaces.

Meanwhile, a few minutes later, in a side street around the corner, the newspaper seller collapsed and died. This, too, was caught on mobile phone camera, sent to the media and uploaded online. The public reaction to the whole incident was one of shock and outrage. Through social networking sites, the suggestion of a 24 hour vigil to mark this deep concern was mooted and organised. Thousands of people flocked to a procession to the spot where Ian Tomlinson had died, wearing black, laying flowers and many staying overnight in pop-up tents. Such roots-led direct action is enabled by digital technology.

The convergence of technology is being used in some contexts to encourage other forms of everyday civic participation. One example is use of phone cameras in alerting local government workers to new graffiti. Passers-by who notice this problem text an image and details to a central point with instant prompt to street cleaning teams who in turn text a picture of the cleaned-up area back to a central point. Before and after are displayed instantly on the local government website. Perhaps even more powerful is the latent capacity of social networking sites such as Twitter in mobilising social movements in response to current affairs.

In Iran in June, 2009, huge public demonstrations were organised through Twitter, protesting against the outcome of the contested presidential elections. With foreign journalists effectively prevented from reporting alternative news stories, social networking sites, and particularly Twitter, took on the role of reporting news in the form of text and images, along with the exploration of reactions in real-time online. The extraordinary contrast between bottom-up mobilisation of collective voice together with top-down attempts to control information led the US State Department to request a delay to planned maintenance work, which would have taken the site down for a critical 90 minutes. Thus, the bottom-up concentration of power focused through the medium of the social networking site made news and had the potential to change history – and was reported in the mainstream press (eg Cardwell, 2009).

The openness of the web combined with the much greater penetration of software, hardware and broadband access means that bottom-up creative concentration of power is now possible in an unprecedented way. Yet, just as creativity itself is devoid of ethical or moral content, so too, digital capability and access, even in its early days, was recognised as having the potential to empower 'revolutionaries, reactionaries and racists alike' (Jenkins and Thorburn, 1996). And yet, more recently, Jenkins (2006a) argues, it is the integration of actual and virtual which is remarkable. Whilst YouTube, Second Life, MySpace, Facebook and other blogs, social networking, content generation and gaming spaces offer the opportunity for participation in production, selection and distribution of specific sets of values, it is their integration with old media which is notable. An example of this, as he notes, was a partnership between YouTube – as a social networking site – and CNN – as a US-based international news agency – during the US Presidential election process, in which members of the public were encouraged to engage in a live televised debate with candidates through YouTube. A further example was the use by some candidates of Second Life as a parallel medium for the election campaign and the use of social networking sites to broadcast podcasts to supporters and arrange meetups.

Characteristic of the interweaving of media and fast, widely available access to user generated content, alongside professional reporting, is the mix of media forms that it is possible to engage with, in forming opinions about current affairs. The speed with which semi-professional and amateur reporting can be uploaded means that conventional forms of reporting, which are subject to greater editorial control, sometimes (as in the case of the death of the London newspaper-seller discussed earlier), follow rather than lead the breaking news.

The remarkable integration of actual and virtual engagement in what Jenkins (2006) calls 'the age of convergence culture' (p275), means that the characteristics of digital media are increasingly characteristic too of childhood and youth in the 21st century. A further aspect of plurality of activity is the collective and collaborative flavour to so much digitally-driven or digitally-enhanced engagement. Children and young people can make ideas happen with relative ease, connecting with others and with the actual and virtual activity of others.

I recently travelled with my family to a small seaside resort in the East of England, hundreds of miles from our home, for a week in a cottage on the edge of the village green. Our two children, then aged eleven and nine, spent some time each day playing with a dozen or so local and visiting children with a dozen or so local children and exchanged digital contact details before they left. They have since been in regular contact with some members of this group, through instant messenger using webcams to arrange meetings and play-dates in specific virtual games, uploading photos of pets and places and comparing notes on the options for a reunion at the same village on a future holiday. The reach of this emergent community of young people has a potency in its collaborative and collective potential, that did not, it seems to me, exist in previous media forms.

The collective and collaborative possibilities inherent in digital media mean that, as Leadbeater puts it (2009), 'the web is the source of our most ambitious hopes for spreading democracy, knowledge and creativity'... (p3). And clearly, digital media make it possible for new ideas to be shared quickly and far afield. Such media have the capacity, as Leadbeater notes, to find solutions to shared challenges 'by allowing us to combine the knowledge and insights of millions of people, creating a collective intelligence on a scale never before possible' (2009:3). Yet, as Leadbeater also notes – this collective and collaborative potential is imbued with risk, offering an open space for 'shadow networks for shadowy purposes' (Leadbeater, 2009:3). Mirroring creativity itself which can be harnessed toward both constructive and destructive ends, digital space offers potential for expanding possibilities and solving problems – as well as reducing, corroding and destroying both virtually (through viruses and worms for example) and actually (through organising acts of terrorism, for example).

Certainly digital space can be an experimental one which raises ethical issues. Exploring the potency of computers as a propositional object (ie as offering the opportunity for what might be), through online gaming, Turkle (1994) highlights the ethical dimension of the relationship between real and virtual. As the space between actual and virtual collides, others are drawn into representations which players may manipulate. Participants in an online game may, for example, present themselves as being other than who they really are (in terms of gender, age, beliefs and so on). The ethics of participation in pretence are intriguing, particularly where the virtual begins to overlap the actual as, for example, in Second Life, and in the consumer behaviour trends reported in the press where increasingly players are willing to spend real money to buy virtual items for their avatar (Guarino, 2009).

The boundaries between reality and virtual reality are set to become increasingly blurred (Harper *et al*, 2008) as augmented reality is developed, enabling people to overlay a digital interface on to their actual experience. This will enable people to experience the online world whilst moving around in the actual one. Digital environments and digital-actual environments have the potential to combine play, learning and socialising in the same spaces. Features of activity named by young people as possible in such digital environments are the anonymity, interactivity and connectivity (Macszewski, 2002). These assist powerful interactions and relations and are experienced very positively by some young people. And along with the anonymity, interactivity and connectivity there are new and creative challenges in terms of reading and constructing symbolic and aesthetically coherent visual material. Reading and offering this material is stretching our conceptions of literacies, as explored in Chapter 7.

Plurality of literacy

Undoubtedly, the digital environment demands facility with a widening range of literacies in which children and young people are increasingly expert. In a compelling early book Tapscott (1998) offered insights into what it means to grow up in what he called the 'net generation [N-Gen]' (p15). He recognised ten new aspects of these widening literacies which by 2009, in a follow-up book (Tapscott, 2009), he had reduced to eight norms:

- *Freedom*: a belief in choice at the click of a mouse – what to buy, who to engage with, how to present oneself – and tapped into, as Tapscott points out, by President Obama whose iconic line 'Yes we can' both summarises and provides a compass for the digital generation. Freedom of choice, suggests Tapscott, is part of the literacy spectrum for children and young people.

- *Customisation*: the expectation that technology will work for them – rather than simply function. Tapscott's studies suggest that the net generation expects to be able to customise devices or schedules for watching for example television programmes, downloading music, even, when they are older, working hours and location norms.

- *Scrutiny*: Tapscott argues that the net generation are sceptical online, using the web to explore the difference between fact and fiction. This is alongside an expectation that information will be available to them for scrutiny. Tapscott suggests that most net geners recognise that information they have placed in the public domain themselves through, for example, social networking sites, is similarly open to scrutiny.

– *Integrity*: the net generation has a strong sense of justice. Net geners can check out with a few clicks what the implications of their actions might be – for example, as a consumer. On the other hand, when it comes to music, he suggests, a large majority of 18-29 year olds download music illegally and the majority of these do not see this as stealing, justifying it within an ethical framework of their own (music should be available, small bands need support, etc). Net geners are quick to mobilise support against injustice when they see it, using the technology to hand.

– *Collaboration*: as later chapters of this book explore, a characteristic of net geners' behaviour is that they collaborate, as Tapscott puts it, 'online in chat groups, play multiuser video games, use e-mail, and share files for school, work, or just for fun' (Tapscott, 2009:89). They like to be in touch, with 'a friend in their pocket' (*ibid*). Wishing to offer and engage with opinions, expecting their views to matter, the net generation also volunteer in huge numbers, and contribute to the development of business ideas and civic action alike.

– *Entertainment*: net geners expect to have fun and to be entertained at work, argues Tapscott, citing examples of companies which provide sports facilities and which tolerate breaks from work through game-playing and social networking whilst at the office. Outside work, entertainment is also key; net geners are both producers and consumers of user-generated content such as edited photos and video material.

– *Speed*: is expected not only in video games but in being able to be connected round the clock and through the week. Instant access to others implies an instant response. Expectations of speed influence the kinds of technologies the net generation use; they are more likely to use instant messenger, for example, or texting, than e-mail.

– *Innovation*: is expected as the norm and, perhaps most significantly, as Tapscott puts it, this 'means rejecting the traditional command-and-control hierarchy and devising work processes that encourage collaboration and creativity' (p95).

Tapscott recognises the challenges which these widening literacies pose to the previous generation of Baby Boomers. As he puts it, the net generation are 'confident, plugged-in, digital-savvy' (1998:2). And yet, being connected and having the potential to be so twenty-four hours a day, seven days a week (24/7) means being intravenously (as it were) connected with vast amounts of information and virtual experiences. How do children and young people learn when to switch off? And how do children and young people learn to sift, make sense of and evaluate all this material, elements of which increasingly find us rather than being sought out by us?

When we consider the implications of the reality-differences between the connected generations (not that this is always age-dependent) and what is on offer in schools, we begin to understand the frustration and bewilderment of the young man whose story about mobile phones opens this book.

Plural implications?

This chapter has discussed ways in which digital environments offer children and young people unprecedented plurality in their dealings with the world around them, from whom they play and work with to where they do these things, as well as how and when. The access and opportunities offered by digital tools are potentially limitless; this however has implications at a number of levels. Already discussed is the question of how to organise and critically scrutinise information and experiences gained in virtual or semi-virtual spaces. This is in part a problem of criticality within an entertaining context which does not necessarily privilege or emphasise critical scrutiny, discussed further in Chapter 7. Pluralities open to children and young people through digital space also raise potential ethical dilemmas in terms of privacy and openness, and the question of who has control, also discussed in Chapter 7. Ultimately we might question whether virtual environments in the end offer children more control, or less.

Perhaps most intriguing is the gauntlet thrown down for educators about how to engage with young learners appropriately. As Tapscott puts it:

> Educators should take note. The current model of pedagogy is teacher focused, one-way, one size fits all. It isolates the student in the learning process. Many Net Geners learn more by collaborating – both with their teacher and with each other. They'll respond to the new model of education that's beginning to surface – student focused and multiway, which is customised and collaborative'. (2009: 91)

But embedded in Tapscott's warning is the assumption that if young people are motivated to be multiple/plural outside school/education then they would want to be so within it. This seems credible but we might question whether this assumption is itself derived from the control or high modernist view of education which lacks diversity, responsiveness and sensitive and appropriate customisation. Recognising not only where we position our-selves but also the embedded assumptions in our provision, are key to how possible futures may be conceived.

4
Possibilities

As explored in the first three chapters of this book, a characteristic of childhood and youth in the early 21st century is the multiple ways in which possibilities are open and malleable, particularly in light of the virtual dimension to young people's lives. Chapter 3 explored several aspects of plurality which living in a digitalised environment makes inherent in the experience of childhood and youth: place, people, personae, activities and literacies. Behind the potency of each are the continuously emerging multiple possibilities, at the intersections between the technology itself, embodied realities and collective human imaginations. The continual transition from what is to what might be, is what I have called 'possibility thinking'. possibility thinking can be seen as at the heart of creativity, whether domain-situated or everyday lifewide creativity, and whether individual or collective. Developed initially as a concept (Craft, 1999, 2000, 2001, 2002), possibility thinking has since become the focus of a four-stage research study (Craft, 2007; Craft, Burnard, Cremin and Chappell, 2008; Craft, Cremin, Burnard and Chappell, 2008; Jeffrey and Craft, 2004). In its simplest form, possibility thinking involves posing in multiple ways the question 'What if?' and thus initiates the shift from the given to the possible – the transition from 'what is this and what does it do?' to 'what can we/I do with this?'

'Possibility thinking': from *what is to what might be*

The multiple transition from what is to what might be seems characteristic of childhood and youth in the early 21st century, played out in a digital environment. This chapter explores first the concept of possibility thinking, then how this can be applied in a variety of ways in understanding the changing nature of childhood and youth, before discussing some of the paradoxes posed by multiple possibilities.

Possibility thinking, the engine of that shift from what is to what might be, was initially proposed as involving questioning, imagination and combinatory play (Craft, 1999, 2000). Empirical work with 3-11 year olds has shown that these are often embodied and non-verbal (Craft and Chappell, 2007; Craft and Chappell, 2009; Chappell *et al*, 2008a, 2008b). Studies of children working creatively in primary school classrooms in England show that possibility thinking involves problem-finding, problem-refining and problem-solving (Jeffrey, 2006; Jeffrey and Craft, 2004).

Possibilities with young children
Qualitative empirical work has been undertaken in the interpretive tradition since 2004 by a team spanning, by 2010, six universities, seeking to understand the nature of possibility thinking in education and to characterise pedagogical strategies which seem to foster it. Involving four overlapping and focused stages of work, the research has involved working with children and young people across the age range 3 to 18. Using participant and non-participant observation by means of video recording, still images, field notes, interviews and other audio recordings, reflective diaries, critical incident charting and learner artefacts, our analytic approach has involved teachers and sometimes pupils.

Each stage of the study has brought a distinctive lens to the analysis, with *Stage 1* (2002-2006) focusing on possibility thinking and pedagogy within the 3 to 7 year old age span. Findings from Stage 1 identified interlinked features of children's and teachers' engagement with possibility thinking. These included: the confirmation of *posing questions* as being a driving force. Other features included play, immersion, innovation, being imaginative, self-determination and risk-taking, as shown in Figure 3 opposite.

Stage 1 also reported on pedagogy which fostered possibility thinking and identified the practices of standing back, profiling learner agency and creating time and space for creative learning, as shown in Figure 4 opposite.

These teachers thus actively valued and therefore encouraged agency, ie children's own choices and ideas. They actively attended to how children engaged with learning opportunities, standing back from the action (albeit in active reflection), and enabling children to take centre-stage. Teachers thus gave the children time and space to develop and realise ideas. Yet these teachers also knew how and when to intervene, provoke, clarify, narrow down, inform, demonstrate, and help children reach conclusions, through closely attentive and sensitive observation. By attending to cues and clues in the children's

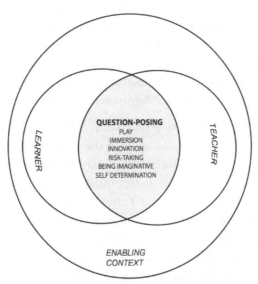

Figure 3: Stage 1 'model of possibility thinking'
Source: Burnard, Craft and Cremin, 2006

Figure 4: Stage 1 model of pedagogy and possibility thinking
Source: Cremin, Craft and Burnard, 2006

engagement, these teachers were able to make a huge success of what Erica McWilliam (2008) calls 'meddling in the middle' (somewhere between being the 'sage on the stage', acting as the source of all knowledge, and the 'guide on the side', who emphasises their facilitation role). Through active meddling in the middle, these teachers encouraged children's constructions of meaning whilst also seeking to channel and hone these when appropriate.

Stage 2 of the Possibility Thinking (PT) study (2006-7) focused on question-posing, with 5-7 year olds exploring both the visual and verbal video data. Stage 2 analysis led to the categorisation of *play* and *immersion* as the context for PT (made visible by specific behaviours). Analysis also indicated that *action/intention* (taking intentional action) and *self-determination* (auto-nomy and agency) were better described as permeating through PT rather than being core components. Being *imaginative, risk-taking, question-posing* and *question-responding* were therefore identified during early Stage 2 as the core components of possibility thinking. *Innovation* was conceptualised as a possible outcome of possibility thinking and thus, potentially, a condition for attributing creative learning (Burnard *et al*, 2008). These relationships are shown in Figure 5.

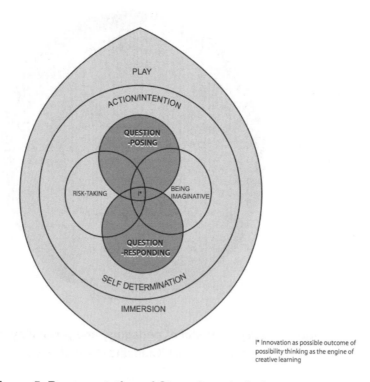

I* Innovation as possible outcome of possibility thinking as the engine of creative learning

Figure 5: Representation of Stage 2 analysis focus

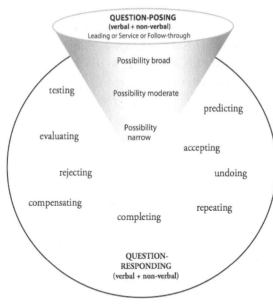

Findings from Stage 2 centre around a taxonomy of question-posing and question-responding (Chappell *et al*, 2008a; Chappell *et al*, 2008b), showing the dynamic relationship between the two, as shown in Figure 6.

This fine-grained taxonomy of question-posing and question-responding was situated within the wider conceptual constellation for possibility thinking, as summarised in Figure 7.

Figure 6: Question-posing and question-responding in relation to one another

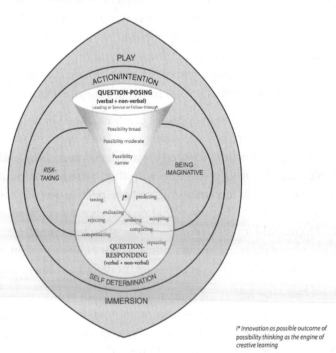

Figure 7: Question-posing and question-responding within possibility thinking

Possibilities with older children

Having confirmed the significance of questioning in the overall conceptual structure of possibility thinking at the conclusion of *Stage 2, Stage 3 (2007-2009)* has extended the focus to 9-11 year olds, returning to the two original research questions in this older age-range context, characterising possibility thinking, and also pedagogical strategies in relation to it. Analysis to date has resulted in a refinement of the conceptual structure of possibility thinking in relation to these older children.

As shown in Figure 6, the analysis reveals that *immersion* at both an individual and a collaborative level provides a context to the other elements. Much more significant for the older children was the role of playful engagement, at a level far more elaborated than seen in younger children. Despite, however, the elaborated playfulness, this stage of the study has demonstrated a lack of risk-taking among the older children. Yet, it has also demonstrated the significance of collaboration between children in this older age group, which was less evident among the younger children.

This collaboration is characterised by children at times shining – developing their own personal ideas, arguments and expressions and seeing those through, persuading others of their worth – what might be described as a dialectic approach to learning with others. At other times the collaboration is characterised by children sharing – negotiating and co-constructing understanding and meaning together, with multiple voices and perspectives in the mix of working together – what might be described as a dialogic approach.

The study reveals that in episodes of shining and sharing, children are deeply absorbed in what they are doing, and both ways of working together are imbued with reflection oriented toward decision-making and therefore action. Particularly intriguing was the way that, whether shining or sharing, the resolution of ideas toward one agreed perspective was not necessary; disagreement was common between children and ways in which possibilities would be developed seldom resolved. This capacity to hold plural ideas alongside each other seems inherent to classrooms where enquiry and imagination are celebrated and multiple perspectives are modelled, as shown in Figure 8 opposite.

Analysis under way at the time of writing (Craft *et al*, in preparation) highlights the significance of the provision of an enabling context and the encouragement of children's questioning – both posing and responding to enquiry, generated largely by children, though often within a framework defined by teachers. The interchange between teachers' and children's creativity is much more evident among these older children, where possibility spaces can be

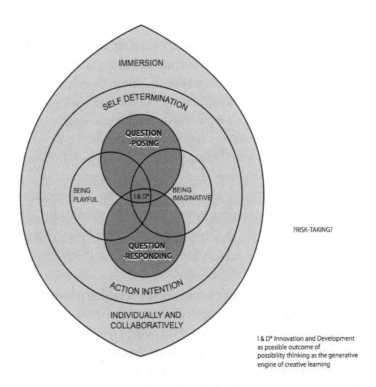

I & D* Innovation and Development
as possible outcome of
possibility thinking as the generative
engine of creative learning

Figure 8: Emergent possibility thinking framework, Stage 3 analysis
Craft *et al*, 2008 (BERA – need reference)

opened and engaged in through close interaction. These are 'inter-mental' (Mercer, 2000) territories, where children and adults learn and think dynamically together, and where meddling characterises the teacher's role rather more than the active standing back characteristic of work with younger children.

The final stage of the study (launched mid 2008) concerns the age span 4-18, and is exploring the nature of possibility thinking in the context of students, teachers and some parents, aspiring together in exploring and nurturing aspiration and evaluating their own steps toward future education systems. Working in a range of sites across England, Stage 4 of the Possibility Thinking study is focusing on characterising possibility thinking in the Aspire activity* of these schools, and on how it is enabled.

---

* Aspire is a learner-led school transformation approach currently based at the University of Exeter. http://education-exeter.ac.uk/aspire

Possibility Spaces

The analysis suggests that in these collaborative and collective contexts possibility thinking emerges through actual, virtual and embodied learning conversations which are characterised by the research team as 'living dialogic spaces' (Chappell and Craft, 2009). Such living dialogic spaces are characterised by openness and dynamic exploration, recognising and working with distinctiveness and difference in perspectives. Their liminal potential is inherent, in other words their potency for chance. Informed by Lefebvre's concept of the 'lived space' (1991), which is a continuous, disordered engagement without closures, where reconstruction and tentative reconstituting occur through interaction, these learning conversations involve a 'radical openness' (Soja, 1999). Such radical openness is harnessed toward co-actioning change, the goal of the Aspire programme; thus we see the enactment of collective possibility thinking.

From the ongoing analysis of the phenomenon of possibility thinking, what is becoming clear from the overall project is that the lived realities of young children involve direct manipulation on many levels in the transformational shift from what is to what might be. It seems that, with age, the transition into possibility may itself become a much more powerful driver of children's increasingly immersed and engaged activity. Our analysis also shows that immersive activity is increasingly characterised with age by sustained playfulness and by a dynamic engagement, through versions of lived dialogic space, particularly at a communal and collective level. This includes openness between students and between students and teachers, in each case holding ajar the potential and reality of difference without necessarily seeing resolution.

Whilst analysis of possibility thinking has not yet been undertaken in digital contexts, it may, nevertheless, turn out to be a useful explanatory concept for the ways in which children and young people engage with possibility in such spaces. Given the increased capacity to take control of decisions in play and social spaces, characteristic of childhood and youth more broadly, this chapter argues that possibility thinking is a useful way of thinking about how the lives of young people are harnessed to and informed by multiple possibilities in their lives more generally.

Multiple possibilities in childhood and youth

Given the affordances of digital environments, an increasingly clear feature of childhood and youth is the capacity to take action – or to demonstrate agency. Digitalised engagement offers accessible means of expressing such agency, or of taking action. Children and young people then are able to act instrumentally at a mouse-click, whether in relation to their social lives, imaginative gaming or in relation to invention of digital content (such as an imaginary creature, a design for a building, a piece of digital art, a powerpoint presentation, edited still or video material etc).

There are four key dimensions of possibility thinking evident in childhood and youth today in digital space which seem particularly potent: possibilities in the breadth and nature of choices, possibilities in terms of who can be involved, possibilities in learning by doing and doing by learning, and possibilities in terms of making ideas happen. I look at these one by one.

1. Breadth and nature of choices

As argued in the previous chapter, children and young people have access to an increasingly wide range of choices because of the virtual contexts in which they can co-exist with their actual activity.

In *gaming*, their choices span playing against pre-determined pre-programmed games where there is a finite number of possibilities in playing, to those where they are playing against and with other people with and through whom they can be imaginative and creative. From hand-held game devices such as PSPs and Nintendo DS, as well as integrated multimedia ones such as mobile phones, to laptop and desktop computers, to static home entertainment systems such as Play Stations or Nintendo Wii, children can engage in virtual imagination with others. What is different in these virtual spaces from the kinds of choices they might make when playing in their front room or back garden, or in the playground, on the beach, in the woods and further afield, is, firstly, that the imagination is made manifest and shared with others in a more literal way in virtual space. If a player decides to create an army of insects with special powers in an online space, they are instantly seen and experienced by other players in a way that they cannot be when children are playing in the back garden (and where the imagination of each child melds with that of others in the stories they co-create). Whilst the imagination is therefore made more tangible in a digital space, it is perhaps less unique for each player than playing without the digital dimension, due to being made manifest as visual and, perhaps, auditory format.

On the other hand, such choices, and consequent decisions are perhaps co-experienced in a more 'dialogic' space (Ravenscroft *et al*, 2007; Wegerif, 2006) than in actual play, and enacted in a mouse click. A further feature of such imaginative digital choices is the way they can be reversed just as quickly as they are first made. And of course the decisions made may affect many other (perhaps thousands) of players instantly, and so the reach of choices is much greater than in an actual play space.

In digital gaming, the nature of choices available to children and young people enable visible and reversible dialogic collaboration, which can reach into a large community. But the choices available are often marketised so that they are harnessed to products or experiences which are purchased. Most virtual games are themselves subscription products, so children and young people are aware of the price of their choices in a different way from play choices in the front room, playground or park. Being thus targeted directly as consumers, children's digital play becomes something they seek agency over as consumers, introducing consumer choice into play in ways distinct from other kinds of gaming or play.

An aspect of the consumer world that can be thus entered into by children and young people is that the consumer experience itself is at once everywhere and nowhere. For players located in China, South Africa, Ireland, Taiwan or USA, the landscape of consumer experience is the same: a ubiquitous Westernised consumer world, which reaches into homes and minds the world over and yet is at the same time entirely virtual. As a consequence, the landscape of con-sumer experience is both larger than the individual imagination yet simul-taneously restricted by its Westernised and ubiquitous framing.

So choices made by children and young people in digital gaming are also marketised and globalised. And, whilst they are in some ways potentially huge choices in terms of their reach, their scope exists within the framework of the game and then in the consumer marketplace. So possibility-broad questions are limited by these game and marketplace frameworks and therefore the scope of what children and young people pose questions and make choices about is self-limited in this way. Yet it seems that asking themselves 'what if?' is very much embedded in the blood and guts of digital game playing.

In *social networking*, choices available extend well beyond one's own im-mediate friendship and contact circles. Social networking sites such as Bebo and Facebook enable people, particularly young people, to keep in touch not only with each other but with friends, so creating a much greater social net-working capacity than can be accessed through being with peers at school, going shopping on the High Street or engaging in sports or leisure activities which involve others. Choices can span far across the globe in terms of whom to befriend, whom to share information with, and how to connect.

And in *content generation*, the tools available to children and young people are diverse. They range from software designed to enable image and sound generation, recording and manipulation to programmes designed to enable the addition of a play piece in a game, or the communication of ideas in a presentation through, for example, Powerpoint. Children and young people face a wide spectrum of choices about what they want to make and how. And the culture of digital engagement encourages the generating of content as a means of communication between people, with a far greater emphasis on the integration of sound, animated movement and image than in previous generations. Jewitt (2002, 2005) acknowledges both the opportunities and the challenges that are posed by the multi-modal literacy which children and young people are therefore engaged in.

Overall, then, choices faced by children and young people in the virtual dimensions of their lives in terms of what and how to engage and with whom, are diverse, despite some limitations. And perhaps what is most striking is that access to such choices is broadening by the day.

2. Possibility thinking with others
Digital environments, then, can offer children and young people multiple opportunities and many possibilities for who can be involved in play, work and learning activities. The democracy and accessibility of gaming, social networking and content generation through both hand-held and fixed technology mean that children and young people can exercise possibility thinking with ease about whom they engage with – with their opportunities ranging from 'possibility broad' (where the possibilities are very open) to 'possibility narrow' (where the options are in some way or ways restricted).

Work in the gaming industry, in particular to explore how embodied and digital experience can collide in playful spaces, is beginning to offer some intriguing combinations. At the time of writing, Microsoft was working on Project Natal, a concept for Xbox, a controller-free gaming and entertainment system. Here the player is able to interact with a virtual player through voice and whole-body movement and, through use of an unobtrusive scanner, actual artefacts can become part of the virtual game world. Such experiments with augmented reality, in which engagement is partly virtual and partly actual, offer the player ways of interacting with a virtual agent who can perceive and react to both the virtual and the actual world. In the context of education, such opportunities to engage with an 'embodied conversational agent', or ECA, may be both motivational and accessible (Wiendl *et al*, 2007).

It is important, as Buckingham notes (2006), to acknowledge differences be-tween categories of children and young people, especially in terms of social class and gender. For example, Livingstone and Bober (2004) found that home internet access for middle-class children in England at the time was 88 per cent, whereas for working-class children it was only 61 per cent. Other (albeit historical) studies suggest a gender imbalance, with boys having greater access to computers, spending more time online and being more interested in doing so (eg Cupitt and Stockbridge, 1996; Jessen, 1999; Living-stone and Bovill, 1999). Indeed computer games are often labelled both by children and by analysts as toys for the boys. Implications of this imbalance include potential impact on employability (Cassell and Jenkins, 1998).

The whole story is not simply about access, however. Whilst access to digital opportunities is increasingly widely available through public spaces such as libraries and schools as well as in the home for those with greater resources, it is the *nature of interaction* online that is increasingly significant; or what Jenkins (2006a) calls participation. Jenkins draws our attention to what he calls the 'participation gap' (2006:23), by which he means not availability but the participatory culture which accompanies skilful mastery of digital com-munication, whether through social networking, gaming or content-genera-tion. And a focus on participation, as opposed to access, evokes a very dif-ferent set of concerns. As he puts it: 'as long as the focus remains on access, reform remains focused on technologies; as soon as we begin to talk about participation, the emphasis shifts to cultural protocols and practices' (2006: 23). Chapter 6 of this book explores dimensions of participation; this chapter considers aspects of possibilities that are open to children and young people, and the surrounding ethos that enables possibility thinking.

Mirroring other social research including the most recent core research work on possibility thinking discussed above, some work focuses on the home con-text and explores what is significant in how children and young people engage online. This research suggests that the ethos and values in the home are very important in relation to the kinds of activities children and young people engage with online. Snyder *et al* (2004), for example, and later Peter and Valkenburg (2006a), showed in a study of Dutch 13-16 year olds that with the same degree of access to ICT, disadvantaged families and affluent families used the technology in different ways – lending support to the concept of 'digital differentiation' in contrast to that of the 'digital divide' (*ibid*:1). Peter and Valkenburg (2006a) report that the more affluent and educated they were, the more parents used the internet for both social activities and information, whereas the lower status the background, the more likely it was that children would use the internet for entertainment.

Equally, personality and gender may be significant in determining perceptions of digital environments and possibilities. Peter and Valbenburg (2006b) report, from a study of how teenagers perceive the reciprocity, depth, breadth and controllability of online communication compared with face to face communication, that younger, lonely and socially anxious teenagers place higher value on the control inherent in digital communication, and that boys recognise greater reciprocity, depth and breadth in this form of communication than girls do. Their study also revealed that those who had most need for affiliation regarded digital communication as offering greater depth.

In addition to socio-economic factors which may influence how children and young people experience the possibilities, the expanding ubiquity of virtual media for learning, playing and working, and especially the increased convergence of hardware and software into portable devices, raise questions as to how degrees of possibility thinking in virtual spaces may develop over time. For, whilst use of digital environments is not universal for all children and young people, the rapidly increasing inclusion of digital opportunities in the lives of children and young people means that a longer reach is built into assumptions made in and beyond such environments about possibilities for involvement. Young people in the early 21st century assume that they may equally well play or socialise with known others from school or other face to face contact spaces, as with people living in another part of the world, who may be experimenting with who they are in terms of, say, gender or age (Smith and Curtin, 1988; Turkle, 1995). Possibilities within gaming include playing with or against entirely fictional and digitalised characters, from virtual pets to hero and super-hero characters, to those derived from other media such as film, to creatures or beings actually created by the player or by others. An example of this latter playmate is the online game, 'Spore' which provides an ecosystem in which players invent creatures with specific characteristics, which live and battle alongside the inventions of other players.

3. Learning by doing and doing by learning
The digital environment is a space which offers many possibilities for learning by doing and doing by learning. In other words, it is a space where projects and ideas can be generated and developed and where mistakes can be made and learned from; it is a space where generating content, such as still or moving images, an animation, a blog piece, an email, an avatar or an artefact in a virtual world, is informed by learning – and *vice-versa*. Learning in the

digital context can be understood as performance (Squire, 2006), in that through integrated contextualised play, networking and content generating, children and young people demonstrate their understanding through performance.

The involvement of so many children and young people in digital media spaces suggests these elicit high motivation. The extent to which this is due to the potential for personal agency, the reward structures and nature of pleasure inherent in different kinds of spaces, and how much it is possible to find and own a personal voice in these spaces is becoming clearer. Inherent in online digital games, for example, is an assumption of interaction with a social and material world embedded in a process of open and closed problem solving, both of which involve participation in 'distributed social organisations' which are often self-organised (Squire, 2006:22). Indeed, most players of digital games describe the experience as a social experience and as offering opportunities to connect with friends (Johnson, 2005) in 'possibility spaces' (Squire 2006:20). Games are designed to provide immersive experience with friends, affinity groups and family, begging questions for some (eg Squires, 2006) about how far educational contexts could learn from such design, for example where students might be offered more enticing opportunities to negotiate and work in teams.

Initial studies of social networking by children and young people suggest that social networking websites offer motivational opportunities to socialise within a defined space, and they are used in similar ways in actual public spaces such as parks or shopping malls. An ethnographic study of American youth (Boyd, 2007) suggests a conscious recognition among young people of characteristics of these settings, ie persistence, replicability, searchability and invisible audiences. This reinforced findings from an earlier study of 11-16 year olds in England (Valentine and Holloway, 2002) which documented ways in which virtual and actual social engagement are mutually constituted. The young people in this study incorporated aspects of their virtual worlds into their actual worlds and *vice-versa*.

Recent investigation of social networking behaviours of young people in North America suggests that social possibilities that emerge in and through digital social networks are defined by the educational level of parents, and by ethnicity, with site populations delineated by distinctive populations (Hargittal, 2007), suggesting differentiated motivation.

4. Making ideas happen

When we make decisions outside a digital environment, these are usually made with reference to others, even if we do not recognise this. For our ideas are both prompted and informed by what we know. This in turn is the result of our active engagement with the culture/s in which we are immersed. Through informal contact, books, teachers and fellow students, through exploration of the actual and digital environment, we build up understanding of and interest in the world around us. One of the drivers of this phenomenon in learning is the depth which human beings are social. So it is no surprise, then, that in a digital environment, we find what Shirky (2009:14) has called 'new leverage for old behaviors'. So, instead of having access to those in one's immediate circle of friends, family and aquaintances as well as to school and public libraries, and to local indoor and outdoor play spaces, children and young people can now navigate personal digital access to, potentially, the whole world. And, unsurprisingly, in digital environments, decisions generated by children and young people are rarely made in isolation. This is in part because the infrastructure itself facilitates opportunities to think with others. As Lead-beater (2009:240) puts it: 'the web invites us to think and act with people rather than for them'. The reach and potency of digital engagement enables what he calls 'a great levelling' (Leadbeater, 2009:xxxv). Leadbeater's argument leads him to suggest new ways of engaging with globalisation, an idea which is discussed in Chapter 6.

Thinking and acting with others in a digital environment has the potential to nurture what Resnick (2007:4) calls 'learning through designing'. Resnick argues that when digital technology fosters creativity (or what I would call possibility thinking), it is harnessed to the interests of each person involved, enables multiple pathways and styles of engagement and encourages use of the familiar in unfamiliar ways. Resnick's research and development work at Massachusetts Institute of Technology (MIT) in the United States focuses on how to support children and young people in fluently realising ideas by using digital technology. It is established on several principles which are focused on putting into practice an integrated transition from what is to what might be, supporting *learning through design*. This entails offering active participation, control and responsibility, encouraging creative problem-solving, encouraging feelings of personal connectedness to the project and the knowledge it requires, bringing together concepts from a range of disciplinary areas, encouraging exploration of how their ideas might be used and offering a context for reflection and discussion.

Resnick and his colleagues argue that digital environments are not of themselves creative but attention to the design elements can contribute to their being so. Once significant elements in digital environments thus become possibility spaces, he and his inter-disciplinary project team, made up of staff from MIT and from two museums, argued for provision of a design element, space for the interests of participants to drive what is designed and developed, creation of an emergent community around the design process, and provision of an environment of respect and trust (Resnick *et al*, 1998).

By 2010, when this book was written, the design principle is arguably for more overtly embedded in social networking, gaming and content generating than it might have been previously. In 2006, Resnick was arguing that we need to understand the computer more as a paintbrush than a television, in other words more as an active tool than a form of passive entertainment; by 2010 we could argue that this constructive and co-constructive element of the technology is pervasive in the experience of children and young people. Indeed by now the interface was able to adapt to the user's requirements (for example, the iPhone).

In addition, the nature of the digital medium means the inter-relationships between individuals in the emergence of possibilities – the transition from what is to what might be – is visible and can be captured. And this, combined with the assumption that information is malleable (Palfrey and Gasser, 2008) in a globally connected context, means the re-working of possibilities is endlessly possible – and thus that young people are endlessly able to engage with relative ease in digital possibility thinking.

Multiple possibilities and the classroom

I have argued that the digital environment in which children and young people may generate ideas and experience the transition from what is to what might be, involves several characteristics. These include the existence of breadth and reach of choices, opportunities to choose from a wide network of co-participants with whom ideas emerge, and learning by doing and doing by learning. I suggested that these may enable a strong sense of personal ownership and relevance and therefore motivation.

How, in the light of its prevalence in many aspects of childhood and youth, is the seed of imagination within possibility thinking manifest within the classroom? The possibility thinking study has paid increasing attention over time to the social context of learning environments (Craft *et al*, 2008), social context and engagement (Chappell *et al*, 2008a, 2008b; Chappell and Craft, 2009). Embedded in the policy and practice discourse in England which increasingly values creativity (alongside the performative outcomes discussed in Chapter 2), the development of the concept of possibility thinking as emergent in social context offers a way of thinking about learner outcomes and about pedagogy. What seems clear is that inherent in the digital environment is potential for creativity; an assumption that children and young people make continual and personally meaningful transitions from what is to what might be, whether that concerns how to present oneself in a social networking space, what route to take through an online game, or how to construct an animation or other piece of content.

Paradoxes for educators

With the digital environment increasingly pervasive, it can certainly be argued that multiple and expanding possibilities are actively available to, and definable and malleable by, children and young people. However, the communal paintbrush aspects of virtual engagement do raise a number of paradoxes, which reflect the perspectives on childhood discussed in Chapter 1 where we explored the concept of childhood as cocooning or empowering.

Clearly there are technical and design issues around the extent to which classrooms may enable young people to integrate virtual and actual learning so that pedagogical energies focus on the nature of use rather than the question of access. Yet the integration of digital opportunities for children and young people to experience and generate multiple possibilities presents practical dilemmas for educators.

Some of these concern implicit values inherent in the integration of technology. For example, whilst digital environments do offer multiple ways in which possibilities may be constructed and co-constructed, it is important to recognise that this is made possible, and nurtured, in a globalised context. The global integration and interdependence of economies, driven by capitalist development, with consequent social, political, technological, cultural, environmental and ethical dimensions, provide the cradle for digital possibility. But we must recognise the potential pathologies in marketised generativity (Craft, 2005; Craft, Gardner and Claxton, 2008). Squire (2006), for example, notes that many digital gaming contexts for example require immersion in specific ideological systems.

As educators, is it sufficient to accept the digital revolution as pervasive, powerful and persuasive, or do we need caution, care and consideration of values and impact? To what extent is it the business of educators to consider the extent to which 'we-think' approaches to learning and living might challenge globalisation's shallower and more destructive faces, to offer what Leadbeater (2009) calls 'a different possible story, one of trust and collaboration built on liberal and enlightenment traditions of peer collaboration in pursuit of better ideas arbitrated on the basis of evidence rather than ideology' (p239). This is something we consider in Chapter 11.

A further contextual dilemma for educators concerns the distinction between 'edutainment' and 'playful learning' (Resnick, 2006). The former is primarily about the provision of a service and more akin to old-style pedagogy and learning; the latter is more focused on providing opportunities for participation. His case is that 21st century connectedness for young people is increasingly able to support playful learning – in my terms, the nurturing of possibility thinking. This means paying careful attention to what can be offered by digital resources. A traditional model dressed up as a digital resource (such as a programme for rehearsing multiplication tables, or for learning vocabulary) may be much less motivating than one which is essentially a gaming or content-generation space.

Other dilemmas faced by educators concern practical issues around privacy and openness, and authority and agency.

Privacy and openness
The accessibility and immediacy of digital engagement means that traditional boundaries on privacy are broached, particularly in social networking sites, where, as Palfrey and Gasser (2008) note, more traces of oneself can be left in public places online. Children and young people can socialise, play and work with a wide range of others, they can reveal a great deal about themselves if they choose to, but there are risks associated with the lack of privacy that can ensue. As Palfrey and Gasser put it: 'At their best, they show off who they aspire to be and put their most creative selves before the world. At their worst, they put information online that may put them in danger, or that could humiliate them in years to come' (p7).

A study undertaken in England by the Institute for Public Policy Research (IPPR) of how 8-18 year olds feel about the invasion of privacy inherent in connectedness, revealed contradictory attitudes. Young people reported a tension between the capacity to connect, to devise and experiment with personae, and to self-advertise (and with this, placed high value on uploading, for example, images of themselves) – and the strong dislike they felt about their social networking profiles being viewed by strangers (Withers and Sheldon, 2008). The study also revealed that dangers which may accompany such a lack of privacy may be under-estimated by children and young people.

Thus, whilst young people were well aware of dangers and tended to use the internet to meet people they already know, and despite the strong norms against using the internet to meet wholly new people, they did communicate with friends of friends on a social networking site. When using cameras to meet, young people express more faith in use of webcams than still images to establish identity, and they report taking a group of friends along with them if meeting someone face to face. The study also reported that cyber-bullying was not recognised among this sample, with the general view leaning toward 'seeing the joke' (Withers and Sheldon, 2008:6); it was offline relationships that determined how cyber-bullying was perceived. Nevertheless, the implications of exposing someone online, for example through posting embarrassing videos or images, were not seen as significant. The implications of such behaviour were thus under-estimated by the young people in this study (Withers and Sheldon, 2008).

Authority and agency

Children and young people are increasingly using media beyond and within schools which support autonomy and co-participative engagement, geared to a 'hands-on, 'let's build it' approach" (Brown 2005:12.2). It may be, as Weigel *et al* (2009) suggest, that 'students are using digital media in ways that might lead them to question approaches that are more teacher-centric, uniform, and passive for students' (p14). How do teachers balance authority and agency in this new era of capacity to take action and to self-direct in childhood and youth?

And, finally, educators are faced with the question of how far the digital and globalised context to their work and the consequent increasing facility children and young people may have as possibility thinkers, implies a digital response in the context of education. To what extent is the inevitable consequence of recognising the world as increasingly connected, a shift of education partially into the virtual? Perkins (2008) points to the increasing 'relevance gap' in today's educational provision and we must ask ourselves as educators to what extent our responses to this can be meaningful without the integration of virtual with actual.

In the next chapter, this question is taken up in the exploration of a further dimension of childhood and youth in the early 21st century, made manifest in particular ways through the integration of virtual and actual engagement: playfulness.

5

Playfulness

In the first four chapters of this book, I highlighted how the lives of children and young people in the 21st century are permeated by opportunities to engage both face to face and online through a variety of media. These are increasingly converging through a single system where it is possible to surf the web, play games against the computer or with other people, communicate, listen to music, watch visual material, use a global positioning system (GPS) in place of a map, manage scheduling and hold directories of contact details. Some media, such as Nintendo DS, Nintendo Wii, Play Station or PSP, are not fully integrated, but others offer increasing convergence, for example fixed, laptop and palmtop computers and, increasingly, mobile phones.

Chapter 3 discussed the plurality of opportunities which characterise childhood and youth in the Western world because of this virtual dimension in their lives. Chapter 4 explored ways in which this dimension brings opportunities to develop possibility thinking, or the capacity to generate and navigate multiple possibilities, in the transition from what is to what might be. I have suggested that the digital dimension to the lives of children and young people offers particularly pervasive and empowered opportunities to use possibility thinking, and thus to operate with imagination and creativity, yet that integration of actual and virtual dimensions of their lives poses some dilemmas for educators.

So far two of the four Ps as key components of early 21st century childhood and youth have been explored: plurality and possibilities. A powerful combination, plurality of opportunities for engagement, together with the potency that active engagement in possibility brings, these two characteristics of childhood and youth demand of educators a clear line on how they view their role in relation to children and young people. For, as providers of learning experiences, educators need to be clear about the extent to which they view their mission as protecting young people from harm, as opposed to empowering young people as active and exploratory agents both now and as adults. During the course of writing this book, I attended a summer course at Harvard University, which included a focus on the digital revolution as it applied to education. I found myself among a group of impressive senior and experienced educators from all over the world, all of us grappling with this question and others. Toward the end of our time together, we each participated in an exercise in which we noted down what had changed in our thinking. Some of these are set out in Figure 9.

I used to think...	Now I think...
The digital revolution was something to be wary of	The digital revolution can be a great opportunity
We should discourage/shut down such technology as Facebook, cell phones etc during school hours	We should consider the ways in which we can teach responsible use of such technologies on campus. As adults, we need to educate ourselves on how we can use these banned technologies to deepen the educational experiences for our students
The digital revolution was a concept that was purely technology	The digital revolution is social in design
That social networking was for the younger generations and that they are okay leading the journey	Educators have a vital responsibility to jump over the digital divide and help guide youth into the future of learning
That the digital revolution was not relevant to me	That the digital revolution is a critical issue for the future of learning. And I, as a future learner, need to understand better the consequences of the digital revolution to improve the ways I teach and learn

Figure 9: Changing views of the future of learning (Harvard Institute, August 2009)

This selective list of statements highlights a range of awareness among that educator group about the significance of the technology in the lives of children and young people. In each case, the educator documents a change of mind from a protective or a dismissive position to one which sees the digital revolution as being not only part of their work but as offering affordances as well as challenges – and the beginnings of a recognition of what it might enable in students by way of their active engagement in learning. What is not highlighted explicitly, however, by this particular set of reflections, is an awareness of the *exploratory drive* that is nourished by digital contexts common in the lives of children and young people, and it is this which underpins the playfulness characteristic of childhood and youth, reaching perhaps longer into the teenage and young adult years than hitherto.

Exploration and Playfulness

The drive to explore is proposed by Laevers (2000) as inherent in young children. He suggests that 'deep-level-learning' in young children harnesses curiosity, imagination, creativity, intuition, self-management, social competence, physical exploration and communication skills. For Laevers, these are developed in educational contexts that encourage deep involvement, driven by exploration or, as he puts it, the 'disposition of curiosity' (p21). As Laevers puts it: 'An exploratory attitude, defined by openness for, and alertness to, the wide variety of stimuli that form our surroundings, makes a person accessible... [and] brings a person into the most intense forms of concentration and involvement' (p21).

Placing high value on the exploratory drive, and thus on play, is implicit in European progressive theories of learning such as those put forward by Pestalozzi and Froebel and leading to the influential work of Montessori (1914), Dewey (1938) and Malaguzzi (1996). All recognised the significance of exploratory, practical hands-on approaches and children's construction of meaning. Built on by others not only in Europe but also in North America and Russia, by researchers of learning such as Piaget (1930, 1951), Bruner (1960, 1995) and Vygotsky (1976, 1978), approaches to learning and teaching in classrooms, especially with the youngest children, have been influenced by the assumption that children actively explore their environments with encouragement and support from adults, constructing meaning in context. Thus, provision of hands-on, active learning opportunities which encompass playfulness, together with careful observation and thoughtful response, intervention and stimulus by education practitioners working with young children is now the norm in many Western classrooms, built on theories developed by

Piaget, Bruner, Vygotsky and others. In this way, intersubjective spaces are developed between players (Wood, 2008).

Play at risk in education...
In many Western contexts, however, this constructivist approach to learning, where children actively make meaning (and thus construct knowledge) in social and cultural context, is eroded as children reach the middle years of primary education, and as the goals of the curriculum becomes much more of a driver. In many parts of the world, although not in the United States, introduction of national curricula alongside universalisation of education has led to a codifying of what subject areas are seen as important. Weigel *et al* (2009) document increasing emphasis on science, technology, engineering and mathematics (known as 'STEM' subjects); this is a global trend.

The privileging of children's exploratory drive is frequently overshadowed, then, in educational contexts, by the increased emphasis from the middle years of primary school onward, on a content-heavy curriculum, and peda- gogy which is frequently 'pointedly teacher-centric' (Weigel *et al*, 2009). But it is also the case that alongside the content-orientated, visible achievement trend are attempts, as discussed in Chapter 2, to raise the profile of creativity within the arts and beyond, together with approaches to teaching and learn- ing that engage the imaginations of children and young people.

This chapter argues that teacher-centred approaches to pedagogy, and a curriculum emphasising content, is at odds with the nature of childhood and youth beyond schools. It extends the warning from Laevers (2000) that 'The challenge for education is not only to keep [the] intrinsic source of motivation alive, but also to make it encompass all domains that belong to reality'. And one of the large dilemmas facing educators is the extent to which the multiple cultures of childhood and youth are engaged with by education; this is not necessarily, in itself, a new problem.

A problem revisited by educators
Whilst writing this book I had a conversation, in the summer of 2009, with my father about the interfaces between youth and school cultures. He reflected on the phenomenon (acknowledged by Weigel *et al*, 2009) that changes in mass media (television, film, radio and so on) have rarely been seen as rele- vant to schools. He recalled that when he was at school in London in the 1940s and 1950s, it was made clear to students that reference to films or comic strips were inappropriate in a school context. The implication was that such media were populist, unreliable and superficial. It struck us both that

there were strong parallels between this and the experience of the boy I referred to in Chapter 1 who wanted to take his phone into school and who could not understand why it was not integrated with his studies, since it was a part of him and his life.

One of the remarkable differences, however, between those days and the early 21st century is that the digital media in which young people are immersed has the potential to encourage an exploratory drive at a collective level, at a time when the cultural context is not of stasis but of massive change. The exploratory drive is nurtured in our collective understandings of and responses to seismic alteration in our environments including climate change, economic interdependence and instability, fundamentalist conflict, revolutions in genetics and biomedical research. The exploratory drive is not solely significant, then, in the learning of young children. Digital media allow us to explore and to play with ideas and with other people, exercising the exploratory drive far into adulthood. Indeed, Chan and Vorderer (2006) report Figureures from 2004 demonstrating a rise of more than 30 per cent in adult online gaming in the previous year, and a 50 per cent higher engagement in online gaming by women than men.

Expansion of play online

It is the playful dimension of this exploratory drive that seems significant in 21st century childhood and youth. The contexts in which children and young people engage could be said to be *highly playful* ones, whether they are actually focused on gaming, social networking or making content. For at the heart of much digital experience is a playful exploration of what might be.

In her book, *Generation Digital*, Montgomery (2007) suggests that an aspect of the digital revolution is that children and young people are getting older younger, ie being exposed to more adult content and engaging in more mature activity than in previous generations. Whilst this may be so, I want to argue that the opposite is also true in terms of playfulness; in other words, children and young people are staying younger older, too. Playful engagement is inherent in many if not most of the online and virtual experiences that form part of their lives. It is possible for young adults to continue to play online until a greater age than formerly. This may be driven partly by characteristics which Tapscott (2009) identifies in the net generation, in particular an expectation of choice and freedom to be and self-express in self-determined ways and, with this, the pervasive sense of agency which accompanies it and which rejects a command and control style which might in former generations have led young people into behaviours more heavily driven by obligation.

Significant aspects of this long-lasting playfulness in the lives of children and young people include extended make-believe in possible worlds, the role of emotions, the complexity and connectedness of playfulness and yet the potential for increasingly networked individualism, and finally, the role of playful consumerism. Each of these is now briefly explored.

Extended make-believe in possible worlds

Bruner (1986, 1991) writes of the construction of 'possible worlds' through narrative. He distinguishes between two dimensions of thought, the 'paradigmatic' (or logical) and the 'narrative' which enables us to make possible realities. Narrative thought, he suggests, is expressed as a story, and thus can be verbalised and sequenced, but it emerges from personal imaging (visual, auditory and also olfactory, tactile, kinaesthetic, gustatory). It is often episodic, emerging from dreams and daydreams, and its object is not the finding or telling of truths, but exploring aspects of the human condition, enabling a deep, symbolic construction of personal and shared meaning. Bruner's argument is that children and young people need to develop both kinds of thought. Many early childhood theorists have studied such symbolic or make-believe play in young children. Traditional studies have explored the ways in which children manifest such play over its peak period, from ages 3 to 6 (Singer and Singer, 2005), exploring ways in which children act 'as if'. Drawing on Vygotsky (1976, 1978), who emphasised the role of the social context in play, early childhood theorists have developed insights into ways in which children's imaginations are fired by one another and where the imaginative world can take precedence over the actual one. As Singer and Singer (2005:28) explain:

> when children use objects to represent other objects in play (using a block to represent a boat), this sets the stage for abstract thought. The child, for example, may envision the bathtub as an ocean filled with boats, submarines, fish, or strange animals of the deep. The ordinary bath now becomes an adventure on the high seas. Getting clean, for the child, is secondary to the pleasure resulting from imaginative play.

Virtual make-believe

Research by Subrahmanyam *et al* (2000, 2001) suggests that computer games can stimulate playfulness and social interaction in make-believe contexts. I suggest that the digital revolution may extend this capacity for 'as if' play well beyond the early years of childhood long into youth, young and older adulthood. Game playing online can both enable and encourage symbolic play in the provision of time, space and raw materials for invention. The ongoing nature of online games means that this extended playful engagement can develop a depth over time within a specific game or in the gaming space in general. So children and adults alike participate in large-scale make-believe games online, playing as if they are characters other than themselves, making and manipulating digital objects as part of their play.

Self-creating online

As far as social networking goes, similar arguments might be made. Whether through wikis, blogs, micro-blogs, Skype or instant messenger communication, or through personal websites or integrated social networking sites, there are, as discussed in Chapters 3 and 4, multiple opportunities to self-create – to choose and experiment with aspects of oneself in social interaction. These, too, could be seen as highly playful possibilities, which begin perhaps slightly later in childhood but which go on until full adulthood.

Thus my contention is that a growing element of the context to childhood, youth and indeed adulthood in the early 21st century involves extended playful interaction, giving expression to the exploratory drive of children and young people across space, place and time.

Playing with feeling

Studies of the brain are revealing the role played by emotion in cognition, acting as a kind of rudder to predict outcomes of possible and actual actions. Immordino-Yang and Damásio (2007) report that research undertaken since the last decade of the 20th century has begun to illustrate the significance of emotions in cognition. Studies have come to help us understand that emotion is 'a basic form of decision making, a repertoire of know-how and actions that allows people to respond appropriately in different situations' (*ibid*:7). We are beginning to understand that the processing enabled by emotion oils the imagination in prediction of possible outcomes to the possibility thinking question, 'what if?' Neuroscience is thus beginning to reveal that emotions provide a rudder to learning, guiding both judgement and action.

Play as enabling learning

At least two important implications for playfulness may stem from this developing understanding of the role played by emotion. First, it suggests that positive – and negative – experiences of the extended playfulness now open to children and young people through digital media may be significant in what is learned from these experiences. Put alongside studies that demonstrate the capture of attention with emotion and the apparent difficulty in disentangling emotional qualities of a stimulus from attention to it (Fox *et al*,

2001), it may be that positive emotional experience in gaming, social networking or content generating virtual environments contribute positively to attention and to learning in this playful digital sphere. Secondly, the transfer of learning beyond the immediate seems likely to be higher. In other words, players may be more likely to seek opportunities to engage playfully in both familiar *and* new contexts, if they have positive experiences of it. And although further studies are needed, researchers have in recent years begun to explore how online simulations (which represent reality in some way), and games in particular (which provide a reality of their own) might be harnessed to the purposes of learning (eg Garris *et al*, 2002; Roussou, 2004).

Garris *et al* (2002) argue that 'the recurring judgment-behavior-feedback loops that characterise game play... can lead to changes in locus of control (the perception that outcomes are a result of one's own control), self-efficacy (perceptions of competence and mastery), and valence (the value placed on the activity)' (p461). They suggest therefore that 'a student that values an activity, believes he or she has the skills to achieve it, and has the capacity to control desired outcomes, is more likely to achieve educational goals (p461). Roussou (2004), studying the immersive environments of virtual reality, suggests that the characteristics of interactivity and narrative are important elements in the enjoyment experienced by children in online games, together with the capacity to create both presence and illusion. Ritterfield and Weber (2006:401) add to this the significance of what they call the 'intelligent reactions' of video games, in particular where the video takes a player's history into account. This could also be said of social networking sites where histories are recorded, and where the system itself remembers some aspects of participants' lives and personae.

Feeling our way with difficulty

Such studies of the role of emotions in digital play highlight challenges. For example, possible gender differences, the problems and ethics of colonising the voluntary playful territory of children and young people, differences in the ways that players perceive games in terms of their relationship to reality, and the relationships between game choices and developmental status. It seems that, for many students, transfer does not necessarily occur unless explicit links are made between one and the other. High amounts of game-playing online may correlate with poor educational achievement (Gentile, Lynch, Linder, and Walsh, 2004; Lieberman, Chaffee, and Roberts, 1988) particularly where the content of games is violent and where parental controls and involvement are absent. However, there is also evidence that games in particular can be tailored to enhance socio-emotional and behavioural skills and also cognitive and metacognitive ones (Ritterfield and Weber, 2006). For it seems that gaming opportunities do harness enjoyment, high involvement, and thus intrinsic motivation.

And, as Immordino-Yang and Damásio (2007) point out, since the studies demonstrate that 'aspects of cognition that we recruit most heavily in schools, namely learning, attention, memory, decision making and social functioning, are both profoundly affected by and subsumed within the processes of emotion', a way of clustering these processes would be to think of them as aspects of *emotional thought*' [original italics] (Immordino-Yang and Damásio, 2007:3). What the studies are telling us is that emotion and thought are inter-twined. Work with people who have sustained brain damage has led to the conclusion that reasoning can become flawed when emotional and social considerations have been compromised (Damásio, Grabowski, Frank, Galaburda and Damásio, 1994; Damásio, Tranel and Damásio, 1990 and 1991). In other words, rational thought and logical reasoning depend on emotional stability in order to be used appropriately and usefully. The concept of emotional thought recognises a large overlap between emotion and cognition. Whilst understanding that learning occurs in a social context is not new, what is new is, as Immordino-Yang and Damásio (2007) put it, the light shed on the 'nested relationships between emotion, cognition, decision making and social functioning' (*ibid*:9). It gives us greater insight into why and how it is possible for children and young people to apply learning from one sphere to another.

The overall message from this neuroscientific work for education is that 'When we as educators fail to appreciate the importance of students' emotions, we fail to appreciate a critical force in students' learning... in fact... we fail to appreciate the very reason that students learn at all' (Immordino-Yang and Damásio, 2007:9). Building from this, my thesis here is that online spaces – gaming, social networking, content generating – are both engaging and appealing by the emotional and social elements. They contrast greatly with what schools can currently provide in this way in being both more personal and more powerful (and therefore more dangerous) at the same time. Schools, on the other hand, tend to problematise and belittle the emotional value experienced through this enticing element of reality by many children and young people. By banning mobile phones and other hand held devices, putting up firewalls, rejecting personal laptops and seeing teachers and other adults in schools as gatekeepers to digital realities, schools may actually or at least appear to reject the online experiences of children and young people as irrelevant and potentially worthless in relation to learning. Such behaviour contributes to the deepening 'relevance gap' (Perkins, 2008) perceived by young people between school and out of school life. Stripped of media and characteristics of media which motivate, many young people simply walk away. In the United States, one third of all young people do not complete high school (Barton, 2005).

Fragmentation and reconstruction?

Although the significance of emotions in learning is challenged by some (eg Furedi, 2009, who argues that the infusion of emotions into education is insidious and inappropriate in creating pseudo 'therapeutic cultures' in schools and denying the key goal of schools which is to transmit culture), it seems to me that neuroscience may provide some explanatory power to the wheel-spin of student disengagement in education. Granted, Furedi's critique of the highly individualised, and marketised world of the early 21st century does alert us to the problems of uncritical acceptance in education of development-orientated globalisation (which I and others have critiqued elsewhere; see for example Craft, 2005; Craft *et al*, 2008). However, Furedi's view that education should not bother itself with the emotions not only ignores evidence from neuroscience about the nature of learning discussed briefly here, but it also implies a hierarchical, command and control model of educating, sidestepping the impact that the web-based capacity for mass innovation (Leadbeater, 2009 and Shirky, 2008) could have on the goals we desire in education.

Given a playfully connected global population, goals in education might begin to reflect a much more open-access style of collective engagement; what Surowiecki (2005:xiv) calls 'the wisdom of crowds'. Surowiecki argues that, given a diverse population, each member of which is making independent decisions which draw on local and specialist knowledge, together with some kind of aggregating system, private views can be turned into a 'crowd judgement' which can, as he puts it, be 'remarkably intelligent' (pxiii). His view is that such groups are 'often smarter than the smartest people in them ... [groups can] reach a collectively wise decision' (pxiii-xiv). The question of how crowd wisdom might change our educational goals and how we go about aspiring toward these, is developed in Chapter 8, whilst here we turn to other characteristics of playfulness in early 21st century childhood and youth: complexity and connectedness, and networked individualism.

Complexity, connectedness and networked individualism

Playfulness in virtual contexts is characterised by its capacity to connect people with one another, in groups or communities, harnessed to self-chosen short and long term goals. As we have already seen from neuroscience, inherent in such processes is learning which is neither 'rational or disembodied' nor 'lonely' (Immordino-Yang and Damásio, 2007:4). Rather it seems that the emotional processes that underpin decision making and learning, both nurture and rely on our capacity to engage socially and to 'perceive and incorporate social feedback in learning' (*ibid*:5); a form of social creativity. Online gaming, networking and content generating spaces can be understood, then, as building playful and emotionally rich foundations for Immordino-Yang and Damásio's notion of 'social creativity that we call morality and ethical thought' (*ibid*:7).

The complexity of play in and through online spaces means a continuous dynamic between the individual and others. Online play, as discussed in Chapters 1, 3 and 4, is frequently a hybrid of actual and virtual, in that play occurs between people but incorporates the computer as a third player. The idea of the 'third place' to summarise this special kind of connectedness was evoked by Wadley *et al* (2003) in their study of Microsoft's Xbox Live system using fixed and portable consoles, which had at that time been introduced in Australia. X-box supports co-operative online gaming, allowing players to engage not only with others present in the room but also with players linked in online. The findings suggest that for players the third place of play offered social opportunities – and that having a sense of other players' identities was important, as were opportunities to communicate through the peer to peer network created within the game and also in linked forums where common interests could be pursued. Interestingly, the demand for simultaneous channels of communication within the same space emerged from this particular study, perhaps suggesting that what may be increasingly significant for children and young people is communicative collaborative play in multiple parallel third places.

Playful networking for learning

The kinds of playful interactions that may occur in a third place may be extended by Soja's (1999) concept of the 'third space'. Soja uses this term to reflect a 'Lived Space' (1999:269) which meshes the First, or 'Perceived Space' (1999:265) and Second, or 'Conceived Space' (1999:266). Influenced by Lefebvre (1999), Soja's third space is one of radical openness, where difference can be held distinctive and present across interactions through a continuous reconstruction. Consequently reconstruction and tentative reconstituting occur through interaction, characterised by lack of closure in difference. Digital playfulness, it seems to me, offers a 'living dialogic space' (Chappell and Craft, 2009) holding liminal potential, and characterised by openness and dynamic exploration, recognising and working with distinctiveness and difference, and offering potency for change.

What we see is a form of playful networked individualism. Far-reaching social networks in parallel third places offer powerful potential for playing through the teens and into adulthood. This phenomenon reflects the distributed social contexts documented by sociologists recognising that, by the 1990s, face to face relationships within the local neighbourhood might be less important than, or at least equal in importance to, those sustained long-distance, increasingly using digital technology. Wellman (2002, 2004) describes this as a shift from 'glocalisation' to 'networked individualism'. Wellman's research group, at Netlab, University of Toronto, Canada, has, over the last ten years or so, researched the means by which the technology has brought people closer together, just as the railways, roads, postal systems and airplanes did. As Wellman puts it: 'the evolving personalisation, portability, ubiquitous connectivity, and wireless mobility of the internet is facilitating a move away from interactions in groups and households, and towards individualised networks... The person has become the portal' (2004:127). Interestingly, his studies suggest that digital communication also goes on within communities (ie between people who live, work and play in real space and time, too) and often spurs a focus on local issues (Hampton and Wellman, 2003).

In considering what this means for children and young people, it seems clear that alongside the best friends, cliques and casual collectives of the playground down the road, the multiply linked social network of the globally-reaching internet enables individual children and young people to connect and intersect across social networks within and beyond gaming contexts. Actual friendships may be tied into the same playful experiences, but what is significant about virtual ones is the control held by the individual player or networker, in choosing how, and whether to, engage with specific others.

The long reach of playful consumerism
A recent survey in the USA (Lenhart, 2009) reported that more than 80 per cent of people use websites for information about films, music groups, sports stars or TV shows, 55 per cent have searched for information about a college or university which they are considering attending, 57 per cent have watched material on a sharing site such as YouTube, 38 per cent have purchased some-

thing (eg books, clothes, music) online and 27 per cent have searched online for health information on, for example, dieting or fitness. What is particularly notable about these activities is that they are driven by consumer needs or desires. As indicated in Chapter 1, the internet offers children and young people the capacity to act as active consumers, from their own palm tops.

But this is a consumerism which is driven by personal perception of need, and thus a social contract which is narcissistically-centred. Take music as an example. Music becomes an increasing focus of this consumer behaviour with young people as they enter mid and later teens, sharing and passing on music for use on portable devices such as MP3 and MP4 players or iPods. But studies show that young people consistently download music illegally at a high rate (Lysonski and Durvasula, 2008), strongly believing that this is not ethically wrong (although they are deterred by the possible social, financial and other costs of getting caught). Downloading and sharing music, and sharing personalised playlists etc are the norm, and 'a generation has come to expect music to be digitally formatted, often free for the taking, and endlessly sharable and portable' (Palfrey and Gasser, 2008:6); this view is particularly prevalent among college-aged students. Whilst this is perplexing the legal profession (Rob and Waldfogel, 2006) and undermining the music recording and distribution business (Zentner, 2006) it remains prevalent behaviour.

Children as active players

My thesis as regards playful consumerism in the marketplace is that children and young people see themselves as active players in it, organising their lives so as to have and to experience what they consider to be valuable. Their frames of reference are determined not only by mass advertising but by what they can afford and by what their peers say to them. This is illustrated by the advice given by a 15 year old boy to the international merchant bank, Morgan Stanley in the summer of 2009 (*The Guardian*, 2009). He claimed that teenagers are keen to expand their use of free media, citing cost and a low tolerance for text-heavy media as reasons for reading news online, cost as a reason for downloading film and music illegally, and high visibility as a reason for using social networking sites such as Facebook rather than Twitter, and for using game consoles such as Wii, which can connect to the internet with a free voice chat option, as a better way of talking to friends than the phone. The boy also claimed that teenagers are discouraged by intrusive advertising, seeing 'adverts on websites – pop ups, banner ads – as 'extremely annoying and pointless" (*The Guardian*, 2009). Yet he suggested that his peers are content to forward on viral marketing since this is often humorous and engaging. The consumerism of children and young people today, it seems, is one where, although their economic spending power may be limited, they experience a sense of agency in making decisions about what to seek out, accept and reject.

So, long-lasting playfulness in lives of children and young people can be understood in terms of extended make-believe, the role of emotions, the complexity and connectedness of playfulness and yet the potential for increasingly networked individualism, and the reach of playful consumerism. This set of characteristics extend existing notions of playfulness and also pose challenges given the digital backdrop.

Challenges for educators

Educators considering the extended characteristics of playfulness and their implications for the classroom in its broadest sense are faced with a range of dilemmas, some at the levels of principle and others at the level of practice.

Principles

Educators need to ask themselves whether it matters that what drives the engagement and motivation children and young people may experience in the extended playfulness, offered especially by gaming contexts but also social networking ones, is driven by market principles. The virtual opportunities which enable extended playfulness, as discussed in this chapter, are underpinned by the profit motive and encourage consumer-oriented behaviour in even very young children. Do educators accept this marketisation as simply part of the context of childhood and youth, and look to ways of narrowing the gaps between the playfulness experienced by children and young people? Or do they find ways of challenging the assumptions of acquisition, development and global degradation – even the capacity to use electricity to be online – which accompany this extended playful reach? Yet education in the Western world is traditionally concerned with issues of equity, ethics, social cohesion and social justice. What role can and should educators play in orientating provision appropriately to intersect with the marketisation of extended playfulness?

These ethical dilemmas intersect with the issue of who is seen as being in charge. Is it the top layer of the command and control model, where the hierarchical structure of the institution both defines and drives authority, or is it the opposite way around, where crowd wisdom is both recognised and welcomed? And what are the dangers inherent in perspectives that seek to empower individual and collective ideas, as opposed to those which seek to provide greater constraint? These are issues that are explored in Chapter 8.

Finally, and linked with this, what role do educators assume – is their primary task about the empowerment or protection of their students? Research about extended playfulness offers a mixed picture to inform this dilemma. For example, one question that could be asked about playfulness might be whether playing in online spaces damages young people's capacities to make positive social relationships. Some evidence (Lo *et al*, 2005) from a study of college-age Taiwanese teenagers, playing for long hours in virtual worlds, suggests that the quality of their interpersonal relationships outside the virtual worlds decreased, whilst the levels of their social anxiety increased, as the amount of time spent playing online games increased. There is evidence of potential for over-use and even addiction (Ng and Wiemer-Hastings, 2005).

Yet there is also evidence that the social dimension and production of social networks through online games is of prime importance to users (Jakobssen and Taylor, 2003), and that they are frequently deeply integrated into offline social lives (Fromme, 2003). It is possible that augmented reality gaming, which blends both physical and digital realities combining both computer generated data and data generated by the physical environment (currently done by use of digital overlays through mobile devices such as phones) may increase this fusion, bringing yet greater opportunities to develop social inter-action within and across the actual and virtual realities experienced by children, young people and adults.

Practicalities

The ways in which the actual and virtual may interface, which augmented reality raises, beg questions about the nature of reality. Where the interfaces mix so closely, what is real and what is virtual? Does it matter for educators? Is the role of the educator to help children and young people distinguish be-tween what is real and what is not? It may be that the extended playfulness typical of childhood and youth demands a playful education where actual and virtual blend more and are seen as different facets of reality, rather than one as real and the other as not.

Once educators begin to consider this possibility, other dilemmas arise. Can playful education be achieved within a command/control structure? How far does the educative process value individual over collective (or vice versa)?

Play on

It seems likely that extended playfulness is going to be an increasing, rather than decreasing, aspect of childhood and youth, as the boundaries between work and play dissolve (Van Eck, 2006). Proponents of digital game based learning argue increasingly for the affordances in learning offered in digital play-based spaces (eg Prensky, 2001a). Yet, in the effort to re-engage the many young people disenfranchised by traditional teaching and learning, seeking multiple information streams and bringing extraordinary visual literacy skills, perhaps the largest challenge for adults working with children and young people as educators is to accept the possibility that playfulness and serious-ness are two sides of the same coin rather than different currencies.

6

Participation

In Chapters 3, 4 and 5, I suggested that a mix of influencing factors including globalisation and the digital revolution means that childhood and youth in the early 21st century is characterised by multiple plurality, broad possibilities and extended playfulness. These are three of the four Ps that I suggest provide both impetus and explanatory power in the way childhood and youth are experienced and understood. In this chapter, I explore the fourth and perhaps the most pervasive P: Participation.

Participation as pervasive

Drawing together implications of the plurality, possibilities and playfulness inherent in young lives, it could be argued that pervading all of these is the quality of high participation in both the potential and lived experience of the children and young people. A particular characteristic of this increasingly active participation is its occurrence in not only social but also *economic* spaces. The reach of the digital marketplace into the homes and pockets of children and young people offers them increasingly powerful access to each other through fast-developing digital spaces for play, networking and idea-realisation. Participation as playmates, friends, performers, audience, authors, makers, is all possible through digital spaces which are economic spheres as well as social ones. Connecting through gaming, making or networking spaces usually involves some kind of subscription or license-enabling download of software, or through sites which carry advertising. Children and young people are thus actively engaged in a digital marketplace and their participation therefore occurs against this backdrop.

High participation online

The combination of powerful marketisation, personal reach, and relevance of offer means that, where children and young people have access to the technology, their participation is high overall. So what is it about the reach and relevance of the gaming and social networking industry which has been so successful in reaching and motivating children and young people? Lyman *et al* (2004) suggest that the technology offers three elements which encourage high participation:

Imagination – providing many contexts in which individuals and groups can engage in 'what if' and 'as if' thinking;

Communication – enabling connection in real and discontinuous time with others, both at one to one level (as in using MSN or e-mail) and one-to-many (as in putting content on the web through for example YouTube or a personal social networking site) or many-to-many (as in an online game or forum);

Cultural production – offering open opportunities to generate and share perspectives on and representations of experience and ideas, and to produce publicly visible ways of playing, working, thinking, understanding and representing which can themselves be evolved by anyone engaging with them – thus enabling cultural production.

The irresistibility of online participation

Multiple opportunities to experience all three of these in exciting ways add up to motivational, enticing, even irresistible experience for many children and young people. Why might this be?

In this chapter I embellish the elements identified by Lyman *et al* (*ibid*), to explore how digital technologies used by children and young people enable and encourage participation through:

- ▨ enacted imagination (building on Lyman *et al's* 'imagination')
- ▨ playful co-participation (extending Lyman *et al's* 'communication')
- ▨ making their voices heard (building on Lyman *et al's* 'cultural production')

These three means of participation are explored briefly next.

Participation through enacted imagination

Lyman *et al* (*ibid*) argued that the fostering of imagination facilitated in digital contexts enables high participation. Certainly it can be argued that working and playing with others and producing digital content gives voice to the imagination (Cheskin, 2002). Hsi *et al* (2005:1) called this the 'enacted imagination', predicting that all children could be 'creators, producers, and generators of imagination if provided with equitable access to digital media, human instructional resources, and technologies to develop digital fluency'.

The interest and capability in 'digital fluency' which Hsi *et al* predicted across childhood, seems to have been exceptionally accurate. And it is this fluency with the enacted imagination which is most remarkable. Through social networking, for example, children and young people can embellish themselves and their lives, organise actual and virtual events, wish for and follow through on getting to know new people, music and other media. They can invent, manipulate, share and broadcast content. In gaming, they can customise avatars, choose pathways and challenges, interactions and, depending on the game, some goals. They can act as if they are a tennis player, golfer, surfer, yoga practitioner or warrior. But perhaps the most potent aspect of this *enacted* imagination, or imagination brought into action, is the opportunity to do these things with others.

By 2006, UNESCO (Asthana, 2006) had published a study of twelve initiatives offering young people access to ICT specifically as journalists or media makers in developing countries (including Mexico, Zambia, India, Ghana, Nigeria, Mozambique, Somalia, Kyrgyzstan, Haiti, and Vietnam); essentially involving enacted imagination. The outcomes of the project indicated that the mix of digital and non-digital media content creation (ie using print, radio, television, video and computers) offered children and young people 'a sense of accomplishment and ownership, both individual and collective' (Asthana, 2006:54) in constructing media content, bringing imagination alive and into action. This report emphasised the significance of communication, not only between young people but also with others:

> The conversations and dialogue between ... these youngsters and their peers, with the adults within the initiatives and larger community pointed to aspects of participation and involvement that otherwise would not have been possible in other media and educational settings. This was a common feature across the various initiatives explored. (Asthana, 2006:54)

The technology had enabled young people to bring to fruition ideas for conveying messages they had synthesised through the media. It also offered them connection, conversation, learning and thus participation with others.

The capacity of the technology to enable enacted imagination and communication with others is documented by researchers studying gaming among children. Dodge *et al* (2008) investigated the pro-social imaginative experiences of 9-12 year olds in a gaming environment which integrated real and digital world activity. Gross (2004) revealed that, for teenagers, *communication* is the most significant aspect of the internet whether through social networking or through gaming. The technical infrastructure enables imagination to be enacted, ie brought to life, both technically and socially. This is confirmed by others (Boneva *et al*, 2006; Greenfield *et al*, 2006; Greenfield and Yan, 2006; Subrahmanyam and Greenfield, 2008a, 2008b).

The potency of digital engagement in enabling social interaction represents rapid change, from a point, documented by Valentine *et al* (2002) where to use a computer in one's spare time as a teenager was seen as 'geeky' or unfashionable, to one where it is less usual *not* to have a digital dimension to one's engagement with others. According to Rogers and Rodden (2010), users of the internet have shot from 650 million to 1.6 billion in ten years. This amounts to around 25 per cent of the world's population being internet users by 2010 – when this book was being completed – up from 11 per cent seven years previously (International Telecommunication Union, 2010). The International Telecommunication Union reported in February 2010 that globally 67 in 100 people now had mobile phone subscriptions, with over 50 per cent penetration in developing countries 'estimated at 57 per 100 inhabitants at the end of 2009' (ITU, 2010:1), and more than double the 23 per cent penetration which had been documented in 2005.

Undoubtedly there are inequalities and there remains a divide between those with high access, expertise and opportunities to use ICT and those with less (Livingstone, 2007). Nevertheless, whilst costs in establishing network infrastructure mean the use of broadband and mobile internet is much lower in developing countries than in the developed world (with only one in twenty people in Africa able to surf the web), overall the picture is one of growing access for children to potential participation in global digital communications. The digital divide, globally, appears to be narrowing, and opportunities to connect, play and construct with others, widening.

Playful co-participation
Interaction with others is assumed, then, by the technology, which allows children and young people both to experience the social environment and to *shape* it along with other participants (Greenfield and Yan, 2006). Lyman *et al* (2004) talked of communication enabling participation. I extend this to argue that the technology enables co-participative forms of communication, where

every participant has some stake in and access to what is being developed. Co-participative interaction is by nature owned by everyone.

For this is a world in which children and young people playfully co-construct their environments, their activity and even, as discussed in earlier chapters, their identity, through instant messaging, blogs, chats, forums, e-mail, gaming, personal and other websites and so on (Subrahmanyam *et al*, 2001). And the opportunities to co-participate playfully exist from gaming to social networking. As Subrahahmanyam and Greenfield (2008b) note:

> In the past couple of years alone, we have seen young people flock to various communication applications such as chat rooms, e-mail, instant messaging, blogs, and most recently social networking sites. Social networking sites such as MySpace and Facebook, have over 100 million users between them, many of whom are adolescents and emerging adults. (p417)

Facebook is a particularly powerful example of how fast this playful co-participation and co-construction can and does grow, given the technological infrastructure which can link millions of people. In 2006, Facebook entailed two people linked to one another in a college dormitory. By 2009, it involved 250 million people and was the seventh most valuable capitalised company in the world (Rodden and Rogers, 2009).

The extent and reach of playful co-participation into the pockets, bedrooms, homes and lives of children and young people is bringing with it shifts in what social participation means in the early 21st century. Observers of digital participation in social and playful spaces highlight paradoxes in what it means to be friends with someone is coming to mean. Friendships in the digital sphere seem to be both more momentary or fleeting, and yet simultaneously more enduring. For whilst online friendships may be focused around shared interests and may involve frequent interaction, they may nevertheless be very superficial and short-lived (Palfrey and Gasser, 2008). At the same time, records of social networking activity, including contributions to web-pages, forums, social networking sites, for example, may exist on the web permanently or semi-permanently and so in this sense the evidence trail of interaction and friendship may have visible or public longevity. And of course friendship online is frequently with people known in real life (Gross, 2004), so adding a further dimension to existing relationships, where the existence of a permanent or temporary history can be both affirming while also, where friendships break down, undermining the embodied, here and now, connections (Brown *et al*, 2006, Gillis, 2006).

Gender differences in participation

In terms of playful co-participation enabled by media, there may be gender differences. Certainly there is evidence that adult women use digital environments more for socialising than men do (Kennedy *et al*, 2003) and that in digital games, children exhibit gendered behaviour. Girls attend to the physical aspects of people and environments to their satisfaction before initiating the game, whilst boys are eager to initiate the game more quickly (Gros, 2005). Gender differentiation among children has been documented in terms of their levels of gaming, boys being far more inclined to playing digital games than girls, and also in terms of seeking information; older boys (14-18 year olds) visiting more websites than older girls (Roberts *et al*, 1999). Some have critiqued the ways in which role playing games in particular have tended to represent girls and women, arguing that such games frequently reproduce sex role stereotyping in an unhelpful way (Kennedy, 2002). The structural demands of computer games have been oriented toward spatial skills, traditionally thought of as strengths of boys and men (Gros, 2007). These structural demands have changed little, despite rapid advances in technology and the capabilities of computer games (Subrahmanyam and Greenfield, 2001).

There is evidence that pre-adolescent girls and boys play differently when with same-sex players. Girls interact more through written dialogue than boys, who tend to interact more through action and rapid, playful exchanges (Calvert *et al*, 2003). When in mixed-gender pairs, however, the same study documents boys writing more and being involved in less playful exchange, and girls writing less and being more active.

It has been argued that the digital games industry serves to reinforce gender stereotypes in the construction and presentation of games (Cassell and Jenkins, 2000). Thus there do appear to be gender differences in the use of the social networks and gaming capabilities of digital technology in particular. Nevertheless participation and co-participation within a digital environment arguably offers children and young people potent opportunities for playful, conversational, open co-construction (Duranti, 1997).

Alongside the recreational and marketised motifs there is recognition that such digital media can be used by young people to participate in political and civic activity (for example, Bentivegna, 2002; Hall and Newbury, 1999; McNeill, 1999) and particularly in developing youth voice.

Participation and children's voices

Lyman *et al* (2004) talked about digital media offering children and young people opportunities for cultural production through public co-representations of experience which can in turn be changed and manipulated or evolved by others online. On one level, such cultural production is an example of enacted imagination. On another level, however, and possibly more fundamentally, cultural production involves the representation of children's voices in a more political sense. For there is evidence that alongside completely playful experiences, the infrastructure does appear to offer serious potential for children and young people to engage politically through peer to peer communication, content creation, sharing and seeking of information and other interactivity (Livingstone *et al*, 2005). The study by Livingstone *et al* did also indicate, however, that although the technology itself encourages both creativity and interactivity in the very process of using it, and many young people are drawn into civic interaction through opportunities offered by the internet, the civic participation evidenced is differentiated, ranging through what the research team called *interactors,* the *civic-minded* and the *disengaged.* These categories they define as follows.

> Interactors: These young people engage the most interactively with websites (for example, filling in a form about themselves online, voting for something or someone on the internet, contributing to a message board and sending an email or text message to a website), and although they are not especially likely to visit civic websites, they are the most likely to make their own webpages.

> The civic-minded: These young people are not especially likely to interact with websites generally, nor are they especially likely to make their own website. Rather, they are distinctive for being much more likely to visit a range of types of civic websites, most of all charity websites and sites concerned with human rights issues.

> The disengaged: These young people are the least active in all three areas of online participation, being much less likely than the other two groups to interact with sites, visit civic sites or make their own webpage. (Livingstone *et al*, p12)

This study by Livingstone *et al* illustrated that age, gender, access to the technology and parental controls on access, all contribute to the extent to which children and young people demonstrate civic engagement. It also showed that whilst children and young people do enthusiastically participate in civic spaces online, seeking and offering advice or opinions, news-seeking, or organising club activities, these kinds of activities are less commonly taken up than, for example, quizzes or sending emails in response to a website-based prompt.

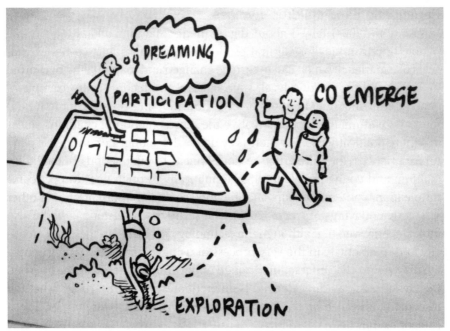

Image part of a larger piece scribed by Andrew Park alongside Anna Craft's Keynote to 2010 CELT symposium, Galway. Full acknowledgement p2, full image p150-151.

Across a range of participation, then, children's voices are heard in unprecedented ways, and participation is experienced as alluring, a means of entertainment and socialising. A key feature of joining in and being heard is the pervasive valuing and welcoming of all into a playful, dialogic space, regardless of experience (Jenkins *et al*, 2006), with implicit and explicit recognition of voice and impact. So, whether it is a forum associated with a game, uploading or downloading digital content and asking for or offering and getting feedback, communicating through MSN or texting, the voices of young people are enabled and demanded by the infrastructure itself. The cultural production made possible by technology is profound.

Participation in playful, plural possibilities?

Once we bring together participation with the other three Ps of playfulness, plurality and possibilities, we can see how the accessibility, ubiquity and personal nature of the digital dimension means that childhood and youth is characterised by unprecedented opportunities for participation. The playful, networking and content-generating spaces in which children and young people spend significant time offer many opportunities for imagining possibilities through 'what if' and 'as if' thinking, and engaging with a plurality of people, places, activity, personae and literacies. It has been argued in this chapter that participation is high in these spaces because imagination is brought alive or enacted, play opportunities involve others, and there are so many ways in which children's and young people's voices can be heard by one another and by others.

Marketised participation

The economic, social and, most significantly, technological changes discussed earlier in the book mean relationships between producers and consumers are far more interactive than ever before. Producers are listening to users and users are also producers. Boundaries between the roles are now more blurred, especially in media production. Children and young people, and therefore childhood and youth, are embedded in the economy in new ways, thus marketising their own participation.

The participation of children and young people is increasingly visible at the level of local, regional, state and other policy making. Whether it be in infrastructure, health, education, youth and community services, social services, social justice, or other provision, the participation of children and young people is increasingly valued.

Being heard

Hart's ground-breaking global analysis for UNICEF of the realities of participation among young people (1992) acknowledged a 'ladder' of participation which continues to provide a useful framing for how children and young people can and do contribute to their communities through having their voices heard. Hart's ladder of participation by children and young people analyses the degrees of participation, with the top as 'Rung 8', as shown in Figure 10 (overleaf).

At the time of its publication, Hart's Ladder of Participation led to debate about which was most appropriate or desirable in relation to community change: level 7 (child-led action) or level 8 (shared decision-making). It influenced community participation projects and approaches, especially in youth and community work and in lifelong learning. And although not necessarily directly influenced by Hart's work, a feature of early 21st century state provision for children and young people, at least in England, has been an increasing recognition of rights of children and young people to be heard and actively involved in shaping their futures (as illustrated in the contribution of children's views in the 2009 review of child protection in England by Lord Laming, 2009, and to the Children's Society report on 'A Good Childhood', Layard and Dunn, 2009), despite the simultaneous 'intensification of control, regulation and surveillance around children' (Prout, 2000:315).

There remain significant issues in parts of the developing world with regard to child poverty, with many countries affected by the fiscal responses to the global economic crisis which unfolded in 2008 (Overseas Development Institute, 2009). Yet the impetus to value the active involvement of children and young people in policy responses to economic crisis is nevertheless advocated by some (eg Harper *et al*, 2009).

Rung 8: children and young people make decisions with adults
Partnership: projects or provision initiated by children or young people, decision-making shared with adults. Children and young people empowered whilst also learning from expertise and life experience of adults

Rung 7: children and young people initiate and lead action
Youth activism: Children or young people initiate and direct a project or provision, adults in a supportive role.

Rung 6: adult-initiated, children and young people invited to share decisions.
Adults initiate provision, decision-making shared with children or young people. May involve participatory action research.

Rung 5: children and young people are both consulted and informed
Children or young people give advice on ways that adults are designing and organising experiences. Children or young people told how their advice will be used and what decisions are made by adults on their behalf.

Rung 4: children and young people are assigned and informed
Children or young people are allocated a specific role, informed why and how this involvement is being established.

Rung 3: children and young people are tokenised
Discrimination: children and young people appear to have been given a voice but in fact have little choice in how they participate.

Rung 2: children and young people are 'decoration'
'Adultism': children or young people used to 'badge' or to help a cause without claiming this cause was inspired or chosen by them.

Rung 1: children and young people are manipulated
A form of 'adultism' (discrimination by adults against children and young people): children and young people used by adults to support causes as if the causes were inspired by children and young people when they were not.

Figure 10: Ladder of Participation, adapted from Hart, 1992

What is striking is the contrast in possibilities for participation when the ladder of participation is considered in the context of digital technology nearly twenty years after Hart's work was published. Content generation, social networking and gaming all offer children and young people many kinds of opportunities to take a lead and to initiate action without having to work through adults as gatekeepers. At the time this book was completed in 2010, children and young people who have access to the technology may not need to share decision making, and therefore power, with adults as they play and connect. Their experience in a digital environment may be one of agency and capability, where they have access to the world's resources in terms of knowledge, playmates and creativity. Whilst, as acknowledged earlier in the chapter, the gap between those with access and those without does remain, there are signs this is closing, so raising the expectation of meaningful participation online.

However, inherent in the very openness characteristic of the digital environment in relation to the enacted imagination, playful co-participation and voice, are tensions and dilemmas.

Tensions and dilemmas in participation

A number of tensions and dilemmas emerge from an open, networked environment which offers multiple interfaces between actual and virtual life, pervaded by ubiquitous opportunities to generate personal content to post into public spaces. Four sets of issues are explored here: the tensions between freedom and control, between privacy and participation, the extent to which children and young people can be seen as agents or objects of change, and clashing perspectives on responsibility and risk.

Freedom or control?

High participation presumes a broader context of freedom, since it is the very openness of the web that encourages and enables high engagement. Yet, for children and young people living in oppressive regimes, not only may access to the technology be restricted, but so might their expression in using it, due to surveillance and censorship. In addition, the openness of digital networks makes them vulnerable to attack and disruption. Whilst I was writing this book, I attended a session at Harvard University on the digital revolution in which the audience and speakers were simultaneously using Twitter. Co-incidentally, during the session, the entire (global) Twitter network was hacked into and brought to a standstill, forcefully reminding us of this simultaneous openness and vulnerability.

This combination of censorship and insecurity has led to increasing use of private peer to peer networks between groups of friends, which offer security and privacy. Based on either group or friend-to-friend principles, varying from local to global in size and reach (some friend-to-friend systems connecting up real life friends only), and varying in their degree of administrative centralisation, these networks allow new people to be introduced with varying degrees of security. In other words, new participants can be immediately visible to all those participating in the private network and *vice versa*, or they may have restricted visibility in each direction (Rogers and Bhatti, 2007; Popescu *et al*, 2004). In some contexts, complete invisibility of the host of the network is important (Bethencourt *et al*, 2007), protecting providers of data, consumers of it and others who may be acting as intermediaries from consequences stemming from oppressive regimes (Popescu *et al*, 2007). In friend-to-friend networks, trust is an important ingredient guiding social interaction (Loukos and Karatza, 2009).

The use of such private networks raises various ethical issues and dilemmas about privacy, access and focus. Although a private network can offer security from a controlling or destructive regime, the technology may offer opportunities for those engaged in questionable or even illegal activities.

But for children and young people playing, learning and socialising in Western contexts, *their* dilemmas are more likely to revolve around privacy, participation and social pressures.

Privacy or participation?

Recent studies indicate that young people experience some tension between the high degree of social participation offered by digital media and the desire for privacy. For example, a study of 13-18 year olds conducted in the London area in 2008 for the Institute for Public Policy Research (IPPR) found that whilst they expressed strong dislike of having their social networking profile viewed by strangers, they nevertheless valued highly the opportunity to place personal details online and to 'self-advertise' (Withers and Sheldon, 2008:6). Young people involved in this study emphasised the importance of adding photographs and personal detail to their online profiles so as to entice friends. Having their profile viewed widely was highly valued. The study suggests that, within the framework provided by social networking, the desire to build a visible friendship network overrides concerns about the possibility of strangers intruding into personal space. Indeed, the IPPR study revealed contradictory patterns in these young people's attitudes toward meeting strangers: despite very strong norms toward socialising online with people they already knew, they were happy to communicate with people they had only met as friends of friends online, for example, being copied into the same chain e-mail or linked through a social networking site.

In addition to this tension, the same study also revealed 'strong norms towards 'seeing the joke' where online behaviour is concerned' (p6). Because of their unwillingness to recognise cyberbullying, the young people were unable to distinguish between embarrassing someone online and actually harming them.

The ethical dimensions of children and young people's online behaviour have been under scrutiny by the GoodPlay project team at Harvard University over the early years of the 21st century. Three of the areas which they identify as hotspots for negotiating ethics of conduct involve relating to others. Identity experimentation, privacy and credibility all raise their own issues. In a recent study (Santo *et al*, 2009) of teenagers, the GoodPlay team and other collaborators revealed that:

> *In terms of identity*, whilst young people see the benefits of experimenting with their own identity online and were focused on not causing harm to themselves, they are less concerned about deceiving others or being misled themselves;

> *In terms of privacy*, whilst young people are aware of the risks inherent in sharing information about themselves, they are much less aware of the issues involved in sharing information about others;

> *With regard to credibility*, young people are aware that the inclusive nature of online spaces mean that anyone can 'have a voice and share their knowledge' (Santo *et al*, p13). They are aware of the issues involved therefore in credibility when accessing information online, but less aware of the issues involved in their own personal credibility or the credibility of others who they might be engaging with (mirroring the prevalent perspective on identity above).

So the evidence suggests that children and young people may have different views from adults on ways in which high participation inherent in digital landscapes impacts on privacy (and indeed what counts as private).

Children and young people as objects or agents of change?

The extent to which adults view digital technology as threatening or enabling depends on how children and young people are positioned. At one extreme, children and young people can be understood as objects of change, reactive to change including that which is technological. At this extreme, children are seen as recipients of adult authority. Furedi (2009), for example, argues that a key challenge for educators is 'the ambiguous status enjoyed by the exercise of adult authority' (p7), or, in his view, its (mistaken) erosion. This perspective of children as objects of change argues vehemently that adults should protect children from what Palmer (2006) calls the toxic elements of childhood: 'a competitive, consumer-driven, screen-based lifestyle' (pxi). The role of educators, parents and other grown-ups, then, is to ensure that adult knowledge and experience is re-established much more firmly as a means of socialisation and discipline. According to this perspective, children are objects of adult-initiated change, and adults know best and better.

At the other extreme, children are seen as active, capable, creative meaning-makers who are able to contribute to decision-making, and who may be agents of change themselves at many levels. Claxton (2008) argues that a successful learner might be seen as a 'confident lifelong explorer and navigator' (p115). Claxton's capable, agentive child co-constructs his or her play and learning world, and is seen as having extensive capability and potential. It is a perspective shared by many commentators, including journalist turned researcher Brooks (2006) who argued, after her close ethnographic study of nine British children, that 'we need to recognise children's evolving competences' (p334).

Clearly these two extremes frame childhood, youth and therefore participation in opposing ways. The traditional perspective privileges the adult and the progressive places much greater emphasis on the child or young person. For the traditionalist who sees children as objects of change, participatory opportunities afforded by digital technology pose potential threats and undermine a good or appropriate life for children and young people. For the progressivist, such opportunities are positive, exciting and empowering elements of key dimensions of childhood and youth – though not the sole elements.

Children may experience, in the varied elements of their lives, a mesh of perspectives. Many children and young people experience greater participation at home than at school, something which traditionalists highlight as problematic (Palmer, 2006). As educators, we have to ask ourselves to what extent it is appropriate to respond to a need for nurturing flexibility, ingenuity and creativity, alongside community spirit, responsibility and vision, in ways that exclude perhaps the most pervasive and commonly held medium in the lives of children, young people and adults alike, and which may give young people some extraordinarily potent means of involvement.

Clashing perspectives on responsibility and risk

A view that sets children in the position of authors or agents of change, and not simply objects of it, foregrounds responsibility over risk, and assumes children are capable of acting responsibly and minimising potential dangers in their social and economic participation online. And yet, as indicated earlier in this chapter, evidence suggests that the technical expertise and confidence of children and young people may far outstrip their awareness of the dangers they engage in online. For example, research with English teenagers cited earlier in this chapter (Withers and Sheldon, 2008) revealed that where they were aware of risks, they were seen in relation to their own behaviour, and 'in terms of immediate, quantifiable consequences' (*ibid*:6) – ie the chances of getting caught. This would include instances of teasing others and of plagiarism. It also revealed 'lack of awareness of the implications of online exposure of themselves and others, a limited concept of the audience who may be viewing their activities online, and the extent to which they are willing to take information accessed online at face value' (p6). All of these findings highlight risks in overstating the role of children and young people as agents of change.

The findings of the IPPR work in relation to risk and responsibility are reflected in the work undertaken in Harvard University's GoodPlay project cited above (Santo *et al*, 2009). As well as the aspects of social networking discussed under the topic of 'privacy and participation' above, the Harvard team found that young people bring distinctive views on authorship and ownership. In making use of digital media to download material illegally, or to re-mix or appropriate creative work made by others, young people were much more inclined than adults to see this as acceptable. Giving credit where it is due appeared for young people in this study to stem from a concern with being caught rather than what is the right thing to do.

Perhaps the most worrying finding from this research was the teenagers' responses to scenarios that would put them or others at risk. The responses suggested highly individualised thinking (in relation to being asked to lie in a gaming context) together with evidence of a lack of agency (in relation to bullying). Again, the Harvard research brings into focus the possible mismatches in potency of medium with maturity of users. Perhaps children are to some degree both agents and objects of change.

The digital environment undoubtedly brings young people unprecedented personal exposure and thus vulnerability. Although a highly participative and thus compelling environment, a progressive perspective which welcomes this is confronted by some evidence that online space assumes a capacity for responsibility in children and young people which may be mis-matched with maturity. This raises questions about how adults nurture responsible participation among children and young people.

Participation and the classroom

We know from studies in recent years that participatory activities can provide excellent contexts for the development of creativity (for example, Beghetto, 2007; Rojas-Drummond *et al*, 2006; Vass, 2007; Wegerif *et al*, 2004; Wegerif, 2005). We also know, as discussed earlier in this chapter, that digital environments offer multiple opportunities for creative involvement. So one question which follows is, how can use of digital technologies enhance participation in the classroom? It has been argued that the lack of integration of digital learning environments into the classroom means there is a gap between the lived experience of children and young people outside school and within it (Kirshner, 2004). To an extent, this reflects the failure of schools to recognise the ways in which children and young people use digital media outside school (Arafeh and Levin, 2003). For, alongside the highly participatory potential offered by digital media, children and young people experience schooling and here adults are very clearly the gatekeepers and at school level, their participation may range from Hart's (1992) 'rung 3' (being tokenised), to 'rung 5' (where they may be both consulted and informed) if they are lucky. This raises challenges for educators and for students, at all phases of learning.

Studies (eg Kuo, 2007) show that digital, game-based learning fosters motivation for learning (although not necessarily achievement). On the other hand, internet use encouraged in a more general sense in the lives of low-income teenagers does seem to be associated with increased performance in standard assessments at school, particularly in reading (Jackson *et al*, 2006). This may be to do with the amount of web-based interaction which is actually text-based, despite the highly visual and audio elements to it.

A more fundamental question to ask is how far children and young people are able to participate in their current classroom experiences, how this might be improved, and what element mobile and fixed digital technology could offer. In a recent visit to a secondary school in the South of England, I noticed students using their mobile phones to send text messages when moving between lessons. It seemed a striking contrast to the school referred to in Chapter 1, where phones are entirely banned. Asked about this, the Head Teacher said that texting in between lessons was fine, but that in lessons their use was confined to calculators. Nevertheless, during the course of the visit, I witnessed students using their phones surreptitiously under tables and hidden by blazers. To what extent could the opportunities afforded by the technology be integrated in ways that harnessed the students' feeling of ownership, relevance, control and innovation? What does limiting use of a far-reaching communication device to that of a mere calculator imply to young people?

The presence of mobile phones in the classroom offers extended and novel opportunities for participation. We know that gaming contexts and involvement in virtual worlds can stimulate high motivation and involvement, enabling creative individuality as well as many levels of collaboration with others (Ward and Sonneborn, 2009). We also know about the motivational effects of children collaborating together within the classroom itself (and not simply across time and space) 'co-locationally', using digital resources (Inkpen *et al*, 1999) rather than just pen and paper.

But how do classrooms and schools respond to this? Egan (2008) puts it like this: 'The bad news, then – to put it crudely – is that we live in a world that requires flexibility in adapting to changing norms, beliefs and values, but evolution has equipped us to be socialised in a manner that creates rigidity and commitment to a particular set of quickly outdated norms, beliefs, and values ... the bad news is ... yes, we can all imagine an ideal society that would encourage endless exploration of possibilities. The problem ... is that [society's] homogenising requirements will always be at odds with the ambitions of our imaginations...' (p14-15).

And yet, perhaps the four Ps of childhood and youth can offer a compass for navigating the uncertain waters of educational provision. It is with this thought that we turn to Chapter 7.

Image part of a larger piece scribed by Andrew Park alongside Anna Craft's Keynote to 2010 CELT symposium, Galway. Full acknowledgement p2, full image p150-151.

7

Extending Literacy and Medium?

The challenge for a creative response to educational provision were laid out in the first two chapters of this book. Chapters 3-6 discussed four key ways in which childhood and youth are changing. Implications for education have been raised in each chapter. What is in no doubt is the need for responses which are both creative and wise (Craft, 2008), responses which motivate and inspire children and young people, and which attend to the development of thoughtful, responsible and sustainable possible futures for themselves and others. Creativity is demanded of educators in imagining and re-imagining provision. But contrary to those who regard the lot of learners as being salient horizons glimpsed by adults who are older and wiser, I argue for a progressive position in which children and young people have a meaningful contribution to make.

Two quests, a landscape and a compass

To do this I return to a challenge I laid out in Chapter 2. I argued the need to develop education which is itself creative, whilst also fostering creativity. And I highlighted three problematic and inter-connected aspects of constructing educational futures:

- is capitalist economic development all there is, with its emphasis on wealth creation and acquisition and inexorable innovation?
- what other responses could there be to social and demographic change, other than those which reify individualism?
- to what extent can and should educational provision be driven by the affordances and opportunities offered by rapidly changing technology?

In this chapter, I argue that a key function of education, however organised, is to offer children and young people opportunities to grapple with the first two of these issues: critical awareness of the consequences of globalised capitalism and extension beyond individualism. This demands imagination of teachers as well of learners.

Whilst neither the re-evaluation of inexorable development and the critique of individualism is, on one level, new, what is novel about these issues in 2010 is the depth, breadth and speed with which the multiple impact of values tied to economic and therefore environmental globalisation is affecting the capacity of Earth to sustain the populations living on it. As a consequence, there is unprecedented urgency in the search for possible futures in terms of alternative or adjusted values. If we are to expect children and young people to embrace and adopt values which may be different from those currently dominant, we might expect at the very least to involve them in scrutiny of the challenges we face, and thus to scan horizons together, setting navigational course just as the adults who teach and care for them are doing.

With critique of these two key issues (capitalism and individualism) in mind, the final two chapters of this book turn to two quests. I build a case for children and young people to have an active role as co-constructors of creative education futures and who are prepared to challenge the basis of our current lifestyles. Along with my two quests, technological change provides both landscape and compass in the project of educational futures.

And it is with the landscape that I begin.

A landscape of playfulness and plurality

The current *digital landscape* in which children and young people learn is characterised, as I have argued, by plurality (of places, people, personae, activities, widening literacies and opportunities for play, learning and socialising) and by playfulness (in terms of make believe, feelings, connectedness and consumerism). These two of the four Ps: plurality and playfulness, are digital realities in the lived experience of the majority of children now being educated in the developed world.

Plurality and playfulness highlight the interactive, engaging, enticing, exciting, and often fun contexts for learning alone and with others that children and young people experience outside of the classroom. They contrast with the much less diverse opportunities that pertain in schools where digital learning plays a smaller role in children's learning lives. The territory of out-of-school, traditionally distinct from formal education, is highlighting multiplicity and fun in new ways through portable digital opportunities. The contrast between out of school and in school is stark and pervasive. Depending on what educators value most (ie education for safety or education for empowerment), the potential for integration within schools is therefore simultaneously both more open and, potentially, more closed.

Participation and possibilities as a navigational tool

Participation and possibilities, the other two of the four Ps, provide a form of compass, or navigational tool for educators in orienting creative education futures. And it is the role of participation and possibility thinking in orienting creative education futures which the remainder of this book mainly explores.

Participation and possibilities can be charted in relation to one another, to acknowledge the spectrum of experience in each, from positive to negative. Doing so highlights the allure of learning environments that nurture high participation and high possibility thinking, through multiple media and thus multiple literacies, as shown in Figure 11.

By showing how participation and possibilities interact, Figure 11 exposes limitations of the 'childhood to be protected' perspective and highlights the advantages of recognising childhood as primarily empowering (see Chapter 1). With digital media in mind and starting in the bottom left-hand quadrant, we can see that the perspective that is especially concerned with childhood at serious risk is likely to place low value on digital literacies. Access to digital media is therefore likely to be restricted. Children are protected from risk (as

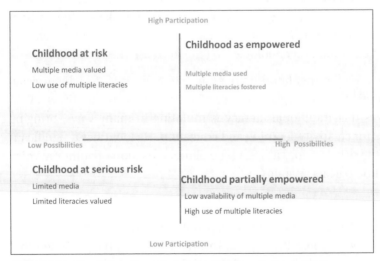

Figure 11: Participation and Possibilities in learning: how views of childhood influence media and literacy

happened to Jake in Chapter 1 where mobile phones were banned). But they are also denied access to an empowering engagement with their learning. Participation and possibility thinking are therefore low.

By contrast, represented in the top right-hand quadrant, is the perspective that sees childhood as empowered. This perspective strongly values multiple literacies, encouraging access to and use of digital media. Opportunities for participation and possibility thinking are therefore high.

In considering how education interfaces more effectively with a greatly empowered landscape for children and young people, it is difficult to imagine how the risk-averse and protective perspective can articulate meaningfully with 21st century living, characterised as it is by pluralities, playfulness, participation and possibilities.

Whilst human-digital interfaces expand how probable and possible education systems can be conceived of, these must change how educators conceive of *literacy*, and the *media* through which learning is nurtured. The remainder of this chapter explores the extending of literacy and medium inherent in the digitisation of 21st century childhood and youth. It explores dilemmas posed by embracing an empowerment perspective yoked to technology, and considers implications for what is learned and how.

Extending literacy and medium

Some of those studying the growth of digital communication have begun to define and shape a whole world of new literacies characterised by their multiplicity and multi-modality, requiring new strategies and skills, offering high personal, economic and civic participation, and changing regularly as new technologies cause older technologies to fade from use (Leu *et al*, 2007).

Researchers and commentators frequently highlight ways in which visual literacy in particular is changing the face of literacy as a concept. Kress (2003) acknowledges that traditional literacy is mutating in many ways, bringing implications for creativity, learning and education. He identifies a significant element in the new territory as being the democratisation of authorial voice through technological capability.

New literacies

The ways in which children and young people interact with their world are changing, as documented throughout this book. In Chapter 1, I noted that Lenhart *et al* (2007), in their survey of American teenagers, highlighted the increasing role of authorship and content generation among 12-17 year olds, with blogging and images being used at that point by 64 per cent of online teenagers surveyed. Content creation also involved conversations about images and text being uploaded, with girls uploading more still images than boys whereas boys uploaded more video material. Whilst it is certainly true that there is unevenness in access and use in relation to class and gender (Livingstone *et al*, 2005), Tapscott (2009) argues that a characteristic which children and young people of the net generation (net geners) share is increased sensitivity in peripheral vision compared with their elders. He also notes that they do not read from the top left hand corner but rather graze across smorgasbords of information presented in diverse ways.

Facer (2007:105-6) described this reading style as randomly accessing screen information. A consequence is that children and young people do not pick up detailed information carried in dense text. The digital screen allows users not only to reflect but also to construct and reconstitute and therefore it co-exists as an organic dimension of the here-and-now. With multiple data sources simultaneously on the same page, moving as well as still, colour as well as monochrome, powerful images telling layered, non-chronological stories are presented that can be accessed at multiple levels. They can be read in any order and may be processed in parallel and very fast – at 'twitch speed' (Facer, 2007). Perhaps most significantly, as discussed throughout this book, authorial voice and audience intermingle as never before.

Visual primacy

The world beyond the screen is increasingly visual. Attention is paid to choice and positioning of objects, signs, symbols in architecture, lighting, public monuments, exhibitions, interior design, dance, film and fashion. Whilst each of these is inherently visual, the significance of the visual in wider culture increased over the later 20th century, and the term 'visual literacy' was devised in 1968 (Debes, 1968). Whether applied to the world beyond the screen or limited to it, visual literacy is increasingly necessary. It encompasses both understanding and experience of sending and receiving visually rich information. It enfolds the capacity to construct meaning from visual communications by being able critically to understand the references they encompass and hence the ways that implicit and explicit messages work (Buckingham, 2003, 2007). Evidence from secondary school classrooms in England suggests that for students, 'the visual appearance of the text acts as a gatekeeper to the text, conveying messages of accessibility or inaccessibility, and affecting readers' motivation to engage with the text: in other words, there is an integral link between the appearance of a text and the degree to which readers can engage in an intellectual way with it' (Maun and Myhill, 2005:13).

Integrated multi-modality

Being aware of the integration of multimodal texts is at one level important for educators. However, making use of them in the classroom means cultivating visual literacy and this entails not only being able to read images in a meaningful way, but also being able to make judgements (Bamford, 2003). Given the increasing significance of the visual in all our lives, there are evident implications for learning. Indeed, it has been argued that 'the need to learn to read visual images is an urgent one that touches at all levels in our society' (Oring, 2000:58). What Oring is arguing for is a depth to interpretation which goes beyond simply reacting to images made by others or even by oneself. Going beyond this, creative classrooms of the future need to support children and young people in critical and knowledgeable visual construction, ie seeing, thinking, noticing, considering, judging and deciding as they make.

For educators, this means attending to ways in which literacy is extending to encompass 'the aesthetic, creative and compositional aspects of the visual' (Jewitt, 2008:48). So it involves embracing a breadth of media in which children and young people can and do develop the capacity to communicate and to construct meaning. Nurturing visual literacy means, as Bamford (2003) notes, attending to:

- syntax (building blocks of images, ie pictorial structure and organisation including scale, motion, depth, colour, light, perspective, balance, manipulation, visual/text relationship, juxtaposition of images and semantics of images)
- semantics (how images represent meanings, which include form and structure, social interaction with images, understanding of cultural values inherent in how symbols and representations are interpreted)

What near universal access to the technology enables is increasing technological capability among children, young people and educators in combining and making sense of visual with other types of data, for example text-based and audio material. Thus the syntax and semantics of visual literacy extend to other media, too.

A key challenge for educators, then, is in *extending literacy* (to acknowledge ways in which visual, text-based and audio data can be woven together and interpreted), combined with *extending medium* (to recognise the many ways in which information is conveyed and therefore meaning made). Extending literacy means recognising that many children and young people are able to multi-task, using multiple media simultaneously. For example, Oblinger and Oblinger (2005) reported of 13-17 year olds: 'students may use more than one medium at a time... it is the norm for children and teenagers to be online whilst simultaneously watching TV, talking on the phone or listening to the radio.' (*ibid*:2.2).

Enabling high participation and possibility

The navigational tool of the participation and possibilities axes offers ways of considering how opportunities to extend literacy to reflect extending media may encourage high participation and high involvement in generating and seeing through possibilities. Provision of socially oriented multiple media and multiple engagement offers inherent excitement, together with key aspects of creativity: relevance, ownership, control and scope for innovation (Woods, 1990). This is shown in the high participation and high possibilities quadrant of Figure 12.

Figure 12 shows how the perspective which highly values individualism in learning (bottom left-hand quadrant) offers low opportunities for participation and possibilities. Limited media and literacies, focused on individualised tasks where control and ownership reside with teachers, will hold narrow opportunities for student innovation and thus narrow, or low relevance for students.

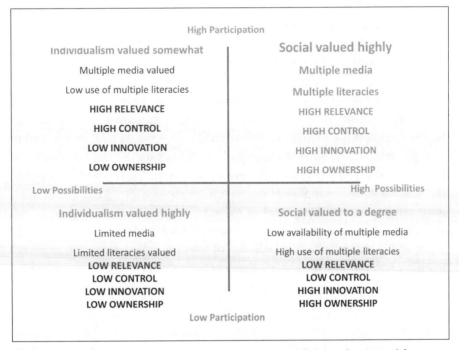

Figure 12: Navigating relevance, control, innovation and ownership

By contrast, the perspective which places high value on social interaction in learning (top right-hand quadrant) is cast as offering high opportunities for participation and possibility. Multiple media and multiple literacies enabling students to work alone and also with others, in virtual and actual space, using, manipulating and producing image, sound and text, all hold opportunities for high control, ownership and innovation and are likely to feel highly relevant to children and young people.

The navigational tool highlights strategies for harnessing motivation and so widening access to learning. It also means recognising that the extension of literacy and medium actually encompasses new and emergent capabilities in children and young people served by the new technology as well as possible limitations (Lankshear and Knobel, 2006). Emergent strengths enabled by technology include holding many ideas alongside and in relation to each other. The art of bricolage (bringing many disparate pieces and references together) can be developed with greater ease in digital media than linear thought (Seely Brown, 2000). The associated tendency to leap from one idea to the other, as one would using hypertext links (Prensky, 2001b, 2005), can be embraced as having advantages. These might include the capacity to take narratives in many directions, to make instant responses while also engaging with those of others and so raising the expectations of engagement.

Clearly, bricolage and moving fast from one idea to another without development and depth may be seen as a weakness. It may reflect difficulty in attending to topics which hold less interest, it may imply an inability to concentrate (as opposed to deciding not to) and it may mean that logical arguments are far more difficult to construct. The educator's challenge is how to enable both multi-layered construction and access and also the capacity to build and understand depth and logic. A similar challenge is posed by the expectation of being connected, immediate, experiential, interactive, multi-sensory and global. Clearly, being connected opens up vast enabling possibilities beyond the traditional individualised, abstracted, mono-sensory, local and longer-term effort-orientated approaches to learning, as discussed earlier. At the same time, the immediate, connected, social learner perhaps loses something of the skill involved in mastery of inward, more abstracted personal learning common in traditional approaches to education. Faced with this dilemma what should the educator do?

The issue in each case is not about how to supplant traditional logic with progressive digital multiply connected thinking but rather how to extend literacy and to extend medium. This means encompassing the traditional as well as the digital. Surveys of undergraduate students' learning preferences undertaken in the USA underline how much students appreciate traditional face to face learning (Kvavik, 2005). But what is also evident from research is that the extent of classroom interaction offering immediate responses to their actions which is expected by children and young people is mismatched with traditional models of classroom interaction (Prensky, 2001b).

The demands for educators of extended literacy and medium

What do extended literacy and media demand of the educator? This book has highlighted how digital technology empowers young people both individually and socially. Children and young people are already empowered by access to technology beyond schools. I suggested that providing multiple media and valuing multiple literacies for collaborative as well as personal learning is likely to encourage both high participation and high possibility thinking. However, as Figure 13 indicates, this is not only about provision. It is also about adults placing their trust in young people to use the technology capably.

Essentially, to extend literacy and medium so that participation and possibilities are optimised means high trust alongside high provision of media (top right-hand quadrant). This is directly contrary to the bottom left-hand quadrant of low media provision, which depicts low trust in children and young people to behave responsibly and safely with new media and technologies.

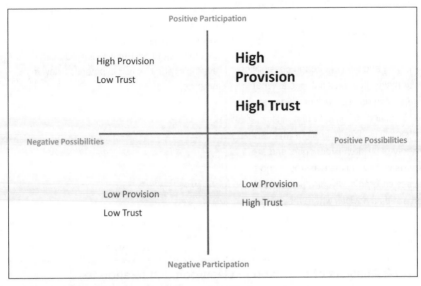

Figure 13: Navigating provision and trust

This is a challenging agenda, as learning opportunities may most commonly reflect other quadrants than the top right-hand one, in Figure 14 below.

High participation, low possibilities	High participation, high possibilities
Characterised by access to multiple (including digital) media for learning hence opportunity for children and young people to participate deeply. However, adult-determined activity and hence low trust in what can be done in these learning spaces by children. Adults emphasise individual engagement. Consequently, potential for imagining and seeing through possibilities, and particularly with others, is low.	Multiple media are valued and provided, and multiple literacies valued and supported. Children and young people are encouraged and valued in working together to have ideas and see these through. This is a high trust environment in which participation is high and so is possibility thinking. It is an empowering, creative experience of learning characterised by a feeling of relevance, ownership of the learning, control over ideas and opportunities to innovate. *This is what the navigational tool is aiming toward.*
Low participation, low possibilities	**Low participation, high possibilities**
Limited media available in which children can learn, and adult-determined boundaries around which literacies are valued. Emphasis by adults on individual engagement. Consequently, the potential for participation is low and restricted mainly to non-digital media and literacy (ie traditional writing and text). The potential for possibilities is also therefore low as identifying and seeing through possibilities occur mainly in non-digital media. What children can do artificially privileges the individual and is limited to non-digital contexts. This does not reflect what the majority of children experience, and are experts in, beyond the classroom and so causes children and young people to be perceived as novices where they could have brought powerful tools to their learning.	Characterised by limited availability of multiple (including digital) media, and yet high emphasis on multiple/ extended literacies. Children and young children are trusted to be able to engage appropriately in and beyond digital media and so possibility thinking potentially high, with children being encouraged to generate 'possibility broad' ideas and to work together on these. But with limited media available, participation is potentially low in practice.

Figure 14: Analysis of provision in classrooms in relation to participation and possibility

Transitioning from low to high participation and possibilities

The transition from low participation, low possibilities, or either of the other two quadrants shown in Figure 14 to the high participation and high possibilities in the upper right quadrant means opening new borders in learning. It challenges educators to consider how each learner's personal resources can be extended by the web and all it offers. It requires recognising a much wider range of settings (many of which may be digital) that can provide learning opportunities. It means making much better use of data about learners and cohorts of learners. It means encouraging cross-border learning through digital learning travel. And it means acknowledging the need for educators to learn, individually and collectively, so as to provide enabling, exciting and relevant experiences for children and young people (Becta, 2010).

From indifference to aspiration

Successful transition into high participation and high possibilities takes children and young people from indifference, disruption, dreaming and coping to aspiring and leadership, as work by Craft and Quaglia (2010) indicates.

Drawn from work with children and young people aged 4-19 in American and English schools, Craft and Quaglia (2010) suggest that student aspiration is harnessed to capacity and motivation to lead learning. Mapping on directly to the participation and possibilities axes, 'positive doing' corresponds to 'high participation' whilst 'positive dreaming' corresponds to 'positive possibility thinking'. High provision and high trust with respect to digital media

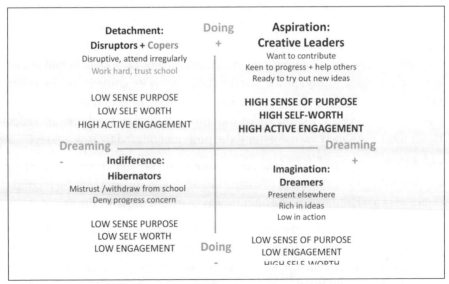

Figure 15: Doing and dreaming (Craft and Quaglia, 2010)

form part (although not all) of the context for student aspiration and leadership in creative education futures – facilitating in students three key guiding principles of high sense of purpose, high engagement and high self-worth. Other aspects of nurturing high participation and high possibilities are considered in the final chapter, while the digital dimension is the focus of the next part of this chapter. What dilemmas are posed for educators in extending literacies and media?

Dilemmas in extending literacy and medium

Five significant dilemmas face educators in extending literacy and medium:

- Can teachers span the gap?
- To what extent is personal private?
- How can criticality be fostered?
- Learning to live with uncertainty
- Is less text more?

Spanning the gap

In a survey for Pew Internet and American Life project, Jones and Fox (2009) report that whilst increasing proportions of American adults were online by 2008 (with a majority using the internet), usage varies greatly across generations. This is shown in Figure 16 opposite.

As the diagram from Jones and Fox (2009) illustrates, most online adults in all generations use email and search engines for research, shopping, health and banking. In contrast, those aged 18-32 are most likely to use the internet to communicate with friends and family and for entertainment, through downloadable music, online games and video, virtual worlds, blogging and social networking sites. Although the survey data shows expanding use by older generations over time (for example the greater use of the internet by older people to download video), there remains a gap. Are teachers, an older generation, equipped to understand the potential offered by technology?

For educators to span the challenges exposed by the gap, they will need to experience a broad spectrum of digital engagement and increase their confidence about what these media offer by way of extending learning and literacy.

This may demand paying greater attention to continuing professional development; it could mean approaching the teaching workforce with greater imagination and flexibility as to who is seen as an appropriate teacher. This would involve understanding and exploring the potential for

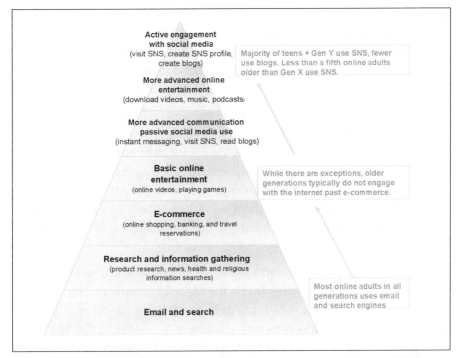

Figure 16: Participation in digital spaces (from Jones and Fox, 2009)

peer teaching and learning, and resolving how partners who are not necessarily solely educators can work with learning systems to nurture students in relevant, personal and extended ways. Spanning the gap, to foster high participation and high possibilities clearly demands that educators have high experience of digital possibilities, and high confidence, as shown in Figure 17 overleaf.

'Myspace is My Space – when I say so'. Is personal private?

To what extent is it appropriate for educators to colonise digital space within education? For whilst it may be visible publicly, such space is experienced in an intensely personal way (Oblinger and Oblinger, 2005). So whilst life online is highly social (Crittenden, 2002), it is also personal and frequently highly emotional. Is this, therefore, private space in a special kind of way? Santo *et al* (2009) documented teenagers' views that whilst sharing and connecting with friends publicly online was positively welcomed, this was seen as a peer-to-peer space. So whilst it may be intensely public space, teenagers appear to see it as clearly demarcated and personal. In addition, as Manuel (2002) has noted, young people may well prefer peers over teachers when it comes to learning. So there may be a powerful sense in which space, whilst open and accessible, should not actually be colonised by professional educators for formal learning. The question is perhaps less about how to provide enticing digital learning spaces for students and more about acknowledging the vast amount of informal learning that occurs beyond educational institutions, much of it online.

The issue of privacy also works the other way, with children and young people increasingly comfortable in contacting staff online through forums, wikis and e-mail, and also in gaming contexts in relation to their learning and with expectations about immediacy of response which may differ from those of adults (Prensky, 2001b). Whereas an adult may view a 48 hour turnaround to a query or communication which arrives at the weekend as perfectly reasonable, this may not be matched by student perception (Oblinger and Oblinger, 2005).

Another dimension of this mismatch is less about privacy and more about the expectation of personalisation. This is the capacity of students to pay attention in contexts where the pace is not as fast as they would expect online and where the response is less personal. There is some evidence that the speed with which young people like to operate means that they tend to disengage if

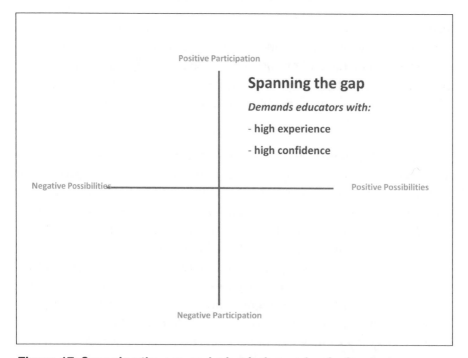

Figure 17: Spanning the gap and what it demands of educators

the pace of a class is too slow or not sufficiently interactive (Prensky, 2001b). And this may sometimes be caused by the technology itself – as one teacher of ICT who read this manuscript in its almost-final form commented, in her experience 'pupils are often 'illicitly' multi-tasking too – sorting e-mail while working; checking facts from another lesson – while waiting for a very slow program, for the current lesson, to load...'

Consequently, there are questions about how differences in perceptions regarding personal boundaries may affect students and teachers. On the part of students, attitudes, practices, learner responses and engagement, and even therefore achievement, may be affected. From the perspective of teachers, enabling children to have greater access to wider resources including other people such as their teachers, outside conventional space and time, may feel like giving away control, may be worrying, and may even be de-motivating for some. A dilemma for educators is how best to respond to such contrasts in perspective. Deepening sensitivity in offering children higher personal control, given the high social visibility involved, means heightened sensitivity to and careful broaching of boundaries.

Figure 18 summarises the qualities which need to be developed in response to the high visibility inevitable in classrooms which welcome extended media and literacies.

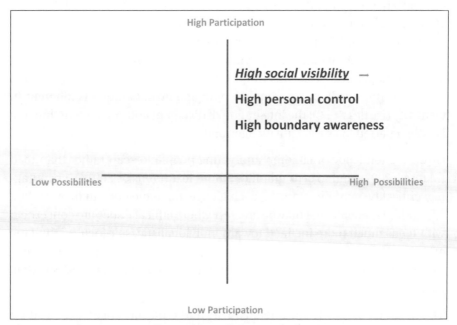

Figure 18: Qualities demanded by high social visibility

Critique and creativity?

A key role for education is to encourage not only creativity but also criticality, including critical appraisal of the broader social values of which the educational process is a part. But there is evidence (Eshet-Alkalai and Chajut, 2009) that critical and creative engagement actually decrease over time as technical competence with digital media increases. In terms of extending literacy and medium, digital literacy includes being able not only to navigate the web, but also to read critically what is found (Burke, 2008). And this poses challenges when what is engaged with is limited in depth or elaboration.

How do educators support children and young people in adopting a critical stance to their learning? This is of particular concern in relation to trust. The study of American teenagers conducted by Santo et al (2009) highlighted differing levels of criticality according to types of information encountered online. So, whilst Wikipedia was understood by teenagers in this study to offer high participation as an editable wiki, it was also recognised as an untrustworthy source. But teenagers tended to be less critical in relation to personal credibility – their own or that of others. Similarly, teenagers' views of intellectual property rights differ from those of older people (Santo et al, 2009) in terms of creative appropriation. So the high-trust learning environment in which students are encouraged and expected to use technology to learn with others globally as well as locally, informally as well as formally, demands criticality of them in evaluating their actions. Without criticality, children and young people not only confuse information with knowledge and risk superficial or misguided understandings, but they are vulnerable because they are visible – an issue highlighted by Withers and Sheldon (2008). So high trust demands high levels of skill in critique, in enabling creativity. A need for high critique is not purely a consequence of digital lives. Critique is inherent in creativity (Parnes, 1992): the integration of divergent and convergent thinking is often referred to as a 'creativity diamond'.

Given the tendency of children and young people to scan rather than read (Manuel, 2002), and to seek graphics before text (Prensky, 2001b), encouraging criticality may be more of a challenge for educators than is at first apparent. This challenge may be greatest where ethical issues are concerned, with teens much more inclined toward individualistic, self-focused thinking and awareness of consequences impacting on them personally, than to considering the perspectives of others (Santo et al, 2009; Withers and Sheldon, 2008).

The dilemma of how to nurture creativity and criticality suggests a need for educators to support children and young people in getting to grips with risks they may face and helping them find ways of negotiating these appropriately. So, rather than adopting the view that risks should be avoided (for example by banning mobile phones or blocking internet sites), which could be seen as akin to and as ludicrous as banning children from crossing roads, an education for risk view would make the technology available but educate children about its dangers alongside is potency.

Developing creativity with criticality means pushing toward depth in how media are used and interpreted. And it means acknowledging that creativity, being value-free, cannot be taken at face value as inherently desirable. Developing sensitivity in the classroom to the impact of creative action means nurturing wisdom. In other words, it means considering the possible impact of ideas and actions from multiple perspectives (Craft, Gardner and Claxton, 2008). This includes the two quests the chapter began with: the current economic system which is built on inexorable development (with possibly irreversible environmental impact) and individualism, the quest for personal success (with possible consequences for community). Critical creative activity means careful scrutiny of values.

High participation and high possibility thinking can thus be fostered through critical creativity. Figure 19 summarises the demands this makes on educators.

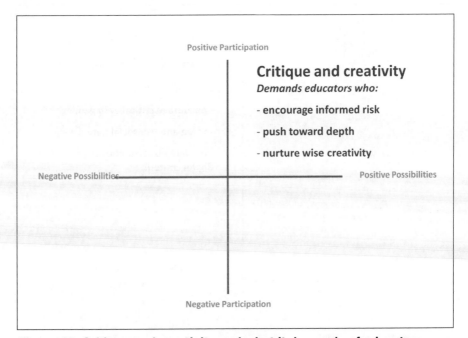

Figure 19: Critique and creativity and what it demands of educators

Living with uncertainty

There is some evidence (Phalen, 2002) that the digital generations are strongly orientated toward achievement, with a tendency to expect some certitudes in the rules of engagement. This phenomenon contrasts with the broader societal and global context for children and young people, because this is characterised by uncertainty and change at many levels including the social, economic, environmental as well as technological, as discussed in Chapter 2. Educators are faced with the question of how to facilitate and nurture their students' confidence in the face of uncertainties as well as a capacity to engage in high achievement.

This is an especially difficult problem. Activity in gaming in particular may inculcate expectations of consistency which are not well-matched with the physical world we inhabit. Gaming is frequently predictable (in being structured and offering personalised feedback), accessible (in making the impossible possible) and speedy (making it possible to make, build, create and construct, far more quickly and more easily than would be possible in real life). The compelling, even addictive, nature of gaming could mean an increasing disjunction between the safety offered by digital games and uncertainties in the real world.

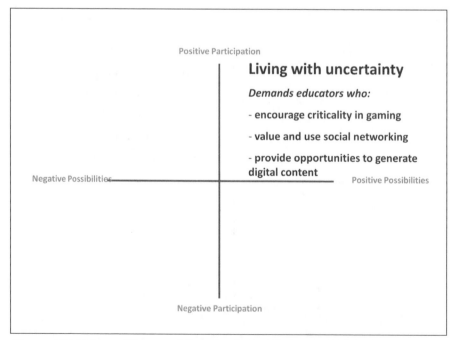

Figure 20: Living with uncertainty and what it demands of educators

Living with uncertainty, driven especially by climate change as well as other changes (Craft, 2006), is part of the landscape of childhood and youth. Social networking and also content generating, with their greater openness and potential unpredictability than current gaming, may offer means of support- ing children and young people in their development of greater confidence in uncertainty. A challenge for educators is how to integrate gaming, networking and generating content across learning as appropriate.

Using digital media, encouraging online learning communities where possibility-broad question-posing is the norm, brings children and young people into contact with contradiction, tensions in perspective and therefore uncertainty. But they are in a position to negotiate new ideas. Some of these digital opportunities may be accessible by the learning group but not by the wider public. Creating, for example, a group blog or wiki focusing over fixed periods on the resolution of distinctive issues, which offer scope for research, synthesis, argument and generating of content, could allow children and young people opportunities to develop voice, critique *and* competence to deal with uncertainty, whilst nurturing high participation and high possibi- lities, as Figure 20 opposite suggests.

Text: where less is more?

Evidence (Manuel, 2002) suggests that young people practised in spending time on the web may find it difficult to read large amounts of text and may even refuse to do so. To what degree is this an issue? Could it be argued that the new literacy inherent in instant messaging, texting and web surfing is not in fact an extended literacy but is actually undermining traditional literacy in school in a way that ultimately disempowers children and young people by robbing them of expressive and appreciative complexity? The skills needed to be competitive in this global economy are rooted in reading and writing, but increasingly in relation to utilising ever-changing technology and resources and less so with conventional books and paper. In education, technology has been linked to literacy due to the decline in literacy rates of traditional texts being connected to today's students spending so much time in front of the television and on the internet.

This may be a seductive argument for some. But there is a compelling story in the possibilities afforded by the constantly and fast-evolving technology which offers far-reaching and deep opportunities to communicate through inter- active multi-media which enable personal and collective creativity in repre- sentation. In this story, less text is understood in the context of more symbolic material in which the learner may have an active role. This is an intertextual

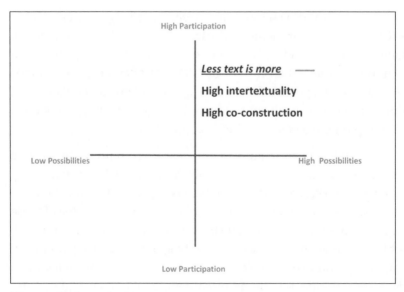

High Participation

Less text is more ——

High intertextuality

High co-construction

Low Possibilities   High Possibilities

Low Participation

Figure 21: Less text is more

literacy which affords and empowers and reaches depth in new ways. And of course the interactivity may mean it is possible to learn alongside those who live many thousands of miles away, to participate in the 'flattening' world (Friedman, 2007) referred to in Chapter 1, where access to computers, and the internet in particular, can mean that two people in different parts of the world can have access to the same information and opportunities. Thus, the combination of intertextual literacy, together with high co-construction of meaning, ideas and artefacts, offers fertile ground for high participation and high evolution of possibilities.

Implications for educators and education

In a context of a shrinking world, and extending literacies and media, where children and young people have increasing agency, and educators grapple with the dilemmas of spanning the gap, privacy and public face, fostering criticality, nurturing capacity to cope with uncertainty, and leaner yet more complex approaches to text, what are the implications for curriculum, pedagogy and assessment? In the last years of the 20th century and the early years of the 21st, governments in many parts of the world have reviewed their approaches to curriculum and have considered how they might approach pedagogy in light of the rapidly changing economic, social, technological and environmental context discussed in this book.

Curriculum

These curricula have to date contained within them elements of traditional knowledge-based material as well as an increasingly significant cross-curricular element of skills or dispositions designed to enable children and young people to co-operate with others, to be creative, critical and responsible global citizens and to cope in and contribute to a world where change is perhaps the only constant. As the world and its challenges have changed, so have the curricula – unsurprisingly for, as Claxton points out, knowledge is relative: it is 'what works' (Claxton, 2008:76). The global and cultural dimension has, therefore, become increasingly significant. So also have critical and creative capability and the capacity to think both independently and with others.

The extension of literacies and media in education in ways which take account of digital dimensions to learning and life, and which are therefore multi-modal (Jewitt, 2006), naturally has implications for the curriculum. What becomes possible in terms of knowledge is now vast, global, multi-lingual and multi-contextual, but it is not only the curriculum which is deeply affected by an extended approach to literacy and media. The curriculum made possible by technology is not only multiple and customisable, but it exists at the touch of the fingers and can be carried around in a pocket.

Pedagogy

So there are far-reaching implications for pedagogy, too. In an information-rich environment, there are open opportunities for teachers to encourage personal and collaborative enquiry, building on and extending the skills and interests of children and young people. Plurality of places, people and ideas are all inherent to these many wide open and yet structured digital learning spaces. It is possible, therefore, to personalise enquiry, to support the co-construction of learning, and so to extend the repertoire of literacies and media core to education, in novel and exciting ways. This is an extensive empowerment perspective.

But the reach of the flattened world brings with it challenges for pedagogy, as teachers (who take on the responsibility of being in *loco parentis* during the school day) strive to find the balance between encouraging learners to explore and ensuring they are safe. This is a challenge which has not yet been satisfactorily resolved by schools as they currently exist. It is in some ways perplexing that educators have been slow to respond to this challenge. This is the 21st century equivalent of ensuring children can cross roads safely, and that they are aware of danger from strangers in the playground or are alert to their privacy and rights among family and friends. Denial of the extensive role

125

of digital play and communication in all our lives is not an adequate response for educators collectively to make. How could school, or educational provision more broadly, respond in ways that both empower and equip children and young people to cope with risk?

Assessment

The digital spaces in which children and young people can socialise, learn and develop demand playful engagement (see Chapter 5). Extending literacy and medium so that play is more prominent brings into question the features and thus possible roles of gaming and simulation in educational provision, as suggested in the discussion of uncertainty. Gaming has, of course, built-in assessment. You don't get to the next level of a virtual game unless you succeed in the mission of the level you are already playing at.

Some researchers have investigated the potential of gaming for education, so as to achieve the depth of involvement or absorption combined with feedback, harnessed to key learning objectives. Exploring the potential of 'the game cycle as a repetitive, compulsive or even addictive process... in which users are engaged in and repeatedly return to game play' (Garris *et al*, 2002: 458), this research team discussed ways in which game features could be paired with 'appropriate instructional content and practice [so as] to achieve desired learning outcomes' (Garris *et al*, 2002:458). Perhaps there are implications for assessment here.

However, Garris *et al* identified a number of concerns: a documented effect whereby simulations lose their effectiveness over time and, perhaps more fundamentally, the possibility of 'violating or corrupting some of the basic principles of games – that play is free and voluntary, nonproductive, and separate from the real world'. They concluded that 'as we adapt games for serious purposes, we must be aware of this tension between the world of play and the world of work', but that 'if we succeed, we will be able to develop games that instruct and instruction that engages the student. If we fail, we end up with games that are dull and instructional programs that do not teach' (Garris *et al*, 2002:459). Such theories highlight ethics and issues surrounding the stealth values inherent in any game-based motivational material. They also open up a possible tension between what Edwards and Usher (2001) call 'unruliness' of knowledge alongside the growth of performativity (Ball, 2003) in education, where teachers are rewarded for pedagogy which yields narrowly constituted outcomes, but not necessarily mastery. And they open up questions about what is assessed, why and what for.

This tension between performativity and mastery, or performativity and *creativity* (Craft and Jeffrey, 2008) means that although plurality and playfulness provide a context of extended and extending media and literacies, these are accompanied by complacency about the values which they reflect. These values are those of of market supremacy and (bizarrely, given the social context of digital childhoods) individualisation.

From past to future

Creative education futures have feet in the present and in the past, but are oriented toward futures and cannot therefore duck either the infrastructural possibilities for learning, curriculum, pedagogy and assessment offered by technology, or the demand to scrutinise inherent values.

Given the high involvement and mastery inherent in playfulness, participation and pluralities in children's digital lives, it seems wholly appropriate that education encourages participatory approaches to learning. The compass of participation and possibilities provides a navigational device not only for providers but also for learners, in a learning landscape transformed by digital potency to one which is increasingly co-constructed and participatory (Barone, 2005; Chappell *et al*, 2008; Jenkins, 2006b).

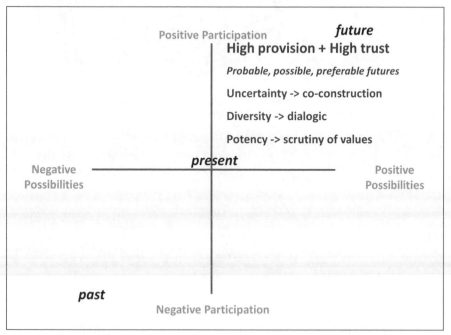

Figure 22: High participation and high possibilities as possible educational futures

Future education, whether seen as probable, possible or preferable, must surely in a digital age involve children, young people and their teachers in high uncertainty, diversity and potency. These principles imply co-constructive dialogic classrooms where values come under scrutiny, as shown in Figure 22.

This emergent landscape for learning contrasts with the landscapes of the past which, I suggest, offered far fewer opportunities for participation and possibility than may be possible or indeed necessary now. Chapter 8 begins with this changing educational landscape and considers how co-construction can begin to address fundamental issues of infrastructure and value.

Image part of a larger piece scribed by Andrew Park alongside Anna Craft's Keynote to 2010 CELT symposium, Galway. Full acknowledgement p2, full image p150-151.

8

Co-creating Education Futures?

Participation and Possibilities: grappling with engagement

This book has challenged the view that the digital medium which increasingly co-exists for young people alongside actual experience is a dangerous mash which has little relevance to, and even pulls against, education. I have argued that, on the contrary, there are four very powerful characteristics (the four Ps) which digital media bring into the lives of children and young people and that these extend how we interact and learn in the 21st century: pluralities, playfulness, possibilities and participation. The immense power and potential enabled by the technology bring with them perspectives on childhood which emphasise what children and young people can do, rather than what they might need to be protected from. I have suggested that whilst protecting children and young people from risk is a key responsibility for society and therefore for educators, this should be undertaken within the discourse of childhood as empowering.

In adopting a view of childhood as empowering, as Chapter 7 showed, educators face implications imbued with paradoxes. It becomes vital that, against a context in which children and young people have access to playful and plural experience through digital media, educators enable continued high participation and high possibility thinking in the classroom. It becomes necessary to think again about policies such as the one in Jake's school, reported in Chapter 1, where mobile phones are banned from the premises. It becomes necessary to re-think policies where children's online experiences are marginalised or even ignored. It becomes necessary to re-think perspectives on learning which seek simply to protect rather than to empower responsibly.

Fostering high participation and high possibilities, two of the four Ps of childhood today, I have argued, is not only desirable but also urgent. Both high participation and high possibility thinking support children's active engagement. Striving for high participation and high possibilities recognises more adequately what children and young people are already able to do beyond the classroom. Designing learning opportunities with high participation and high possibility thinking in mind means learning is better framed to stretch learners' capabilities.

Pedagogy which fosters high participation and high possibilities expects, encourages and rewards high learner engagement. It assumes that engagement is malleable and therefore can be influenced (Fredricks *et al*, 2004). And this means acknowledging that, as Claxton (2008) points out, a significant challenge to many educators is the extent to which students see school as relevant in their lives, and overcoming the perception shared by many young people of dissonance between their lives beyond school and lives within. But developing student engagement is much more than a matter of having good intentions.

Creative, emotional, empowered learners

Many initiatives in schools and school systems, as they currently operate, focus on attempting to improve engagement among students, in response to claims of declining motivation and insufficiently high achievement. Findings synthesised from a recent thematic review of the literature (Fredricks *et al*, 2004) suggest that the behavioural, emotional and cognitive elements of engagement are equally significant. The study highlights the need for better understanding of potential gaps between the lifestyle, expectations, experience and capabilities of children and what happens in the classroom. It illustrates that nurturing engagement in the classroom involves sensitivity to the whole context in which children and young people operate within and beyond school. This means tapping in to their emotional experience of learning and it means bringing thinking and action together. It means protecting and empowering together.

Truly grappling with engagement means involves adopting a view of children as empowered and creative and emotional. It means acknowledging their capabilities and their feelings, offering multiple opportunities for them to extend these. It means respecting their experiences beyond the classroom as well as within it. It recognises children and young people as curious, capable, powerful learners, able to work alone and with others. It means recognising they have a right to fuller engagement in how their educational provision is organised and enacted.

All of these are characteristic of the 'empowerment' perspective on childhood and youth discussed in Chapter 1, which recognises the power and potency of children and young people. But it does not ignore the fact that the young in any society are inherently vulnerable and even more so in a society with increasingly permeable boundaries.

As discussed in Chapters 4-7, the digital landscape is open in terms of space and time. Children and young people can play and learn with others who are located in different geographic locations and time zones. It is open in terms of people with whom they can interact, and their own potency in what they can make visible about themselves in spaces which are open to all and in which they may leave permanent digital footprints. In such open space, young people are, as acknowledged throughout this book, more at risk than they might be in traditional face to face play situations. Nurturing engagement means attending to how to sensitise children and young people to inherent risks and dangers to themselves and others. And it means ensuring that they are resilient in responding to these dangers.

From risk to resilience to reconstruction
Adopting a perspective that empowerment is both inherent and desirable in childhood and youth means working actively with children and young people to support them in developing a sophistication in recognising and managing risk. And it raises questions about how learner and teacher roles can interact with children and their families to offer greater scope for them to make their own contributions to their learning – and in which adults can contribute to decisions young people make.

Although Palfrey and Gasser (2008:10) argue, parents and teachers carry huge responsibility, '...too often, parents and teachers aren't even involved in the decisions that young people are making', such are the opportunities that are available to them online.

The culture of online experiences can bring a different, co-participative dynamic to the classroom and to the school if adults are willing to see this as worthwhile.

Virtual learning spaces and activities offer a lens for learning that prioritises recognition of children as empowered and yet vulnerable. Through this lens they are seen to be highly participative and potent possibility-thinkers. And online spaces and activities reframe the idea of social capital in education away from being produced and delivered by the institution, with the consent of parents. When childhood and youth are seen as empowered and potent, education makes a quantum shift from being what children and young people benefit from as a result of adult actions, to being to some degree co-produced with others.

The compass of participation and possibilities offers a new and necessary direction of travel for education. Meanwhile, the characteristics of playfulness and pluralities permeating childhood and youth are substantially altering the landscape of learning. This landscape inherently challenges educators and our education system to reconsider what is offered by way of social capital or value, and how this is done.

Pluralities and playfulness: changing social capital

The traditional argument surrounding the social capital offered by schools is that teachers and others in educational institutions offer children and young people access to a range of resources by way of attitudes, example, knowledge, guidance etc which can alter their life chances.

Evidence suggests that for the most disadvantaged students, teachers in conventional schools provide 'cultural capital' (Bourdieu, 1977, 1984, 1986; Bourdieu and Passeron, 1977; Di Maggio, 1982) which affects the choices young people make and which effectively empower them. An American study undertaken by Croninger and Lee (2001), for example, which drew on data from the US National Educational Longitudinal Study (NELS), explored whether social capital reduced the likelihood of school drop-out. They studied a cohort of 11,000 teenagers in over 1,000 high schools to determine the students' beliefs about their teachers, and the teachers' reports on what guidance they offered to students. The study concluded that 'teachers are an important source of social capital for students. These teacher-based forms of social capital reduce the probability of dropping out by nearly half.' (*ibid*:548) The authors also concluded that 'students who come from socially disadvantaged backgrounds and who have had academic difficulties in the past find guidance and assistance from teachers especially helpful' (*ibid*:548) and that this seems to help keep young people involved in learning. There is evidence overall that the ethos of the school is very significant (Lee and Burkam, 2003). This concurs with a long line of research (for example, Craft, 1970; whose work highlighted the impact of dissonance between school cultural practices and norms and behaviours in the home; and Di Maggio, 1982; Lareau, 1987).

But the effectiveness of the traditional transfer of social capital is now under challenge (Claxton, 2008; Egan, 2008). Claxton argues for the 'learning gym' (p194) where children 'learn by doing', and for discovery and exploration. Egan (2008) argues that what is needed is new approaches to teaching and learning which foster the imagination. What neither emphasises is new depths of playfulness in the ways that, beyond school, children and young people engage with technology, and the pervasive access to pluralities of both being and of being part of, which it affords them. This, it seems to me, is vitally important in beginning to change the landscape of education.

The extensive pluralities in where interaction goes on, and with whom, and the multiple identities can be developed, adopted and shared (as discussed in Chapter 3), together with the vast array of activity and accompanying literacies that children and young people experience (as discussed in Chapter 7) can contribute to the emergence of new forms of social capital transfer. Digitally enhanced childhood and youth bring new opportunities for social capital to be generated and passed on by adults and children in collaboration, rather than produced by adults and consumed by children.

The meaning of 'social capital' is thus changing and also being changed by opportunities to think together, often playfully (as discussed in Chapter 5), and to imagine new possibilities (as discussed in Chapter 4). We are seeing the emergence of a new kind of social capital which is enabled through the high participation (discussed in Chapter 6) of digital technology. The new social capital acknowledges the role of shared and co-constructed knowledge made possible through plural engagement (discussed in Chapter 3).

Possible education futures: the social responsibility of all

With changing social capital comes new and powerful opportunities and responsibilities for making collective action. Recognising and welcoming the co-construction of knowledge it reflects shifts in how change happens and enables dynamism in learning systems. Possible educational futures in which education both reflects and generates social capital could be characterised by opening up who is involved in social responsibility, innovation and choice-making. In his book about how digital technology is supporting collective and collaborative thinking for action, Shirky (2008) talked about the potential that technology offers for 'epochal change' (p321) through online networking tools. He argues that 'the important questions aren't about whether these tools will spread or reshape society, but rather *how* they do so' (p308) (my emphasis).

What does this mean for possible education futures? Surveying educational provision from the past to the future in a rather general way, we can see evolution occurring. When charting this evolution, I consider four distinctive principles which seem to be embedded within it: trust, certainty, reality itself and innovation. Education provision in England is discussed next in terms of three broad eras or time-envelopes: the pre-1950s, then a very long envelope from 1950s to the 1990s, and finally an extended envelope of possible education futures from the start of the 21st century and projecting forward.

Trust, certainty, reality and innovation

Figure 23 summarises ways in which each of these time-envelopes for education reflects changing views on trust, certainty, reality and innovation.

Each of these changing sets of views is now discussed.

Trust

It could be argued that educational provision prior to the 1950s reflected wider societal values. Teachers were seen as authority figures and students were expected to listen, take note, remember and do as they were told, and student responsibility was framed in terms of behaving appropriately within the adult norms. The dominance of teachers' authority in the classroom implied low trust in students.

Pre-1950s	*1950s to end1990s*	Possible education futures: *2000 onward*
TRUST Low trust	**TRUST** High trust possible	**Trust** High trust valued
CERTAINTY Certainty passed on by adults	**CERTAINTY** Uncertainty alongside certainty	**CERTAINTY** Uncertainty means co-construction
REALITY Singular realities thus dialectic	**REALITY** Multiple realities increasingly evident	**REALITY** Diversity thus dialogic approach
INNOVATION Innovation valued regardless of impact	**INNOVATION** Innovation concerns due to impact	**INNOVATION** Potency acknowledged, values scrutinised

Figure 23: Evolution, continuity and discontinuity in education: four trends

By contrast, education from the 1950s to the end of the 1990s brought higher trust learning approaches in which students were expected to internalise and use knowledge and skill, defining and taking on a degree of responsibility for their learning.

The shift in learning approaches was informed by the work of learning theorists such as Piaget (for example, 1955), who emphasised the importance of hands-on exploration of the physical environment, and Vygotsky (for example, 1978), who highlighted the significance of social interaction. Hands-on, active, higher-trust approaches to classroom learning evolved, it must be remembered, in the wider context of increasingly commercialisation and the rise of the individual consumer in general, and of children as increasing consumers, as media, particularly television, entered the home (see Chapter 1).

Classrooms of the 1950s, 1960s, 1970s and early 1980s were increasingly characterised by child-centred approaches to learning, curriculum, class-room management and organisation. Despite criticism of these approaches at the time and subsequently (Darling, 1994), child-centredness was highly prized, influencing architecture as well as pedagogy. Although the extent to which this was surface or deep practice was contested at the time (Galton *et al*, 1980), the espoused values emphasised high trust in children and young people. Evidence of such child-focused practices is still visible in classrooms today at the end of the first decade of the 21st century, although Galton's later study revealed persistent cracks and crevices between espoused values and practice (Galton *et al*, 1999).

However, from the end of the 1980s educational legislation began to take a parallel route and parallel tracks emerged with respect to trust. With a continued emphasis on student enablement came an additional requirement for students to be able to achieve highly in standardised assessments and public examinations. The funding and popularity of schools became tied to results.

Technicist strategies explaining to teachers how to support children and young people to achieve results, along with what was perceived by schools to be a punitive inspection regime, reflected a low trust view of teachers (Jeffrey and Woods, 1998) and, by implication, of pupils. Yet alongside these technicist measures, from 1999 the role of creativity in education was increasingly emphasised. This stemmed from the publication of the report of the Government-commissioned National Advisory Committee on Creative and Cultural Education (NACCCE, 1999), which generated two parallel discourses: the performative one (Ball, 2003) and the creative one (Craft, in press, a, Craft in press, b; Craft and Jeffrey, 2001; Craft and Jeffrey, 2008) with energy, emphasis and resource expended on both.

Thus, intriguingly, by the end of the 20th century, attitudes encouraging high trust and low trust toward children and young people (and to a degree their teachers) were *both* visible in the policy and practice of the English class-room, whether primary or secondary. And this was in spite of the decline in low trust in society generally over a forty-year period.

And yet from the start of the 20th century, enabled by pervasive and increas-ingly ubiquitous technology, we see the start of a leap-change, with higher trust being increasingly valued. Whether triggered by serious concerns about engagement in education (so a desperate measure to entice children and young people back to formal learning) or inspired by the potential which is so evident in changing childhood, participation and voice are increasing features of education provision. Emergent and therefore possible education futures may, it seems, offer children and young people, as well as the adults they learn with, high trust learning which values collaboration, participation and involvement, and where everyone is an author of present and future.

Such high trust is evident through campaigning organisations, for example in the work of the English Secondary Students' Association (ESSA), which in 2009 launched a competition for ideas for change for the future. Ideas submitted by students included better use of technology, reducing class size, extending curriculum to include the environment, economic news, ideas of British and global identity and placing greater emphasis on cross-curricular skills and ESSA partnered Channel 4 to produce videos broadcast on television to help co-produce possible futures.

Such high trust is evident, too, in the work of Aspire, a national movement led since 2007 from Exeter University, which actively seeks to offer young people co-leadership in educational futures in and beyond their schools (Chappell *et al*, 2008). It is also evident in the RSA's Education Charter launched in 2008 (Taylor and McGimpsey, 2008) discussed later in this chapter.

Alongside these campaigning iniatives, higher trust is also implied in the grow-ing value placed on student voice and participation in policy and practice underpinned by the work of researchers such as Ruddock and Flutter (2000, 2004) and Fielding (2004). Student voice work holds expanding potential for changed relationships with power (Taylor and Robinson, 2009) – although it runs the danger of complacency (Ruddock and Fielding, 2006).

Certainty

Past educational provision was characterised by adults passing on to young people and children certainties about the world, be they related to grammatical rules, laws of science or social values. Whilst knowledge in many domains did develop over time, and values did shift, for example with regard to gender, race/ethnicity and class, the pace of change which fuelled these principles was slow enough for educators to be able to convey some certitude in their teaching. The role of the teacher, pre-1950, was perhaps typically to convey to children and young people facts about how the world operated and to socialise the learners in their charge to acquire this knowledge. As the pace of change in all aspects of the world has speeded up, so certitudes have melted away (Craft, 2005).

Whilst education during the period from the 1950s through to the late 1980s was characterised by certainties (for example about key continuous content of the curriculum such as English and mathematics) alongside uncertainties (for example, reflecting changing views about the British Empire, or perspectives on ethnicity, or increasing aspiration for girls and young women), by the late 1990s a leap-change can be seen.

From the start of the 2000s *uncertainty* became pervasive. Uncertainty was present at many levels in all our lives, from predicting and experiencing the effects of climate change to the geographical and social mobility increasingly characterising family life, to the economic instability prompted by de-regulated financial foundations of globalisation that makes it possible for a multi national company to be wealthier than a nation state (Somerson, 1999; Harvey, 2010). One effect of uncertainty is perhaps the continuous impetus toward interpretation and explanation. Personal and collective stories about how things happen and why become lenses for interpreting and explaining uncertainty and instability. Framing ideas about possible future change, therefore, means engaging in comparison, co-construction and shared development of explanatory narratives.

Predicting and bringing into being educational futures involves negotiation of multiple perspectives and the collaborative construction of possibilities. Pervasive uncertainties in the social, economic, environmental context, rapid technological change and increasing digital reach, are a potent mix. They demand and enable the emergence of new roles in possible future education provision for both learners and educators, where potential for co-construction of educational provision becomes a reality.

Reality

As any researcher is aware, we each carry round with us implicit beliefs about the nature of reality. Whilst these are personal, they also reflect the fashionable beliefs of the time and space in which we go about our lives. Our views on the nature of reality affect what we think of as possible and desirable, and consequently they drive what we do in relation to other people. When it comes to education, views on reality are particularly powerful because they underpin how education is offered.

Views of reality reflected in education prior to around the 1950s were inclined to imply reality as singular and objectified. The role of education was to socialise learners into this dominant set of values which were seen hierarchically as preferable over other perspectives. Education, like society as a whole, was much more prone to consensus which reflected, and gave legitimacy to, the prevalent (ie ruling) ideology in society.

Italian Marxist political analyst Gramsci, imprisoned for his ideas by Mussolini in the mid-1920s, called this permeation of values, beliefs, attitudes and morality throughout society, 'hegemony'. As Boggs (1976) noted, the collective internalisation implied by hegemony meant that the culture and values of the ruling elite became seen by the mass population as 'common sense'. For Gramsci, the system of schooling provided a key element of ideological hegemony, in socialising children and young people into a commitment to maintaining the *status quo*. Writing from prison, he advocated the restructuring of the very hierarchical Italian system of education (which he saw as reproducing and perpetuating social difference) into a comprehensive learning system (Gramsci, 1971).

In England in the post-war years, the tripartite system of schooling which from the 1940s to the 1960s offered very intellectually able children an academic approach, vocationally orientated children a vocational pathway and others a general secondary education, could be seen as reproducing values in exactly the ways Gramsci wrote of. Although the adherence to democracy and free speech remained a vital principle in society in the aftermath of the second world war, and so in this sense diversity was encouraged (and although the selective grammar school system offered children from impoverished backgrounds access to cultural capital they would otherwise not have had), at the same time the tripartite system in education did largely perpetuate social distinctions and inequalities, through social consensus.

The approach to values promulgated and reflected through education in the first half of the 20th century could be said simplistically to have suggested a single dominant framework of reality which reflected a view of reality as objectified and thus of existing 'out there' as opposed to 'in our perceptions'. The didactic classroom stance typically adopted placed the teacher's values as those to aspire to, and perhaps implied dialectic relationships with reality. In other words, the establishment of a dominant, majority set of values perhaps underpinned classroom practices in which the (externalisable) truth was uncovered through dialectic, or counter-pitted logical reasoning. Dialectic reasoning, initially conceptualised by Hegel (eg 1975), frequently involves the pitting of one argument over another, with one overcoming the other, and characterised by a thesis, counter-argument or antithesis and then synthesis.

This use of dialectic, and domination through the dialectic process of the singular reality of the past, contrasts greatly with the multiple realities increasingly evident from the 1950s onward. Social and geographical mobility and the increased volume and diversity in immigration, together with a near-universal comprehensive education strategy from the 1960s, the changing role of women, and the growth of youth culture, meant a greatly diversified population, and therefore dominant cultural values. From the 1960s until the present day, communities and therefore schools in most although not all parts of England experienced multiple realities which jostled alongside one another in classrooms. Educators, policy makers and researchers poured energy into understanding, celebrating and encouraging diversity in relation to gender, disability, race/ethnicity and other values. Curriculum, pedagogy and assessment rapidly became more inclusive and the notion of there being a singular reality quickly dissipated as multiple realities evidenced themselves in schools as learning communities.

With reality recognised fashionably as reflecting multiple perspectives on truth, the traditional notion of hegemony was being eroded and transformed. Alongside the former hegemonic values, however, there emerged a tradition of classroom practice consciously seeking to encourage distinctiveness and diversity within a democratic framework. It can certainly be argued that these practices played out a neo-liberal agenda in harnessing education to a globalising capitalist economy (Craft, 2005). Thus in some important ways, they lacked diversity. Nevertheless *dialogic* approaches to learning began to take root alongside dialectic approaches, with a powerful emphasis on diversity and multi-voiced approaches both with and without technology (Alexander, 2008; Wegerif, 2007; Wells, 1999).

Dialogic approaches, in contrast to dialectic, recognise multiple co-existing differences in perspective and do not seek the dominance of one perspective over others. Dialogic approaches therefore assume relativism of reality, in acknowledging the personal and contextual lenses that shape the versions of reality we are able to share with others. A dialogic approach to education assumes a continuous dynamic, which is socially constructed by students and teachers together rather than a fixed set of ideas which is passed on – or perhaps more precisely, down – by teachers.

Possible education futures, then, are built on foundations of multiple realities, diversity rather than uniformity, and a celebration of dialogic approaches to classroom practice which recognise many points of view and so do not seek for one to win out over others. The increasingly emphasised global dimension to education at policy level, for example in the primary and secondary school curricula, not only in England but elsewhere, too, together with far greater awareness of sustainability, bears witness to the multiple versions of reality which have a key role in education, present and future.

When we aggregate the three elements: the technological landscape, connected, empowered and capable children and young people; and this diversification of reality and ways of engaging with it, we have in our hands a potent mix for co-development of education futures. The challenge for educators is to allow the guillotine of censorship and protection to hover high enough and permissively enough to enable children and young people to bring versions of reality (which teachers may be less aware of) into learning spaces, but to do so in a way which minimises risk and maximises critical engagement in developing creative education futures.

Innovation

Over time we have seen shifts occur in how we understand innovation. From a past perspective where innovation was seen as a good thing, by the end of the 20th century there was much greater awareness of the impact of innovation and therefore of values inherent in it (Craft, Gardner and Claxton, 2008). By the start of the 21st century we see the potency of innovation acknowledged and values scrutinised. And this applies to ways in which possible education futures are explored.

Inayatullah (2008), for example, puts forward six foundational concepts which frame our thinking about the future, which essentially invite us to surface six sets of implicit values. These he calls the used future, the disowned future, the alternative future, alignment, models of social change and uses of

140

Image part of a larger piece scribed by Andrew Park alongside Anna Craft's Keynote to 2010 CELT symposium, Galway. Full acknowledgement p2, full image p150-151.

the future. His analysis invites critical scrutiny of each set. Similarly, in his analysis of futures studies, Slaughter (2008) highlights the role of values in his 'integral' approach to futures innovation.

Social networking, gaming and content generating enabled by technology assumes high trust, uncertainty, co-construction, diversity and dialogic colla-boration, and frames the kinds of innovation that we can nurture in possible education futures as highly creative and with a long reach. We are capable of powerfully shifting our educational provision to encompass changing child-hood and youth, keeping a close eye on the values implicit in such changes. And yet perhaps it is the very potency of values-aware innovation that is res-ponsible for a collective lack of agency, urgency, ownership and determination in facilitating root and branch innovation in relation to possible education futures. The job of transformation may just be too huge. But the shifting land-scape is unforgiving in its demands for just such change.

From fire to ice
William Butler Yeats is famously attributed for likening education to the light-ing of fires (as opposed to filling a pail). The metaphor implies a shift from passive to active, from satiation to voraciousness, from boundaries to bound-

lessness. And, perhaps, also signifies shifts from low to high trust, certainty to uncertainty, singular realities to multiple and recognition of the impact of innovation or change. But how appropriate is the fire-lighting metaphor for creative education futures? After all, whilst the metaphor of lighting fires holds within it terrific potential for transformation, so too it brings with it the almost inevitable potential for widespread and virtually unstoppable, irreversible destruction (until such time as it is possible to start again from scratch).

As I was finishing this book, I made a visit to Iceland, the so called 'land of fire and ice' – to visit colleagues and work with doctoral students. A few weeks before I flew out, one of the active volcanoes began to erupt. Two days after my return, it began to spew out huge amounts of steam and volcanic ash. Situated as it is underneath a glacier, the surrounding area was almost instantly flooded and the whole of European air space was closed for a week to all commercial aircraft because of the perceived danger of the drifting ash cloud disrupting jet engines.

The ensuing chaos was extraordinary. Passengers were stranded all over the world, some for weeks. Friends, family and colleagues were stuck variously in China, Finland, France, Germany, Italy, Portugal, the USA and elsewhere. With many work and other commitments scaled back or undertaken in unexpected and new ways, it was clear that, in this unexpected crisis, pocket-based access to the internet enabled collaborative problem solving.

My sister returned overland from Berlin with her family, with the help of a team. Within minutes of the closure of the airport in Berlin on the day of their departure, she was online to me and our mother via her i-phone and our desktop computers, laptops and mobile phones. I happened to be in the open-plan office space at The Open University that day, rather than in my conventional office at Exeter University. As the news came in on my mobile and desk-top computer, the colleague I was chatting to became drawn into the drama. Within moments, and without being asked, she had pulled up on her own desk-top ash-cloud prediction maps, airport updates and car hire schedules; I had meanwhile located the boat crossing information on my own desktop. My mother was checking trains on her laptop in London whilst my sister was using her i-phone in Berlin to extend her hotel bookings, whilst her husband and two teenage children used their mobiles to locate possible coach tickets back to London. Within hours, during which time I travelled back the 200 miles from Milton Keynes to Exeter where we live, logging in to my laptop and checking my phone for progress as I went, she and her family had secured emergency temporary accommodation and a new route back to

England. Five adults and two teenagers, based in four cities in two countries, had, between them, collaborated to find a solution. They could not have done this so quickly or effectively without the technological capability offered by mainly portable digital media. They all assumed it could be done, and that they would work together to work it out.

What has this to do with creative education futures? It may be that, in the early 21st century, a better metaphor for creative education futures than the lighting of fires is the concept of seismic shifts and volcanic eruption with its attendant sense of crisis, combined with human resourcefulness in making something of all this.

Seismic shifts

Just as the geographic plates on which the continents of the world sit, shift and grate against and move past each other, making unpredictable and yet permanent changes to the landscape, so the digital dimension to all our lives is permanently altering how we go about our lives. What we know about plate tectonics and fault lines in geology and vulcanology affords regular citizens the knowledge that certain geographic regions are more likely than others to experience extreme and permanently life-changing geological activity, although we may not know how to predict the details.

Similarly, as regular citizens we are aware that the digital dimension to our lives is constantly shifting and altering the landscapes in which we live, work and learn. Natural events such as earthquakes and volcanoes can trigger other major landscape changes which may have a vast impact: tsunami waves, avalanches, floods and landslides. In a similar way, the changing digital landscape has already shifted how we build understanding, how we identify and solve problems, how we conceive of who we are, relate to others, make choices, live our lives. It has altered, and continues to alter, our maps of what is possible.

From time to time there is a digital earthquake such as the introduction of the internet, which has very quickly changed how entertainment, work and learning is or can be experienced – being able to travel to us at our beckoning, with greater speed, complexity and variety. Or the introduction of the mobile phone, which has put vast tracts of Africa on the digital map. There are continuous localised events, rather like volcanic eruptions, such as the invention of the Nintendo Wii game console, or the i-phone, or MP3 players, satellite navigation systems for cars or media applications allowing the viewer to listen to or watch a broadcast in their own time. Each of these has the potential to cause a flood, tsunami, landslide, avalanche which again changes the landscape. Mobile phones have caused a landslide away from fixed phone use. Email and personal cloud technology has flooded workplaces, removing a significant degree of paper communication together with the need for secretarial and clerical support as previously conceptualised.

The ease with which we adapt to and harness each localised and seismic event is notable. Nobody asked my colleague to find out about options for my stranded sister, but she assumed that, because it was needed and because she could do it, she would – typical of online behaviour.

Where the metaphor of the earthquake or volcano loses its explanatory bite, however, is that it does not involve human choice and activity in its initiation. For what is really powerful about the creative possible education futures we face is the capacity we have collectively to trigger seismic shifts.

Creative education futures: triggering seismic shifts

I have argued in this book that pervasive technology in the early 21st century has already made significant changes in the landscape of childhood and youth. Characterised by participation, playfulness, pluralities and possibilities, children and young people bring to classrooms of the future the capacity to experiment and co-create – and to do so not only in response to change but also to trigger it. Teachers and other adults, too, have access to the people, tools and places that could see creative education futures extend not only as a mirror but also as a lamp (Jones, 2008), in pushing out the boundaries of how we learn. So – whilst, as far as we know, earthquakes and volcanoes do not change the landscape with the kinds of intention characteristic of human beings, we do have the capacity to embrace, reject and transform the landscape of learning: effectively, to trigger our own seismic shifts. To alter, contribute to and so develop the social capital that education offers. And to do so creatively, we need squarely to address the changing ends, or goals, as well as the means of education.

Goals of education

What are the goals of possible education futures? Clearly, one key role for education is to offer a means of socialisation of the young into the norms of society. And yet, as Egan (2008:15) notes: 'if socialisation is really successful, the result is someone who is indoctrinated'. In Chapter 1, I argued that education urgently needs to make creative responses to what children and young people bring into formal learning spaces, including their digital connectivity. But in Chapter 2, I argued that a world characterised by uncertainty and multiple realities demands that creativity is enabled by education. And so it seems to me that the intersection of probable, possible and preferable futures must surely privilege the fostering of creativity. Not only the creativity of students, but of teachers, too.

In doing so, it appears that educators face three fundamental challenges.

What's the story?

The first challenge is to be clear about the major message of education. What is the narrative for education? For, as noted in Chapter 2, there seem to be two competing agendas running at present, which have been with us for at least a decade and probably much longer.

Is the education narrative about understanding, or about creativity, or about both? Whilst policy makers the world over insist it is both, the reality is that standards – which more or less translates to 'understanding' in key areas of learning, win out every time, measured and compared through standardised tests. We have failed, collectively, up until now, to step up to the plate and find a way of valuing creativity equally with understanding. This is puzzling, since we can only be creative if we have knowledge, and our knowledge is only of use to us if we can apply it in novel contexts, ie if we can be creative with it. Just after this book was completed, the British General Election held in early May led to a new coalition government, committed to a programme of deep public spending cuts, and a much more conservative vision of education involving 'relentless focus on the basics' (Department for Education, 2010). Whilst it is still, in autumn 2010, early days to know what this means in practice for educators, it looks likely that the integration of creative generativity with traditional forms of knowledge will provide even more of a challenge than previously.

Those providing and developing possible educational opportunities face a huge challenge. It is to find ways of mapping, tracking, talking about and developing creativity which recognises its integral relationship with knowledge. This is no small task. Work is under way in the USA (EdSteps, 2010) to explore how creativity can be recognised in any disciplinary area, together with how development might be described.

We do already have some models of what progression in specific areas might look like. One example in England is the Arts Award, operated outside formal education and offering progression from bronze through silver to gold level awards to young people choosing to amass evidence of their performance in a chosen art form. However, there are few examples from within schools and there is a real sense in which many teachers and school leaders the world over do not really know what creative progression looks like unless it is tied to a product outcome. There is pressure always to be aware of the need for a publishable, public outcome, and perhaps even more so that this should reflect well on the students, teachers and school. This means that divergent, unusual and critical work is often modified or even rejected (Craft, in press). Nevertheless, we face confusion about how to evaluate creative work in the face of perceived pressure to teach to the standardised test in a discourse which could be described as if spoken with 'forked tongue' (Craft, 2010) where it is not clear what is really of value.

Whose story is it?

Perhaps even more important than the main narrative of education is the second challenge, which is being clear whose story this is, and therefore what infrastructures are in place to enable the telling of that story. For this is no longer a story of low trust and of certitudes. It is not one of singular realities and unproblematic innovation by the few. It is a collective story involving multiple realities and parallel existences, virtual and actual. It is a story which is shifting from providing 'one size fits all' education to 'one size fits one' (Tapscott, 2009:139). It is, as Surowiecki (2005) would have it, a period in history in which we are capable of collective wisdom at an extraordinarily intuitive level, if four conditions are satisfied:

- *Diversity of opinion* (each person draws on their own private and personal information even if this is simply their own idiosyncratic interpretation of known facts)
- *Independence* (each person has their own point of view and does not allow this to be influenced or determined by those of others)
- *Decentralisation* (it is possible to specialise, drawing on local knowledge)
- *Aggregation* (there must be some mechanism for turning private judgements and ideas into a collective decision).

Applied to possible education futures, the story is diverse. It is every person's. It no longer belongs to the government, the local authority, the head teacher or governing body of the school, or the teacher. It belongs to children and young people, their families and all who work with them directly and indirectly. It is a story that therefore needs to *privilege independence* and to allow the technology to offer both *decentralisation and mechanisms for shifting ideas into action,* locally and beyond.

146

Since education is every person's story, there is a need to transform rather than to improve. Hargreaves and Shirley (2009) argue for a 'Fourth Way' of educational change which affords high trust to those involved in day-to-day teaching and learning and living (teachers, parents, students). As they put it, 'the fourth way pushes beyond standardisation, data-driven decision making and target-obsessed distractions to forge an equal and interactive partnership among the people, the profession, and their government' (*ibid*:71). They call for six pillars of purpose and partnership to forge an equal and interactive partnership:

- an inspiring and inclusive vision
- strong public engagement
- achievement through investment
- corporate educational responsibility
- students as partners in change, and
- mindful learning and teaching
  (Hargreaves and Shirley, 2009:73)

They identify three principles of professionalism: high quality teachers, positive and powerful professional associations, and lively learning communities (p88), yet the role of the digital is virtually absent from their vision of 'resilient social democracy'. They propose four catalysts that offer coherence in such educational change, namely: sustainable leadership, integrating networks, putting responsibility before accountability and prioritising differentiation and diversity. Yet the thrust of their approach continues to lay the responsibility on the shoulders of adults.

By contrast, in 2008, a year earlier than Hargreaves and Shirley's book, the Royal Society of Arts, Manufacture and Commerce (RSA) launched its Education Charter through Creativity, Culture and Education, arguing that there are two choices facing education at this point. 'One is to do more of the same only better. The other is to go back and reconsider our purposes and aims, and then think afresh about how we can successfully deliver the core business of education' (Taylor and McGimpsey, 2008). The RSA's Education Charter highlights *multiple aims for education* (encompassing creativity, independence, confidence, happiness, aptitude for work and capacity to self-regulate emotional, physical and mental well-being). It re-asserts the *right of every young person to develop to their full potential* (and not to be dependent on particular talent or background), with education offering a range of abstract and practical knowledge. It argues that *education professionals must be trusted* to create creative, innovative environments for learning and to design appropriate curricula. And, perhaps most significantly, *it emphasises the need for partnership with children and young people, their families and educators playing a role in designing learning.*

It is this last point which is really key; this is a collaborative venture, and children and young people have a vital role to play in it. As Tapscott argues (1998), young people are 'learning, playing, communicating, working and creating communities very differently than their parents. They are a force for social transformation' (p2). Taylor and McGimpsey amplify this point by noting that: 'young people bring with them the expectation not just to sit and listen, but to participate, to interact, and to shape' (p8).

Adults can learn a great deal from children and young people, especially in terms of how new media may affect governance. This is a new phase of cultural reproduction. Like the avalanches which may follow geographic seismic shifts, we are seeing a disruption of cultural reproduction. But we have the active choice of stamping our feet together and starting the avalanche. Partners in change extend far beyond the traditional ways we have conceived for schools. Education is everyone's story, partnership in developing creative education futures is therefore key. But we need sensitivity to the dangers of disconnects discussed in Chapter 3, of which one was how appropriate it may be for children's leisure spaces to be in effect colonised by education spaces and agendas.

Going back to Yeats, to what extent is the fire of personal choice and motivation inherent in gaming extinguished by harnessing games to instruction? It could certainly be argued that if forced to play a game, it is no longer truly play, and that the fun inherent in games is what makes them so intensely absorbing, and therefore powerful (Huizinga, 1950). So as Garris *et al* argue (2002), it is an oxymoron to refer to a game as 'instructional'.

Finding the balance between motivation and privacy is not easy. Not only are there disconnects inherent in gaming for learning, but there may be opposition within the contemporary teaching profession itself as currently configured. As I completed this book, one of the largest teacher unions in England, during its annual conference, raised the issue of student voice and participation in schools as problematic. During a fringe meeting in which delegates were told that their union had set out six guiding principles which assumed that constructive, effective student voice activities should be drawn on to raise standards, a clear line was drawn relating to activities which students should not be permitted to be involved in. These included observing lessons, involvement in recruiting staff, and becoming involved in the governance of the school. Whilst the union was overall strongly supportive of student voice, at the most fundamental level it appeared to challenge the idea of real partnership between students and teachers (NAS/UWT, 2010).

How are these stories developed?

The third and final challenge we face is in how infrastructures can support the multiple creative education stories in possible education futures, as the formal and the informal blur. The curriculum itself needs to reflect the extending literacies of children and young people and in particular their rapidly developing visual literacy, as argued in Chapter 7 (Oblinger and Oblinger, 2005; Prensky, 2005).

Current work in England by Becta, a government body promoting technology in learning, is exploring five key themes from 2010 – 2011, as part of its 'Fit for the Future' programme. The initiative includes research and development exploring how the personal can integrate with education, how learning can occur beyond a single setting, considering how to make the best use of data, what kinds of new knowledge skills need to be developed through education, and embracing the global dimension in learning which is offered by technology (Becta, 2010). The ideas emerging from the programme could contribute to our feeling far more comfortable with the seismic shifts which have taken place in the learning landscape.

The tools of the classroom need careful consideration. We have seen vast changes in learning tools over the last 100 years – from past approaches to education discussed in this chapter, to the brink of possible creative education futures. Slates were replaced by blackboards, these in turn by whiteboards, by digital projectors and by interactive whiteboards. DVDs replaced VHS tapes. Internet and open-source video clips, which include those collected by teachers and students, are starting in turn to replace DVDs. Computers have replaced DVD players and VCRs; MP4 Players, IPods, Blackberries and other mobile phones have replaced vinyl records, tapes and even CDs. Email and texting increasingly replace phone calls. Online open blogs, together with notebooks, replace diaries. Hand held gaming devices and hybrid physical-technology games replace, to a degree, the front room, playground and street. The boundaries between self and other are more blurred than previously.

During a recent talk I gave in Galway, Ireland, about the context, dilemmas and possibilities opened by the playfulness and the pluralities in the digital landscape, together with the compass of possibilities and participation, Andrew Park, of Cognitive Media http://www.cognitivemedia.co.uk/ was tasked to create a visual image of the ideas. Andrew's graphic representation of these

ANNA CRAFT
CREATIVITY IN EDUCATION

UNLEASH CREATIVITY IN YOUNGER LEARNERS

CHILDHOOD YOUTH

2005
½ WERE US[...]
SOCIAL N[...]

SOCIAL NETWORKING

GAMING

WEB

CONTENT GENERATION

CREATIVITY IS IN EVERYTHING WE DO
→ DRAMA VIDEOS
IN ROLE

WHAT IF?

AS IF

Possibility
Participation
Playfulness
Plurality

→ THINKING & ACTION
IMMERSION PROVIDES A CONTEXT

I WANT TO TURF THE CLASSROOM
↓
WHAT IF THE OUTSIDE WAS INSIDE?

THE 20TH CENTURY PUNCTURE[...] TELEVIS[...]

I'm OBSERVING

→ GETTING OLDER YOUNGER
GETTING YOUNGER OLDER

WHO HAS CONTROL?

R[...] AB[...]

STAND BACK ALMOST BECOME INVISIBLE

ONE SIZE DOESN'T FIT ALL

I CAN'T SEE

EXPOSURE & VULNERABILITY

DREAMING
PARTICIPATION

EXPLORATION

CREATIVITY IN SCIENCE

POSSIBILITY THINKING
IN BIBLICAL TIMES CREATIVITY WAS SEEN AS MYSTICAL

AS WELL AS ART

MEASURING CREATIVITY

ORKING

BUILDING IDENTITIES
PARTICIPATION
INTERACTION
ENGAGEMENT

RISK
PROTECTION
CONTROL
PRIVACY

EMPOWERMENT
OPEN
MULTIPLICITY
PT

BUY THIS WAY OF LIFE!

NEEDS TO BE LESS MARKETISED

WHO'S IN CHARGE?
WHAT'S REAL?

IS IT A DEMOCRATIC SPACE?

WHICH DISCOURSE?

SECOND LIFE "SCOME"

ARGH I PROGRAMMED A SCONE!

FEAR

FIREWALL

PIGGY

WE NEED JAM!

HIGH PERSONAL AGENCY

BECOMES BY AGE 9

CHOICES
↳ CONTENT GENERATION
LEARNING BY DOING... DOING BY LEARNING

THINK

ERGE

CREATIVITY: IS THERE MORE IN THE DIGITAL WORLD?

THIS IS A HUGELY EMPOWERING ENVIRONMENT

ANALOGUE WORLD

DIGITAL WORLD

IT'S NOT AN EITHER/OR

issues and our possible responses to them are skilfully captured in the image overleaf.

What Andrew's image highlights in particular is the new 'bottom line' of co-authorship.

Co-authoring creative education futures

As argued throughout this book, with the tools come new literacies. Education needs both to reflect, and to prepare students for, fluency in this much wider range of literacies, in which children and young people are particularly engaged. We need to be better aware of possible gaps between not only the potentially low demands of technology and the need for a high standard of engagement but also between potentially low demands in face-to-face classrooms compared with the highly creative demands made possible by using technology.

Perhaps the biggest challenge of all is to find ways of developing creative education with wisdom, to maintain keen awareness of who owns this stuff, who gains from it and what its ultimate values are. Creative educational futures involve engaging with pluralities, playfulness, possibilities and participation which permeate the lives of children and young people.

It is up to us as global citizens to work out when we really do need new solutions to new challenges, and what our own roles are in the seemingly unstoppably shifting landscape of our interconnected lives.

References

Alexander, R. (2008) *Toward Dialogic Teaching: Rethinking Classroom Talk.* Thirsk: Dialogos.

Armstrong, S. and WARLICK, D. (2004) The New Literacy www.techlearning.com/shared/printable Article.php?articleID=47102021 (Accessed 30th April 2010).

Arafeh, S. and Levin, D. (2003) The Digital Disconnect: The Widening Gap Between Internet-Savvy Students and their Schools. In C. Crawford *et al* (eds), *Proceedings of Society for Information Technology and Teacher Education International Conference, 2003:* 1002-1007. Chesapeake, VA: AACE. Retrieved from http://www.editlib.org/p/18081 (Accessed 30th April 2010).

Asthana, S. (2006) *Innovative practices of youth participation in media: A research study on twelve initiatives from around the developing and underdeveloped regions of the world.* United Nations Educational, Scientific and Cultural Organization

Baer, J. and Kaufman, J. (2006) 'Creativity research in English-speaking countries', in J.C.Kaufman and R.J.Sternberg (eds), *The International Handbook of Creativity*, New York: Cambridge University Press

Ball, S J (2003) The teacher's soul and the terrors of performativity. *Journal of Education Policy* 18(2): 215-28 Mar-April

Bamford, A. (2003) The Visual Literacy White Paper. Uxbridge: Adobe Systems. Available at: www.adobe.com/uk/education/pdf/adobe_visual_literacy_paper.pdf (Accessed 1 May 2010).

Banaji, S., Burn, A. and Buckingham, D. (2006) *The Rhetorics of Creativity: A review of the literature.* London: Arts Council England.

Barton, P. (2005) One Third of a Nation: Rising Dropout Rates and Declining Opportunities. *Policy Information Report, Educational Testing Service*, February 2005, www.ets.org

Barone, C. (2005) The New Academy. *Educating the Net Generation.* Boulder, Colorado.: Educause, 2005), e-book, available at http://www.educause.edu/educatingthenetgen

Beck, U. (1992) *Risk Society: towards a new modernity.* London: Sage.

BECTA (2010) *Fit for the Future: Education Across Borders. Draft Response, March 2010.* Paper in draft, April 2010.

BECTA (2010) *Fiit for the Future.* Available at: http://events.becta.org.uk/display.cfm?andresID=41547 (accessed 28th April 2010).

Beghetto, R. (2007) Does creativity have a place in classroom discussions? Prospective teachers' response preferences. *Thinking Skills and Creativity*, 2 (1): p1-9.

Bell, W. (2003) *Foundations for Futures Studies 1: History, Purposes, Knowledge.* New Brunswick, NJ: Transaction Publishers

Bentivegna, S. (2002) 'Politics and New Media', in Lievrouw, L. and Livingstone, S. (eds) *The Handbook of New Media: Social shaping and consequences of ICTs*, London: Sage, pp. 50-61.

Bethencourt, J., LOW, W.Y., Simmons, I. and Williamson, M. (2007) Establishing darknet connections: an evaluation of usability and security. *ACM International Conference Proceeding Series, Vol. 229. Proceedings of the 3rd symposium on usable privacy and security*. New York: ACM. Available at: http://portal.acm.org/citation.cfm?id=1280700 (Accessed 22nd August 2009).

Boggs, C. (1976) *Gramsci's Marxism*. London: Pluto Press.

Boneva, B. S., Quinn, A., Kraut, R. E., Kiesler, S. and Shklovski, I. (2006) Teenage communication in the instant messaging era. In Kraut, R. Brynin, M. and Kiesler, S. (eds), *Information technology at home*. Oxford: Oxford University Press, p.612-692.

Bourdieu, P. (1977) Cultural Reproduction and Social Reproduction. In: Karabel, J., and Halsey, A. H. (eds) *Power and Ideology in Education*. New York: Oxford University Press, p.487-511.

Bourdieu, P. (1984 [1979]) *Distinction: A Social Critique of the Judgement of Taste*. Richard Nice (tr). Cambridge, MA: Harvard University Press.

Bourdieu, P. (1986) The Forms of Capital. In: Richardson, J. G. (ed) *Handbook of Theory and Research for the Sociology of Education*. New York: Greenwood Press, p.241-258.

Bourdieu, P. and Passeron, J.-C. (1977 [1970]) *Reproduction in Education, Society and Culture*. Richard Nice (tr). London: Sage Publications.

Boyd, B. (2005) Caught in the headlights. Paper presented at ESRC Seminar, Documenting Creative Learning, Strathclyde University, October 2005. Available online at: http://opencreativity.open.ac.uk/recent.htm#previous_papers (Accessed 10 July 2008).

Boyd, D. (2007) Why Youth Social Network Sites: The Role of Networked Publics in Teenage Social Life. In Buckingham, D. (ed) (2007). *Youth, Identity, and Digital Media* (John D. And Catherine T. MacArthur Foundation Series on Digital Media and Learning). Cambridge, MA MIT Press. pp 119-142.

Brooks, L. (2006) *The story of childhood: growing up in modern Britain*. London: Bloomsbury Books.

Brown, K., Jackson, M. and Cassidy, W. (2006) Cyber-bullying: Developing policy to direct responses that are equitable and effective in addressing this special form of bullying. *Canadian Journal of Educational Administration and Policy*, 57: 8-11.

Brown, M. (2005) Learning Spaces. In educating the net generation, Edited by Oblinger, G.D. and Oblinger, J.L. 12.1-12.22 Educause: http://www.educause.edu/educatingthenetgen/5989 (Accessed 30th April 2010).

Bruner, J.S. (1960) *The Process of Education*. Cambridge, MA: Harvard University Press.

Bruner, J.S. (1986) *Actual Minds, Possible Worlds*. Cambridge, MA: Harvard University Press.

Bruner, J.S. (1991) The Narrative Construction of Reality. *Critical Enquiry*, 18 (1), Autumn 1991: 1-21.

Bruner, J.S. (1995) *The Culture of Education*. Cambridge, MA: Harvard University Press.

Buchner, P. (1990) 'Growing up in the Eighties: Changes in the Social Biography of Childhood in the FRG', in Chisholm, L., Buchner, P., Kruger, H-H and Brown, P. (eds), *Childhood, Youth and Social Change: a Comparative Perspective*. London: Falmer Press.

Buckingham, D. (2006) Children and New Media. In Lievrouw, L.A. and Livingstone, S. (eds). *The Handbook of New Media: Updated Student Edition*. London: Sage.

Buckingham, D. (2007) *Beyond Technology. Children's Learning in the age of digital culture*. London: Polity Press.

Buckingham, D. and Jones, K. (2001) New Labour's cultural turn: some tensions in contemporary educational and cultural policy, *Journal of Education Policy*, 16(1): 1-14.

Buckingham, D. (2003) *Media education: literacy, learning and contemporary culture*. Cambridge: Polity Press.

Buckingham, D. (2007) *Beyond technology: children's learning in the age of digital culture.* Cambridge: Polity Press.

Burke, J. (2008) *English Teacher's Companion.* Portsmouth, NH: Heinemann.

Burnard, P., Craft, A. and Grainger, T. *et al* (2006) Possibility Thinking, *International Journal of Early Years Education,* 14 (3), October 2006: 243-262.

Burnard, P. and White, J. (2008) Creativity and performativity: counterpoints in British and Australian education. In *British Educational Research Journal, Special Issue: Creativity and Performativity in Teaching and Learning,* 24 (5), October 2008: 667-682.

Calvert, S.L., Mahler, B.A., Zehnderi, S.M., Jenkins, A. and Lee, M.S. (2003) Gender differences in pre-adolescent children's online interactions: symbolic modes of self-presentation and self-expression. *Applied Developmental Psychology* 24 (2003): 627-644.

Cardwell, S. (2009) The Twitter Timeline of the Iran Election. *Newsweek.* Available at: http://www.newsweek.com/id/203953 (Accessed 10th August 2009).

Cassell, J. and Jenkins, H. (1998) 'Chess for girls? Feminism and computer games', in Cassell, J. and Jenkins, H. (eds), *From Barbie to Mortal Combat: Gender and Computer Games.* Cambridge, MA: MIT Press pp2-45.

Cassell, J and Jenkins, H (2000) (Eds) *From Barbie to Mortal Kombat: Gender and Computer Games.* Cambridge, MA: MIT Press.

Chan, E. and Vorderer, P. (2006) Massively Multiplayer Online Games. In Vorderer, P. and Bryant, J. (eds) *Playing Video Games: Motives, Responses and Consequences.* Mahwah, New Jersey: Lawrence Erlbaum Associates, Inc.

Chappell, K. and Craft, A. (2009) What makes a creative learning conversation? Presentation prepared for *British Educational Research Association* conference, Manchester, September 2009.

Chappell, K., Craft, A., Rolfe, L. and Jobbins, V. (2009) Dance Partners for Creativity: choreographing space for co-participative research into creativity and partnership in dance education. Special Issue of *Research In Dance Education on Creativity* 10 (3) November 2009: 177-198

Chappell, K., Craft, A., Burnard, P. and Cremin, T. (2008a) Features of 'possibility thinking' in fostering creative learning. Paper given at *American Educational Research Association annual meeting,* New York, April 2008.

Chappell, K., Craft, A., Burnard, P. and Cremin, T (2008b) Question-posing and Question-responding: the heart of 'Possibility Thinking' in the early years. *Early Years,* 28(3), October 2008: 267-286.

Chappell, K. and Craft, A. with Jonsdottir, S. and Clack, J. (2008) *Aspire South West.* Report to Qualifications and Curriculum Authority, December 2008.

Cheskin Research (2002) *Designing Digital Experiences for Youth.* Market Insight Series. Fall 2002.

Christensen, P. and James, A. (2000) *Research with Children: perspectives and practices.* London: Falmer Press.

Claxton, G. (2006) Creative Glide Space. In Bannerman, C., Sofaer, J. and Watt, J. (2006) (eds), *Navigating the Unknown.* London: Middlesex University Press.

Claxton, G. (2008) *What's the point of school? Rediscovering the heart of education.* Oxford: Oneworld.

Claxton, G., Craft, A. and Gardner, H. (2008) Concluding Thoughts: Good Thinking – Education for Wise Creativity. In Craft, A., Gardner, H., Claxton, G. et al (2008) *Creativity, Wisdom and Trusteeship. exploring the role of education.* Thousand Oaks: Corwin Press.

Clouder, L., Oliver, M. and Tait, J. (2008) Embedding CETLs in a performance-oriented culture in higher education: reflections on finding creative space. In *British Educational Research Journal, Special Issue: Creativity and Performativity in Teaching and Learning,* 24 (5), October 2008: 635-650.

155

Cochrane, P. and Cockett, M. (2007) *Building a Creative School: a dynamic approach to school Development.* Stoke on Trent: Trentham.

Cochrane, P., Craft, A. and Jeffery, G. (2008) Mixed messages or permissions and opportunities? Reflections on current policy perspectives on creativity in education. In Sefton-Green, J. (ed) (2008), *Creative Learning.* London: Creative Partnerships.

Cole, H. and Griffiths, M.D. (2007) Social Interactions in Massively Multiplayer Online Role-Playing Gamers. *CyberPsychology and Behavior.* August 2007, 10(4): 575-583. doi:10.1089/cpb.2007. 9988.

Cordes, C. and Miller, E. (2000) Fool's Gold: A Critical Look at Computers in Childhood. www. allianceforchildhood.net (Accessed 30th April 2010).

Corsaro, W.A. (1997) *Sociology of Childhood.* Thousand Oaks, CA: Pine Forge Press.

Craft, A. (1996) 'Nourishing Educator Creativity: a holistic approach to CPD', *British Journal of In-service Education,* 33 (3): 309 – 322.

Craft, A. (1997) 'Identity and Creativity: educating for post-modernism?' *Teacher Development.* 1 (1) March 1997, p.83-96.

Craft, A. (1998a) 'Holistic Postgraduate Learning: evaluation of a UK-based innovation', *Analytic Teaching,* 18 (2): 19-30.

Craft, A. (1998b) 'UK Educator Perspectives on Creativity', *Journal of Creative Behavior,* 32 (4): 244-257.

Craft, A. (1999) Creative development in the early years: some implications of policy for practice. *Curriculum Journal,* 10(1): 135-150.

Craft, A. (2000) *Creativity across the primary curriculum: Framing and developing practice.* London: Routledge.

Craft, A., (2001a) *An analysis of research and literature on creativity in education.* Report prepared for the Qualifications and Curriculum Authority.

Craft, A. (2001b) Little c Creativity, in Craft, A., Jeffrey, B. and Leibling, M. (eds), *Creativity in Education,* London: Continuum. Pp 45-61.

Craft, A. (2002) *Creativity and Early Years Education.* London: Continuum.

Craft, A. (2005) *Creativity in Schools: tensions and dilemmas.* London: Routledge

Craft, A. (2005) *Creativity in Schools: Tensions and Dilemmas.* Abingdon: Routledge.

Craft, A. (2006) Creativity and Wisdom? *Cambridge Journal of Education,* 36 (3), September 2006: 336-350

Craft, A. (2007) Possibility Thinking in the Early Years and Primary Classroom, in Tan, A.G. (ed), *Singapore Handbook of Creativity.* Singapore: World Scientific Publishing.

Craft, A. (2008) Tensions in Creativity and Education: Enter Wisdom and Trusteeship? In Craft, A., Gardner, H., Claxton, G. *et al* (2008) *Creativity, Wisdom and Trusteeship. exploring the role of education.* Thousand Oaks: Corwin Press.

Craft, A. (in press) Interview with Shakantula Banaji, publication in press

Craft, A. (2010). Teaching for Possibility Thinking: What is it, and how do we do it? *Learning Matters,* 15(1): 19-23, Melbourne: Catholic Education Office

Craft, M. (ed) (1970) *Family, Class and Education: a reader.* Harlow: Longman.

Craft, A., with Burnard, P., Cremin, T. and Chappell, K. (2008) Creative Learning and Possibility Thinking. Paper given at *American Educational Research Association 2008 annual meeting,* New York, March 2008.

Craft, A. and Chappell, K. (2009) Fostering Possibility Through Co-Researching Creative Movement with 7-11 Year Olds. In Blenkinsop, S. (ed), *The Imagination in Education: Extending the Boundaries of Theory and Practice.* Cambridge Scholars Publishing.

Craft, A., Cremin, T., Burnard, P. and Chappell, K. (2008) Possibility Thinking, in Craft, A., Cremin, T. and Burnard, P. (eds) (2008), *Creative Learning 3-11 and How We Document It.* Stoke-on-Trent: Trentham Books.

Craft, A., Cremin, T., Burnard, P. with Chappell, K., Alderson, D. and Ting, M. (in preparation). Possibility Thinking in 9-11 year olds. MORE

Craft, A. with Dyer, G., Dugal, J., Jeffrey, R. and Lyons, T. (1997) *Can You Teach Creativity?* Nottingham: Education Now Books.

Craft, A., Gardner, H. and Claxton, G. (eds) (2008) *Creativity, Wisdom, and Trusteeship: Exploring the Role of Education.* Thousand Oaks, CA: Corwin Press

Craft, and Jeffrey, B. (2001) 'The Universalization of Creativity', in Craft, A., Jeffrey, B., Leibling, M., *Creativity in Education,* London: Continuum, p.1-13.

Craft, A. and Jeffrey, B (2008) Creativity and performativity in teaching and learning: tensions, dilemmas, constraints, accommodations and synthesis. *British Educational Research Journal,* 34 (5), October 2008: 577-584

Craft, A. and Quaglia, R. (2010) Creativity and Aspirations: Working Together in the Digital Age. Keynote given at International Symposium on learning in the digital world, Council of Chief State School Officers and Pearson Publishing, London, June 2010.

Cremin, T., Burnard, P. and Craft, A. (2006) Pedagogy and Possibility thinking in the early years, *Thinking Skills and Creativity,* 1(2), Autumn 2006: 108-119.

Crittenden, S. (2002) 'Silicon Daydreams: Digital Pastimes of the Wired Generation,' virginia.edu, vol. VI, no. 2 (fall 2002), <http://www.itc.virginia.edu/virginia.edu/fall02/daydreams/home.html>.

Croninger, R. and Lee, V.E. (2001) Social Capital and Dropping out of High School: Benefits to At-Risk Students of Teachers' Support and Guidance. *Teachers' College Record* 103 (4), August 2001: 548-581.

Csikszentmihalyi, M. (1994) The Domain of Creativity. In Feldman, D., Csikszentmihalyi, M., Gardner, H. (eds) (1994). *Changing the World: A Framework for the Study of Creativity.* Westport: Praeger.

Csikszentmihalyi, M., (1996) *Creativity: Flow and the psychology of discovery and invention,* New York: HarperCollins.

Csikszentmihalyi, M., (1999) 'Implications of a systems perspective for the study of creativity', in Sternberg. R.J. (ed) *Handbook of creativity,* Cambridge: Cambridge University Press.

Cunningham, H. (1995) *Children and Childhood in Western Society Since 1500.* London: Longman.

Cunningham, H. (2006) *The Invention of Childhood.* London: BBC Books.

Cupitt, M. and Stockbridge, S. (1996) *Families and Electronic Entertainment.* Sydney: Australian Broadcasting Corporation/Office of Film and Literature Classification.

Curtis, P. (2007) England Plunges in Ranking for Reading. *The Guardian Newspaper,* 29 November 2007. Available online at: http://www.guardian.co.uk/uk/2007/nov/29/schools.booksnews (Accessed 30th April 2010).

Damasio, A.R., Tranel, D. and Damasio, H. (1990) Individuals with sociopathic behaviour caused by frontal damage fail to respond automatically to social stimuli. *Behavioral Brain Research,* 41: 81-94.

Damasio, A.R., Tranel, D. and Damasio, H. (1991) Somatic markers and the guidance of behavior. Theory and preliminary testing. In Levin, H.S., Eisenberg, H.M. and Benton. A.L. (eds). *Frontal Lobe Function and Dysfunction,* New York: Oxford University Press, p.217-229.

Damasio, H. Grabowski, T., Frank, R., Galaburda, A.M. and Damasio, A.R. (1994) The return of Phineas Gage: Clues about the brain from the skull of a famous patient. *Science,* 264: 1102-1105.

Darling, J. (1994) *Child-centred education and its critics*. London: Paul Chapman.

Department for Culture, Media and Sport (DCMS) and Department for Education and Skills (DfES) (2006a) *Nurturing Creativity and Young People*. London: HMSO.

Department for Culture, Media and SPORT (DCMS) and Department for Education and Skills (DfES) (2006b) *Government response to Nurturing Creativity and Young people*. London: HMSO.

Department for Culture, Media and Sport (DCMS), Department for Business, Enterprise and Regulatory Reform (BERR) and Department for Innovation, Universities and Skills (DIUS), (2008) *Creative Britain: New talents for the creative economy*. London: DCMS.

Department for Children, Schools and Families (DCSF) (2009) *Your child, your schools, our future: building a 21st century school system*. London: DCSF.

Department for Education (DFE) (2010) *National Curriculum*. http://www.education.gov.uk/curriculum (accessed 12 July 2010).

Devine, D. (2000) Constructions of Childhood in School: Power, Policy and Practice in Irish Education. *International Studies in Sociology of Education*, 10(1), March 2000: 23-41(19)

Dewey, J. (1938) *Experience and Education*. New York: Macmillan.

Di Maggio, P. (1982) Cultural Capital and School Success: The Impact of Status Culture Participation on the Grades of US High School Students. *American Sociological Review* 47: 189-201.

Dodge, T., Barab, S., Stuckey, B., Warren, S., Heiselt, C. and Stein, R. (2008) Children's sense of self: learning and meaning in the digital age. *Journal of Interactive Learning Research*, 19(2) April 2008: 225-249.

Downes, S. (2002) The New Literacy http://education.qld.gov.au/learningplace/onlinelearning/courses/sdownessept.html (Accessed 30th April 2010).

Duranti, A. (1997) *Linguistic anthropology*. Cambridge, MA: Cambridge University Press.

Ecclestone, K. (1999) Care or control? Defining learners' needs for lifelong learning. *British Journal of Educational Studies,* 47(4), Dec 1999: 332-347.

Edsteps (2010) http://www.edsteps.org (27th April 2010).

Edwards, R. and Usher, R. (2001) Lifelong Learning : A Postmodern Condition of Education? *Adult Education Quarterly*, 5(4): 273-287.

Egan, K. (2008) *The Future of Education. Reimagining Our Schools from the Ground Up*. New Haven and London: Yale University Press

Eshet-Alkalai, Y., and Chajut, E. (2009) Changes Over Time in Digital Literacy. *CyberPsychology and Behavior.* 12(6): 713-715.

Facer, K.. (2007) Schools Without Frontiers, London, 6 Feb 07 PowerPoint presentation: www.p4s.org.uk/documents/Futurelabpresentation060207.ppt (Accessed 6th February 2008).

Facer, K., Furlong, J., Furlong, R. and Sutherland, R. (2001a) 'Constructing the child computer user: from public policy to private practices', *British Journal of Sociology of Education*, 22 (1): 91-108

Facer, K. Furlong, J., Furlong, R. and Sutherland, R. (2001b) Home is where the hardware is: young people, the domestic environment and access to new technologies. In Hutchby, I. and Moran-Ellis, J. (eds). *Children, Technology and Culture*. London: Falmer pp13-27.

Feldman, D. and Benjamin, R. (2006) 'Creativity and education: an American retrospective', *Cambridge Journal of Education*, 36(3):319-336

Fielding, M. (2004) 'New wave' student voice and the renewal of civic society. *London Review of Education,* 2(3), Nov 2004: 197-217.

Forrester, V., and Hui, A. (2007) 'Creativity in the Hong Kong classroom: What is the contextual practice?' *Thinking skills and creativity,* 2(1): 30-38.

France, A. (2007) *Understanding Youth in Late Modernity*. Maidenhead: Open University Press.

Frasca, G. (2003) Simulation Versus Narrative: Introduction to Ludology. In M. J. P. Wolf and B. Perron (eds). *The Video Game Theory Reader*. London: Routledge .

Frechette, J. (2006) 'Cyber-censorship or cyber-literacy? Envisioning cyber-learning through media education', p149-71 in D. Buckingham and R. Willett (eds), *Digital Generations: Children, Young People and New Media*. Mahwah, NJ: Lawrence Erlbaum.

Fredriks, J.A., Blumenfeld, P.C. and Paris, A.H. (2004) School Engagement: Potential of the Concept, State of the Evidence. *Review of Educational Research*, 74(1): 59-109.

Friedman, T.L. (2005) *The World is Flat a Brief History of the Twenty-First Century*. New York: Farrar, Strauss and Giroux.

Friedman, T. (2007) *The World is Flat*. New York, NY: Picador.

Fromme, J. (2003) Computer Games as Part of Children's Culture', Game Studies, 3, 1 (online journal), at http://www.gamestudies.org/0301/fromme/ (Accessed 30th April 2010).

Fryer, M., (1996) *Creative teaching and learning*, London: Paul Chapman Publishing Ltd.

Furedi, F. (2009) *Wasted: Why Education isn't Educating*. London: Continuum.

Galton, M., Hargreaves, L., Comber, C. and Wall, D. with Pell, A. (1999) *Inside the Primary Classroom: 20 years on*. London: Routledge.

Galton, M., Simon, B., Croll, P. (1980) *Inside the Primary Classroom*. London: Routledge and Kegan Paul.

Gardner, H. (1993) *Creating Minds*. New York: BasicBooks.

Gardner, H. (2008) Creativity, Wisdom, and Trusteeeship. In Craft, A., Gardner, H. and Claxton, G. (eds). *Creativity, Wisdom, and Trusteeship Exploring the Role of Education*. Thousand Oaks, CA: Corwin Press.

Garris, R., Ahlers, R. and Driskell, J.E. (2002) Games, Motivation and Learning: A Research and Practice Model. *Simulation Gaming*, 33: 441. DOI: 10.1177/1046878102238607 Available at: http://sag.sagepub.com/cgi/content/abstract/33/4/441 (Accessed 14 August 2009).

Gee, J.P. (2003) *What Video Games Have to Teach Us About Learning and Literacy*, New York: Palgrame McMillan.

Gentile, D.A., Lynch, P.J., Linder, J.R. and Walsh, D.A. (2004) The effects of violent video game habits on adolescent hostility, aggressive behaviors and school performances. *Journal of Adolescence*, 1, 5-22.

Giddens, A. (2003) *Runaway world: how globalisation is shaping our lives*. New York: Routledge.

Gillis, C. (2006) Cyberbullying is on the rise. Who can stop it? *Maclean's*, 119(2): 35.

Gosling, W. (1994) *Helmsman and Heroes*. London: Weidenfield and Nicholson.

Gramsci, A. (1971) *Selections from the Prison Notebooks*. London: Lawrence and Wishart.

Greenberg, E.H. and Weber, K. (2008) *Generation We: How Millenial Youth are Taking over America and Changing the World*. Emeryville, CA: Pachatusan.

Greenfield, P. M., Gross, E. F., Subrahmanyam, K., Suzuki, L. K. and Tynes, B. (2006) Teens on the internet: Interpersonal connection, identity, and information. In R. Kraut, M. Brynin, and S. Kiesler (eds), *Information technology at home* (p.185-200). Oxford: Oxford University Press.

Greenfield, P. and Yan, Z. (2006) Children, Adolescents, and the Internet: A New Field of Inquiry in Developmental Psychology. Developmental Psychology Copyright 2006 by the American Psychological Association 2006, 42(3): 391-394.

Gros, B. (2005) Adolescentes y videojuegos: el juego desde el jugador, *Comunicación y Pedagogía*, 208: 62-64.

Gross, E. F. (2004) Adolescent Internet use: What we expect, what teens report. *Journal of Applied Developmental Psychology*, 25: 633-649.

Gruber, H.E. and Wallace, D.B. (1999) 'The case study method and evolving systems approach for understanding unique creative people at work'. In R.J. Sternberg (ed), *Handbook of Creativity*, Cambridge: Cambridge University Press.

The Guardian (2009) Twitter is not for teens, Morgan Stanley told by 15-year-old expert. *The Guardian*, 13 July 2009. Available at: http://www.guardian.co.uk/business/2009/jul/13/twitter-teenage-media-habits (accessed 13 August 2009).

Guarino, M. (2009) Four ways technology will change advertising in 2010. *Christian Science Monitor*, 29 December 2009. Available at: http://news.yahoo.com/s/csm/20091229/ts_csm/271215_1 (Accessed 19 January 2010).

Hakim, C. (2000) *Work-Lifestyle Choices in the 21st Century: Preference Theory*. Oxford: Oxford University Press.

Hall, R. and Newbury, D. (1999) 'What Makes You Switch On?: Young people, the internet and cultural participation', in J. Sefton-Green (ed), *Young People, Creativity and New Technologies*, London: Routledge, p.100-110.

Halsey, A.H., Lauder, H., Brown, P. and Wells, A.S. (1997) *Education, Culture, Economy and Society*. Oxford: Oxford University Press.

Hampton, K. and Wellman, B. (2003) Neighboring in Netvill: how the internet supports community and social capital in a wired suburb. *City and Community*, 2(3) Fall 2003: 277-391.

Harden, J. (2000) There's No Place Like Home. *Childhood*, 7(1): 43-59.

Hargittal, E. (2007) Whose space? Differences among users and non-users of social network sites. *Journal of Computer-Mediated Communication*, 13(1), article 14. http://jcmc.indiana.edu/vol13/issue1/hargittai.html

Hargreaves, D. (2007) *System Redesign – The road to transformation in education*. London: Specialist Schools and Academies Trust.

Harland, J., Kinder, K., Haynes, J. and Schagen, I. (1998) *The Effects and Effectiveness of Arts Education in Schools: Interim Report 1*. Slough, Berkshire: National Foundation for Educational Research.

Harper, C., Jones, N. and McKay, A. (2009) *Including Children in Policy Responses to Economic Crises: Lessons from the Past and Policies for a Sustainable Future*. ODI and UNICEF synthesis conference paper.

Harper, R, Rodden, T., Rogers, Y. and Sellen, A. (2008) *Being Human: Human-Computer Interaction in the Year 2020*. Cambridge: Microsoft Research Ltd.

Hart, R. (1992) *Children's participation: from tokenism to citizenship*, Florence: UNICEF International Child Development Centre.

Harvey, D. (2010) *The Enigma of Capital and the Crises of Capitalism*. London: Profile Books.

Hegel, G.W.F. (1975) *The Logic of Hegel* (W.Wallace, Trans.). Oxford: Clarendon Press.

Hendrick, H. (1997) Construction and reconstruction of British childhood: an interpretative survey, 1800 to the present. In James, A., Prout, A. (eds). *Constructing and Reconstructing Childhood: Contemporary Issues in the Sociological Study of Childhood*. 2nd Edition. London: RoutlegeFalmer.

Himmelweit, H.T., Oppenein, A.N. and Vince, P. (1958) *Television and the child: an empirical study of the effect of television on the young*. London: published for the Nuffield Foundation by Oxford University Press.

Hope, A. (2009) CCTV, School Social Surveillance and Social Control. *British Educational Research Journal*, 35(6), Dec 2009: 891-907

Horan, T. A. (2000) *Digital Places: Building Our City of Bits*, Washington, DC: Urban Land Institute.

Horan, T.A. (2001) Digital Places: Design Considerations for Integrating Electronic Space with Physical Place. DISP 144. Available at: http://scholar.google.co.uk/scholar?q=HORAN,+T.A.+(2001).+Digital+Spaces:+Design+Considerations+for+Integrating+Electronic+Space+with+Physical+Placeandhl=enandas_sdt=0andas_vis=1andoi=scholart [A2]

House of Commons Education and Skills Committee (2007) *Creative Partnerships and the Curriculum. Eleventh Report of Session 2006-07. Report, together with formal minutes, oral and written evidence.* London: The Stationery Office Limited.

House of Commons Children, Schools and Families Committee (2008) *Creative Partnerships and the Curriculum: Government Response to the Eleventh Report from the Education and Skills Committee, Session 2006-07.* London: The Stationery Office Ltd.

Hsi, S., Pinkard, N. and Woolsey, K. (2005) *Creating equity spaces for digitally fluent kids.* Available at: http://www.exploratorium.edu/research/digitalkids/Digital_equity_paper.pdf (Accessed 20th August 2009).

Hutchby, I. and Moran-Ellis, J. (eds), (2001) *Children, Technology and Culture: the impacts of technologies in children's everyday lives.* London: RoutledgeFalmer.

Immordino-Yang, M.H. and Damasio, A. (2007) We feel, therefore we Learn: The Relevance of Affective and Social Neuroscience to Education. *Mind, Brain and Education*, 1 (1): 3-10.

Inayatulla, S. (2008) Mapping Educational Futures. Six foundational concepts and the six pillars approach. In Bussey, M., Inayatullah, S., Milojevic, I. (eds) (2008). *Alternative Educational Futures: pedagogies for emergent worlds.* Rotterdam/Taipei: Sense Publishers.

Inkpen, K.M., Ho-Ching, W-L., Kuederle, O., Scott, S.D. and Shoemaker, G.B.D. (1999) This is fun! We're all best friends and we're all playing: supporting children's synchronous collaboration. *Proceedings of the 1999 conference on Computer Support for Collaborative Learning.* Palo Alto, California.

International Telecommunication Union (2010) *Measuring the Information Society, 2010.* Geneva: ITU.

Jackson, L.A., Von Eye, A. and Biocca, F. (2006) Children and Internet Use: Social, Psychological and Academic Consequences for Low-income Children. APA Online: *Psychological Science Agenda.* available at: http://www.mindlab.org/images/d/DOC797.pdf (Accessed 13 August 2009).

Jakobsson, M. and Taylor, T.L. (2003) The Sopranos Meet EverQuest. *Social Networking in Massively Multiplayer Online Games, Melbourne DAC – the 5th International Digital Arts and Culture Conference*, School of Applied Communication Melbourne [website] <http://hypertext.rmit.edu.au/dac/papers/index.html>. Accessed 14 August 2009.

Jeffrey, B. (2003) Countering student instrumentalism: a creative response. *British Educational Research Journal* 29(4): 489-504

Jeffrey, B (Ed) (2006) *Creative learning practices: European experiences*, London: Tufnell.

Jeffrey, B. and Craft, A. (2004) Teaching creatively and teaching for creativity: distinctions and relationships. *Educational Studies* 30(1): 77-87.

Jeffrey, B. and Craft, A. (2006) Creative Learning and Possibility Thinking. In Jeffrey, B. (ed), *Creative Learning Practices: European Experiences.* London: The Tufnell Press, p.73-91.

Jeffrey, B. and Craft, A. (2001) 'The Universalization of Creativity', in Craft, A., Jeffrey, B., Leibling, M., *Creativity in Education,* London: Continuum, p.1-13.

Jeffrey, B., Troman, G. and Philips, E.Z. (2008) Creative and Performativity Policies in Primary Schools. Keynote Symposium, *British Educational Research Association Annual Conference*, Edinburgh, 2008.

Jeffrey, B. and Woods, P. (1998) *Testing teachers: The effects of school inspections on primary teachers.* London: Routledge/Falmer.

Jeffrey, B. and Woods, P. (2003) *The creative school: A framework for success, quality and effectiveness.* London: Routledge/Falmer.

Jeffrey, B. and Woods, P. (2008) *Creative Learning in the Primary School.* Abingdon, UK: Routledge.

Jenkins, H. (2006a) *Convergence Culture: Where Old and New Media Coincide.* New York and London: New York University Press.

Jenkins, H. (2006b) *Fans, bloggers and gamers: Exploring participatory culture.* New York: New York University Press.

Jenkins, H. and Thorburn, D. (1996) The Digital Revolution, the Informed Citizen and the Culture of Democracy. In Ludlow, P. (ed) *High Noon on the Electronic Frontier: Conceptual Issues in Cyberspace.* Cambridge: MIT Press

Jessen, C. (1999) *Children's Computer Culture: Three Essays on Children and Computers.* Odense: Odense University.

Jewitt, C. (2002) The move from page to screen: the multimodal reshaping of school English. *Journal of Visual Communication,* 1 (2): 171-196.

Jewitt, C. (2005) Multimodality, 'reading' and 'writing' for the 21st century. *Discourse: Studies in the Cultural Politics of Education,* 26(3), Sept 2005: 315-331

Jewitt, C. (2006) *Technology, Literacy and Learning: A Multimodal Approach.* London: Routledge.

Jewitt, C. (2008) *The visual in learning and creativity: a review of the literature. A report for Creative Partnerships.* London: Arts Council England.

Jones, S. and Fox, S. (2009) Generations online in 2009. A Report for the Pew Foundation. Available at: http://www.pewinternet.org/Reports/2009/Generations-Online-in-2009.aspx (Accessed 1 May 2010).

John-Steiner, V. (2000) *Creative Collaboration.* New York: Oxford University Press.

Johnson, S. (2005) Your brain on video games: Could they actually be good for you? *Discover,* 26(7). http://www.discover.com/issues/jul-05/features/brain-on-video-games/ (Accessed 16th November, 2006).

Jones, G. (2008) Education: A Mirror or a Lamp? *Art Monthly.* 1st October, 2008. Available at: http://www.thefreelibrary.com/Education:+a+mirror+or+a+lamp%3F-a0187326528 (Accessed 27th April 2010).

Joshi, H. and Hinde, A.P.R. (1993) Employment after Childbearing in Post-War Britain: Cohort-Study Evidence on Contrasts within and across Generations. *European Sociological Review,* 9(3): 203-227.

Kennedy, H (2002) Lara Croft: Feminist icon or cyberbimbo? On the limits of textual analysis. *Game Studies,* (2)2. Available online: http://www.gamestudies.org/0202/kennedy/

Kennedy, T., Wellman, B. and Klement, K. (2003) Gendering the digital divide. *IT and Society,* 1(5) Summer 2003: 72-96.

Kiili, C., Laurinen, L. and Marttunen, M. (2008) Students Evaluating Internet Sources: from versatile evaluators to uncritical readers. *Journal of Educational Computing Research,* 39(1): 75-95

Kirshner, P. A. (2004) Design, development, and implementation of electronic learning environments for collaborative learning. *Educational Technology Research and Development, 52(3): 39-46.*

Kress, G. R. (2003) *Literacy in the new media age.* London: RoutledgeFalmer.

Kuo, M-J. (2007) How does an online game based learning environment promote students' intrinsic motivation for learning natural science and how does it affect their learning outcomes? *Proceedings of The First IEEE International Workshop on Digital Game and Intelligent Toy Enhanced Learning (DIGITEL '07)*. p.135-142. Available at: http://www.informatik.uni-trier.de/~ley/db/conf/digitel/digitel 2007.html (Accessed 3rd May 2010).

Kvavik, R. (2005) Convenience, Communications and Control: How Student Use Technology. *Educating the Net Generation* T(Boulder, Colo.: Educause, 2005), e-book, available at http://www. educause.edu/educatingthenetgen (Accessed 1st May 2010).

Laevers, F. (2000) Forward to the Basics! Deep-level-learning and the experiential approach, *Early Years Journal,* 20(2): 20-29.

The Lord Laming (2009) *Protection of Children in England: A Progress Report. March, 2009.* London: The Stationery Office.

Lankshear, C. and Knobel, M. (2006) *New literacies: Everyday practices and classroom learning* (2nd edition), p65, New York: Open University Press and McGraw Hill.

Lareau, A. (1987) Social Class Differences in Family-School Relationships: The Importance of Cultural Capital. *Sociology of Education,* 60(2): 73-85.

Lash, S., and Urry, J. (1994) *Economies of Signs and Space.* London: Sage.

Lau S., Hui A. N. N., and Ng G. Y. C., (ed.) (2004) *Creativity: when East meets West*, Singapore: World Scientific.

Layard, R. and Dunn, J. (2009) *A Good Childhood: searching for values in a competitive age.* London: Penguin.

Leadbeater, C. (2000) *Living on Thin Air: The New Economy with a Blueprint for the 21st Century.* London, Penguin.

Leadbeater, C. (2009) *We-think: Mass innovation not mass production* (2nd edition). London: Profile Books Ltd.

Lee, J. (2001) The extensions of childhood: technologies, children and independence. In Hutchby, I. and Moran-Ellis, J. (eds) *Children, Technology and Culture: The impacts of technologies in children's everyday lives.* London: RoutledgeFalmer

Lee, V.E. and Burkam, D.T. (2003) Dropping out of High School: The Role of School Organization and Structure. American Educational Research Journal, 40(2): 353-393.

Lefebvre, A, H. (1991) The Production of Space. Oxford and Cambridge MA, Blackwell (trans. by Donald Nicholson-Smith of Lefebvre (1972) *La production de l'espace.* Paris: Anthropos. Massey, D., Allen, J. and Peters.

Lenhart, A. (2009) Cyberbullying: What the research is telling us... *Pew Internet and American Life Project presentation to NAAG Year of the Child*, Philadelphia, USA.

Lenhart, A. and Madden, M. (2007) Social Networking Sites and Teens. *Pew Internet and American Life Survey* available at: http://www.pewinternet.org/~/media//Files/Reports/2007/PIP_SNS_Data_ Memo_Jan_2007.pdf.pdf (Accessed 30th April 2010).

Lenhart, A. and Madden, M., MacGill, A.R., Smith, A. (2007) Teens and Social Media: the use of social media gains a greater foothold in teen life as they embrace the conversational nature of interactive online media. *Pew Internet and American Life Survey* available at: http://www.pew internet.org/~/media//Files/Reports/2007/PIP_Teens_Social_Media_Final.pdf.pdf (Accessed 30th April 2010).

Leu, D. J., Zawilinksi, L., Castek, J., Banerji, M., Housand, B. C., Liu, Y., and O'Neil, M. (2007) What is new about the new literacies of online reading comprehension?. In *Secondary School Literacy: What Research Reveals for Classroom Practice*, p.43. Retrieved from http://teachers.westport. k12.ct.us/ITL/wkspmaterials/NCTE%20chapter.pdf (1st May 2010).

Lieberman, D.A., Chaffee, S.H. and Roberts, D.F. (1988) Videos, mass media, and schooling: functional equivalence in uses of new media. *Social Sciences Video Review,* 6: 24-241.

Lin, Y.S. (2009) Teacher and Pupil Responses to a Creative Pedagogy: Case studies of two primary sixth-grade classes in Taiwan, Unpublished doctoral thesis, University of Exeter, April 2009.

Livingstone, S. (2003) Mediated Childhoods: A Comparative Approach to Young People's Changing Media Environment in Europe. In Turow, J. and Kavanaugh, A.L. (eds). *The Wired Homestead. An MIT Press Sourcebook on the Internet and the Family.* Cambridge, MA: MIT Press.

Livingstone, S. (2007) Gradations in digital inclusion: children, young people and the digital divide. New Media and Society Vol. 9 No. 4: 671-696. Available at: http://nms.sagepub.com/cgi/content/abstract/9/4/671 (Accessed 20th August 2009).

Livingstone, S. (2009) *Children and the Internet.* Cambridge: Polity Press.

Livingstone, S. and Bober, M. (2004) *UK children go online: surveying the experiences of young people and their parents [online].* London: LSE Research Online. Available at: http://eprints.lse.ac.uk/archive/00000395 (Accessed 30th April 2010).

Livingstone, S. Bober, M. and Helsper, E. (2005) 'Internet literacy among children and young people: findings from the UK children go online project', http://personal.lse.ac.uk/BOBER/UKCGOo nlineLiteracy.pdf CHECK

Livingstone, S., Bober, M. and Helsper, E, (2005) Active participation or just more information?: young people's take up of opportunities to act and interact on the internet [online]. *London: LSE Research Online.* Available at: http://eprints.lse.ac.uk/1014. Available in LSE Research Online: May 2007. (Accessed 20th August 2009).

Livingstone, S. and Bovill, M. (1999) *Young People, New Media.* Report of the Research Project 'Children, Young People and the Changing Media Environment'. London: London School of Economics and Political Science. Available at: http://psych.lse.ac.uk/young_people (Accessed 30th April 2010).

Lo, S-K, Wang, C-C. and Fang, W. (2005) Physical interpersonal relationships and social anxiety among online game players. *CyberPsychology and Behavior.* February 2005, 8(1): 15-20. doi:10.1089/cpb.2005.8.15.

Loukos, F. and Karatza, H.D. (2009) Reputation-based friend-to-friend networks. *Peer-to-Peer Networking and Applications.* 2(1) March 2009: 13-23.

Lyman, P., Billings, A., Perkel, D., Ellinger, S. and Finn, M. (2004) *Literature Review: Kids' Informal Learning and Digital-Mediated Experiences.* Commissioned paper for the MacArthur Foundation.

Lysonski, S. and Durvasula, S. (2008) Digital piracy of MP3s: consumer and ethical predispositions. *Journal of Consumer Marketing,* 25 (3): 167-178. DOI 10.1108/07363760810970662 .

McMaster, Sir B. (2008) *Supporting Excellence in the Arts: from measurement to judgement.* London: Department for Culture, Media and Sport.

McNeill, S. (1999) 'Moving Towards Participation on the Internet: New Radio Initiatives for Children and Young People', in C. von Feilitzen and U. Carlsson (eds), *Children and Media: Image, Education, Participation,* Göteborg, Sweden: Nordicom, p.347-353.

McWilliam, E. (2008) Unlearning how to teach. *Innovations in Education and Teaching International,* 45 (3): 263-269.

McWilliam, E. and Haukka, S. (2008) Educating the creative workforce: new directions for twenty-first century schooling. In *British Educational Research Journal, Special Issue: Creativity and Performativity in Teaching and Learning,* 24(5): 651-666.

McWilliam, E. and Jones, A. (2005) An unprotected species? On teachers as risky subjects. *British Journal of Educational Research,* 31 (1): 109-120

Macszewski, M. (2002) Exploring Identities through the Internet: Youth Experiences Online. *Child and Youth Care Forum,* 31(2): 111-129

Magaluzzi, L. (1996) *The Hundred Languages of Children, Catalogue of the Exhibition*. Reggio Emilia, Italy: Reggio Children.

Manuel, K. (2002) Teaching Information Literacy to Generation Y (New York: Haworth Press, 2002), <https://www.haworthpress.com/store/ArticleAbstract.asp?ID=32857>.

Marsh, J. and Bearne, E. (2008) *Moving Literacy On: Evaluation of the BFI Lead Practitioner Scheme for moving image media literacy*, Sheffield: University of Sheffield and United Kingdom Literacy Association http://www.ukla.org/downloads/moving_literacy_on.pdf (Accessed 30th April 2010).

Marshall, D. (1997) 'Technophobia: video games, computer hacks and cybernetics. *Media International Australia*. 85: 70-78

Maslow, A. (1987) *Motivation and Personality*, 3rd Edition. New York: Harper and Row.

Massey, D. (1999) Spaces of Politics. In Massey, D., Allen, J., Sarre, P. (eds), *Human Geography Today*. Cambridge: Polity Press.

Maun, I. and Myhill, D. (2005) 'Text as design, writers as designers', *English in Education*, 39(2): 5-21.

Mercer, N. (2000) *Words and minds: how we use language to think together*. London: Routledge.

Milojevic, I. (2008) Developing Futures Literacy, Bussey, M., Inayatulla, S., Milojevic, I. (eds), *Alternative Educational Futures*. Rotterdam, The Netherlands: Sense Publishers.

Miners and Pascopella (2007) *The New Literacies* www.districtadministration.com/viewarticlepf.aspx?articleid=1292 (Accessed 30th April 2010).

Molesworth, M. and Denegri-Knott, J. (2005) The Pleasures and Practices of Virtualised Consumption in Digital Spaces. *Proceedings of DiGRA 2005 Conference: Changing Views – Worlds in Play*. Available at: http://www.digra.org/dl/db/06276.33335.pdf (Accessed 24th July 2009).

Montgomery, K.C. (2007) *Generation Digital: politics, commerce and childhood in the age of the internet*. Cambridge, MA: MIT Press.

Montessori, M. (1914) *Dr Montessori's Own Handbook*. London William Heinemann.

Murphy, S.C. (2004) 'Live in Your World, Play in Ours': The Spaces of Video Game Identity. *Journal of Visual Culture,* 3(2): 223-238.

NAS/UWT (2010) Report from Fringe Meetings 2010 http://www.nasuwt.org.uk/Whatsnew/NASUWTNews/Nationalnewsitems/FringeMeetings/index.htm (last accessed 28 April 2010).

National Advisory Committee on Creative and Cultural Education (1999) *All Our Futures: creativity, culture and education. Report to the Secretary of State for Education and Employment and the Secretary of State for Culture, Media and Sport*. Sudbury, Suffolk: Department for Education and employment.

Newburn, T. (1996) 'Back to the future? Youth crime, youth justice and the rediscovery of 'authoritarian populism', in J. Pilcher and S. Wagg (Eds) *Thatcher's Children? Politics, Childhood and Society in the 1980s and 1990s*. London: Falmer.

Ng, A. K. and Smith, I. (2004) 'Why is there a paradox in promoting creativity in the Asian classroom?', in S. Lau, A. Hui and G. Ng (eds) *Creativity: when East meets West*, Singapore: World Scientific.

Ng, B.D. and Wiemer-Hastings, (2005) Addictions to the internet and online gaming. *CyberPsychology and Behavior,* April 2005, 8(2): 110-113. doi:10.1089/cpb.2005.8.110.

Nicholl, B. and McLellan, R. (2008) 'We're all in this game whether we like it or not to get a number of As to Cs.' Design and technology teachers' struggles to implement creativity and performativity policies. In *British Educational Research Journal, Special Issue: Creativity and Performativity in Teaching and Learning*, 24(5): 585-600.

Oblinger, D. and Oblinger, J. (2005) 'Is It Age or IT: First Steps toward Understanding the Net Generation,' in Diana G. Oblinger and James L. Oblinger, (eds), *Educating the Net Generation* T(Boulder, Colo.: Educause, 2005), e-book, available at http://www.educause.edu/educatingthenet gen (Accessed 1 May 2010).

Oring, S. (2000). A Call for Visual Literacy. *School Arts*. April, pp58-59.

Orr, D. (1999) Rethinking Education. *The Ecologist*, 29(3): 232-234.

Overseas Development Institute (ODI) (2009) *Raising the game: mainstreaming children's rights, Briefing Paper November 2009*. Available at: www.odi.org.uk (last accessed 22nd March 2010).

Palfrey, J. and Gasser, U. (2008) *Born Digital: understanding the first generation of digital natives*. New York: Basic Books

Palmer, S. (2006) *Toxic Childhood: How the modern world is damaging our children and what we can do about it*. London: Orion

Parnes, S. (ed), (1992) *Source Book for Creative Problem Solving: A Fifty Year Digest of Proven Innovation Processes*. Buffalo, New York: Creative Education Foundation.

Perkins, D.N. (2008) *Making Learning Whole: How Seven Principles of Teaching Can Transform Education*, San Francisco: Jossey-Bass.

Peter, J. and Valkenburg, P.M. (2006a) Adolescents' Internet Use: Testing the 'disappearing digital divide' versus the 'emerging differentiation' approach. *Poetics, 34*: 293-305.

Peter, J. and Valkenburg, P.M. (2006b) Research Note: Individual Differences in Perceptions of Internet Communication. *European Journal of Communication*. 1 (2): 213-226.

Perkins, D. (2008) 'Knowledge Alive', *Educational Leadership*, 62:1, 14-19

Phalen, K. (2002) 'Self-Assured, Stressed, and Straight: Millennial Students and How They Got that Way,' virginia.edu, vol. VI, no. 2 (fall 2002), http://www.itc.virginia.edu/virginia.edu/fall02/student/home.html .

Piaget, J. (1930) T*he Child's Conception of Physical Causality*. New York: Harcourt, Brace.

Piaget, J. (1951) *Plays, Dreams and Imitation in Childhood*. London: Routledge and Kegan Paul

Piaget, J. (1955) *The Child's Construction of Reality*. London: Routledge and Kegan Paul.

Popescu, B.C., Crispo, B. and Tanenbaum, A.S. (2004) Safe and private data sharing with Turtle: Friends team-up and beat the system. In *12th International Workshop on Security Protocols, Cambridge, UK*, April 2004.

Postman, N. (1983) *The Disappearance of Childhood*. London: W.H.Allen.

Prensky, M. (2001a) *Digital Game-Based Learning*. PLACE? McGraw-Hill.

Prensky, M. (2001b) 'Digital Natives, Digital Immigrants, Part II: Do They Really Think Differently?' On the Horizon, vol. 9, no. 6: p.15-24; available from <http://www.marcprensky.com/writing/>.

Prensky, M. (2005) 'Engage Me or Enrage Me': What Today's Learners Demand,' *Educause Review*, vol. 40, no. 5 (September/October 2005): 60-65, <http://www.educause.edu/er/erm05/erm 0553.asp>. (Accessed 30th April 2010).

Prout, A. (2000) Children's participation: control and self-realisation in British late modernity. *Children and Society*, Vol. 14, No. 4, September 2000, p.304-315(12).

Ravenscroft, A., Wegerif, R. and Hartley, R. (2007) Reclaiming thinking: Dialectic, dialogic and learning in the digital age. *Learning through Digital Technologies*, 39-57.

Resnick, M. (2006) Computer as Paintbrush: Technology, Play, and the Creative Society. Singer, D., Golikoff, R. and Hirsh-Pasek, K. (eds). *Play = Learning: How play motivates and enhances children's cognitive and social-emotional growth*. Oxford University Press, 2006.

Resnick, M. Rusk, N. and Cooke, S. (1998) The Computer Clubhouse: Technological Fluency in the Inner City. In Schon, D., Sanyal, B., Mitchell, W. (eds). *High Technology and Low-Income Communities*. Cambridge: MIT Press, 1998.

Rhyhammer, L. and Brolin, C. (1999) 'Creativity research: historical considerations and main lines of development', *Scandinavian Journal of Educational Research*, 43(3): 259-273.

Ritterfield, U. and Weber, R. (2006) Video Games for Entertainment and Education. In Vorderer, J. and Bryant, J. (Eds). *Playing Video Games: Motives, Responses, and Consequences.* Lawrence Erlbaum Associates.

Rob, R. and Waldfogel, J. (2006) Piracy on the High C's: Music Downloading, Sales Displacement, and Social Welfare in a Sample of College Students. *The Journal of Law and Economics*, Vol. 49, April 2006. DOI: 10.1086/430809 (accessed at http://www.journals.uchicago.edu/doi/abs/10.1086/430809 on 13 August 09).

Roberts, D. F., Foehr, D. G., Rideout, V. I., and Brodie, M. (1999) *Kids and media at the new millennium: A comprehensive national analysis of children's media use.* Menlo Park, CA: A Kaiser Family Foundation Report.

Rogers, M. and Bhatti, S. (2007) How to Disappear Completely: a Survey of Private Peer-to-Peer Networks. Available at: http://www.cs.st-andrews.ac.uk/~saleem/papers/ 2007/space2007/space 2007-rb2007.pdf (accessed 21 August 2009).

Rogers, Y. and Rodden, T. (2010) *Being Human: The future of learning in a world suffused with technology.* Presentation at ESRC Seminar on Educational Futures, held at University of Exeter, 11th March, 2010. Summary available at: http://edfutures.futurelab.org.uk/ (accessed 21 March 2010).

Rojas-Drummond, S., Mazon, N., Fernandez, M. and Wegerif, R. (2006) Explicit reasoning, creativity and co-construction in primary school childrens collaborative activities. *Thinking Skills and Creativity,* 1(2): 84-94.

Rose, N. (1990) *Governing the Soul: Shaping of the Private Self.* London: Routledge.

Roussou, M. (2004) Learning by doing and learning through play: an exploration of interactivity in virtual environments for children, *Computers in Entertainment.* Vol 2, Isssue 1, January 2004. p.10-10. Available at: http://doi.acm.org/10.1145/973801.973818 (accessed 14th August 2009).

Ruddock, J. and Fielding, J. (2006) Student voice and the perils of popularity. *Educational Review*, 58 (2): 219-231.

Ruddock, J. and Flutter, J. (2000) Pupil Participation and Pupil Perspective: 'carving out a new order of experience'. *Cambridge Journal of Education*, 30(1): 75-89

Ruddock, J. and Flutter, J. (2004) *How to improve your school: giving pupils a voice.* London: Continuum.

Rudowicz, E. (2004) 'Creativity among Chinese people: beyond Western perspective', in S. Lau, A.N.N. Hui and G.Y.C. Ng. (eds) *Creativity: when East meets West*, Singapore: World Scientific.

Santo, R., James, C., Davis, K., Katz, S.L., Burch, L. and Joseph, B. (2009) *Meeting of Minds: Cross-Generational Dialogue on the Ethics of Digital Life.* Cambridge, New York, San Francisco: Project Zero, Global Kids, Inc and Common Sense Media.

Seely Brown, J. (2000) 'Growing Up Digital,' Change, vol. 32, no. 2 (March/April 2000), p.10-11, <http://www.aahe.org/change/digital.pdf>.

Seltzer, K. and Bentley, T. (1999) *The Creative Age: knowledge and skills for the New Economy.* London: Demos

Shirky, C. (2009) *Here Comes Everybody: How Change Happens when People Come Together.* London: Penguin Books.

Simmons, R. and Thomson, R. (2008) Creativity and performativity: the case of further education. In *British Educational Research Journal, Special Issue: Creativity and Performativity in Teaching and Learning*, 24(5): 601-618.

Singer, D. G. and Singer, G. J. L. (2005) *Imagination and Play in the Electronic Age.* Cambridge, MA: Harvard University Press.

Slaughter, R. (2008) What Difference does Integral Make? *Futures* 40 (2): 120-137.

Smith, R. with Curtin, P. (1988) 'Children, computers and life online: education in a cyber-world.' In I. Snyder (ed). *Page to Screen: Taking Literacy into the Electronic Era.* London: Routledge. p.211-33.

Snyder, I., Angus, L. and Sutherland-Smith, W. (2004) 'They're the future and they're going to take over everywhere': ICTs, literacy and disadvantage. In Snyder, I. and Beavis, C. (eds) *Doing Literacy Online: Teaching, Learning and Playing in an Electronic World (New Dimensions in Computers and Composition).* Cresskill, NJ: Hampton Press, p.225-44.

Soja, W.S. (1999) Thirdspace: Expanding the Scope of the Geographical Imagination. In Massey, D., Allen, J., Sarre, P. (eds), *Human Geography Today.* Cambridge: Polity Press.

Somerson, W. (1999) A Corporate Multicultural Universe: Replacing the Nation State with 'Men in Black'. *Narrative,* Vol. 7, No. 2, Multiculturalism and Narrative (May, 1999) p.213-234.

Squire, K. (2006) From Content to Context: Videogames as Designed Experience. *Educational Researcher,* 35(8): 19-29.

Sternberg, R.J. (2003) 'Background work on creativity', in R.J. Sternberg (ed), *Wisdom, Intelligence and Creativity Synthesized,* Cambridge: Cambridge University Press.

Sternberg, R.J. and Lubart, T.I. (1999) 'The concept of creativity: prospects and paradigms', in R.J. Sternberg (ed), *Handbook of Creativity,* Cambridge: Cambridge University Press.

Subrahmanyan, K. and Greenfield, P. M. (2001) The impact of computer use on children's and adolescent's development. *Journal of Applied Developmental Psychology,* 22(1): 7-30.

Subrahmanyam, K., and Greenfield, P. M. (2008a) Communicating online: Adolescent relationships and the media. *The Future of Children; Children and Media Technology,* 18, 119-146.

Subrahmanyam, K. and Greenfield, P.M. (2008b) Virtual Worlds in Development: Implications of Social Networking Sites. *Journal of Applied Developmental Psychology* 29 (2008) 417-419.

Subrahmanyam, K.P., Greenfield, M., Kraut, R. and Gross, E. (2000) The impact of home computer use on children's activities and development. *The Future of Children* 10:123-144.

Subrahmanyam, K.P., Greenfield, M., Kraut, R. and Gross, E. (2001) The impact of computer use on children's and adolescents' development. *Journal of Applied Developmental Psychology* 22: 7-30.

Subrahmanyam, K., Kraut, R., Greenfield, P. M., and Gross, E. F. (2001) New forms of electronic media: The impact of interactive games and the Internet on cognition, socialization, and behavior. In D. L. Singer and J. L. Singer (eds), *Handbook of children and the media.* Thousand Oaks, CA: Sage pp 73-99.

Surowiecki, J. (2005) *The Wisdom of Crowds.* New York: First Anchor Books.

Tapscott, D. (1998) *Growing Up Digital: The Rise of the Net Generation.* New York: McGraw Hill

Tapscott, D. (2009) *Grown Up Digital: how the net generation is changing your world.* New York: McGraw Hill.

Taylor, M. and McGimpsey, I. (2008) *Thinkpiece: Introducing the Education Charter.* Newcastle-upon-Tyne: Creativity, Culture and Education. Available at http://www.creativitycultureeducation.org/data/files/cyl-thinkpiece-58.pdf (accessed 25 July 2009).

Taylor, C. and Robinson, T. (2009) Student voice: theorising power and participation. *Pedagogy, Culture and Society,* 17(2): 161-175.

Thompson, L. and Walker, A.J. (1989) Gender in Families: Women and Men in Marriage, Work and Parenthood. *Journal of Marriage and Family,* 51(4): 845-871.

Troman, G. (2008) Primary teacher identity, commitment and career in performative school cultures. In *British Educational Research Journal, Special Issue: Creativity and Performativity in Teaching and Learning*, 24(5): 619-634.

Turkle, S. (1984) *The Second Self: Computers and the Human Spirit.* New York: Simon and Schuster.

Turkle, S. (1994) Constructions and Reconstructions of Self in Virtual Reality: Playing in the MUDS. *Mind, Culture and Activity*, Vol. 1, No. 3, Summer 1984, p.158-167 Available at: http://web.mit.edu/people/sturkle/pdfsforstwebpage/ST_Construc%20and%20reconstruc%20of%20self.pdf (Accessed 30th April 2010).

Turkle, S. (1995) *Life on Screen: Identity in the Age of the Internet.* New York: Simon and Schuster.

Turner, V. (1992) Morality and liminality. In E. Turner (ed) *Blazing the Trail: Way Marks in the Exploration of Symbols,* p.132-62. Tucson: University of Arizona Press.

Valentine, G. and Holloway, S. (2001) 'Technophobia'. In Hutchby, I. and Moran-Ellis, J. (eds) *Children, Technology and Culture: The impacts of technologies in children's everyday lives.* London: RoutledgeFalmer.

Valentine, G. and Holloway, S.L. (2002) Cyberkids? Exploring Children's Identities and Social Networks in On-Line and Off-Line Worlds. *Annals of the Association of American Geographers*, 92(2): 302-319

Valentine, G., Holloway, W. and Bingham, N. (2002) The Digital Generation? Children, ICT and the Everyday Nature of Social Exclusion. *Antipode,* 34(2): 296-315.

Valentine, G. and McKendrick, J. (1998) Children's outdoor play: Exploring parental concerns about children's safety and the changing nature of childhood. *Geoforum*, 28(2): 219-235

Van Eck, R. (2006) Digital Game-Based Learning: It is Not Just the Digital Natives Who Are Restless.... *Educause Review*, 41(2) (March/April 2006)

Vandewater, E.A., Rideout, V.J., Wartella, E.A., Huang, X., Lee, J.H. and Shim, M-S (2007) Digital Childhood: Electronic Media and Technology Use Among Infants, Toddlers and Preschoolers. *Pediatrics*, 119(5): 1006-1015.

Vass, E. (2007) Exploring processes of collaborative creativity-The role of emotions in children's joint creative writing. *Thinking Skills and Creativity,* 2: 107-117.

Voydanoff, P. (1988) Work role characteristics, family structure demands, and work/family conflict. *Journal of Marriage and the Family*, 50 (3): 749-61.

Vygotsky, L.S. (1976) Play and its role in the mental development of the child. In J.S.Bruner, A.J. Jolly and K.Sylva (eds) *Play: its role in development and evolution.* New York: Basic Books, Inc. p.537-554

Vygotsky, L.S. (1978) *Mind in Society: the development of higher psychological processes.* Cambridge, MA: Harvard University Press

Wadley, G., Gibbs, M., Hew, K. and Graham, C. (2003) Computer Supported Cooperative Play, 'Third Places' and Online Videogames. In S. Viller and P. Wyeth (eds), *Proceedings of the Thirteenth Australian Conference on Computer Human Interaction (OzChi 03)* (Brisbane, 26-28 November 2003), University of Queensland, 2003, p.238-241.

Wallace, J. (1995) Technologies of 'the child': towards a theory of the child-subject. *Textual Practice*, 9 (2): 285-302.

Wallace, P. (1999) *The Psychology of the Internet.* New York: Cambridge University Press

Wallace, D. and Gruber, H. (1989) *Creative People at Work: Twelve Cognitive Case Studies.* Oxford: Oxford University Press.

Ward, T.B. and Sonneborn, M.S. (2009) Creative Expression in Virtual Worlds: Imitation, Imagination and Individualized Collaboration. *Psychology of Aesthetics, Creativity and the Arts*, 2009, 3(4): 211-221.

Wegerif, R. (2006) A dialogic understanding of the relationship between CSCL and teaching thinking skills. *Computer Supported Collaborative Learning*, 2006, 1: 143-157.

Wegerif, R. (2007) *Dialogic Education and Technology: Expanding the Space of Learning*. New York: Springer.

Wegerif, R., Littleton, K., Dawes, L., Mercer and N. Rowe, D. (2004) Widening access to educational opportunities through teaching children how to reason together. *Westminster Studies in Education*, 27(2): 143-156.

Wellman, B. (2002) Little boxes, glocalization, and networked individualism. In B.Wellman (ed). *Lecture Notes in Computer Science*. Berlin, Springer-Verlag

Wellman, B. (2004) The Three Ages of Internet Studies: Ten, Five and Zero Years Ago. *New Media Society* 2004; 6; 123-129. DOI: 10.1177/1461444804040633.

Wells, G. (1999) *Dialogic Inquiry: towards a sociocultural practice and theory of education*. Cambridge: Cambridge University Press.

Weigel, M., James, C., Gardner, H. (2009) Learning: Peering backwards and looking forward in the digital era. *International Journal of Learning and Media* 1(1): 1-18.

Wiendl, V., Dorfmüller-Ulhaas, K., Schultz, N. and André, E. (2007) Integrating a Virtual Agent in to the Real World: The Virtual Anatomy Assistant Ritchie. *Lecture Notes in Computer Science*. Berlin/Heidelberg: Springer.

Withers, K. and Sheldon, R. (2008) *Behind the Screen: the hidden life of youth online*. London: Institute for Public Policy Research.

Wood, E. (2008) Everyday play activities as therapeutic and pedagogical encounters. *European Journal of Psychotherapy and Counselling,* 10(2): 111-120

Woods, P. (1990) *Teacher Skills and Strategies*. London: Falmer Press.

Yantzi, N.M. and Rosenberg, M.W. (2008) The contested meanings of home for women caring for children with long-term care needs in Ontario, Canada. *Gender, Place and Culture: A Journal of Feminist Geography*, 1360-0525, 15(3): 301-315.

Zentner, A. (2006) Measuring the Effect of File Sharing on Music Purchases. The Journal of Law and Economics, Vol. 49, April 2006. DOI: 10.1086/501082 Available at: http://www.journals.uchicago.edu/doi/abs/10.1086/501082 (last accessed 13th August 2009).

Ziehe, T. (1994) From living standard to life style. *Young: Nordic Journal of Youth Research*, 2 (2): 2-16.

Index

academic standards 145
adult education 36
Africa 90, 143
ageing population 22
Alliance for Childhood 12
art 19
Australasia 24, 30, 36, 81
avatar 23, 37, 40, 48, 63, 89

'baby boomers' 49
Beveridge Report 3
British Film Institute 13
Bruner 73, 74, 76

Canada 24, 30, 82
capitalism 24, 106, 139
CCTV 24, 36
censorship 97-8, 140
certainty 134, 137
change
    children as agents of 35,
    97*ff*
    children as objects of
    97*ff*
child-centred education 135
childhood
    and digitisation 7, 9-11,
    108
    discourses of 8-9, 16-17
    and the economy 5, 21
    and empowerment 8-9,
    11, 14*ff*, 27, 35, 67, 72,
    85, 107-8, 125, 129,
    130-1

and the home 3*ff*, 14,
    37, 62, 100
and risk 7, 8, 12, 14-17,
    35*ff*, 68, 85, 101, 107,
    125, 129, 131
and the social 22
and technological
    change 9*ff*, 22
and television 4*ff*, 74
'marketisation' of 5-8, 29,
    84
China 60
climate change 29, 30, 75,
    123, 137
CNN 46
comprehensive education
    139
continuing professional
    development 116
control 8, 12, 23, 36, 38, 46,
    49-50, 58, 63, 65, 75,
    78, 80, 82, 84/5, 93, 95,
    97*ff*, 103, 111*ff*, 119
creativity
and the arts 20, 25, 26, 74
    and the curriculum 28
    and the digital age 7,
    9-11, 23-24, 48, 61-62,
    65-66, 68, 76-77, 80, 94,
    123
    and the economy 21
    and cultural variation 20
    and social change 22

and technology 22-24,
    27
    shifting conceptions 19-
    20
Creative Partnerships 27
creative industries 22
critical awareness 106
criticality 120*ff*
curriculum 125
cultural capital *see* social
    capital
cultural production 88, 93-4

Dalai Lama 20
developing countries 89-90,
    96
dialogic approach 41, 56,
    58-60, 134, 139*ff*
digital gaming 9-10, 46*ff*,
    59*ff*, 64, 75, 76, 78-79,
    81, 85, 87, 92, 122-3,
    126, 141, 148
digital landscape 33, 131,
    106*ff*, 143
'digital natives' 13-14, 43
digital revolution 7, 11-13,
    33, 67, 72-3, 75, 87, 97
'digital revolution' and risk
    47
disability 139
discourses
    of creativity 27-28
    of education 135

ecological balance 24
Educational Futures
    research group 29
Einstein 20
emotion, role of 77*ff*
employability 62
empowerment 7-8, 11, 17,
    27, 35, 85, 107-8, 125,
    131
engagement 130-1
English Secondary
    Students' Association
    136
ethics 12, 39, 42, 47, 78, 4,
    99, 126
ethnicity 137, 139
Eurocentric analysis 30
exploratory drive 33, 72, 75,
    77

Far East 24
four Ps, the 33, 35, 72, 87,
    103, 106, 107, 129
    participation 87*ff*
    playfulness 71*ff*
    pluralities 35*ff*
    possibilities 51*ff*
freedom 1-2, 37, 43, 48, 75,
    97
Freud 20
Froebel 73

Gandhi 20
Gates Foundation 24
gender 4, 44, 62, 63, 78,
    92, 137, 139
generation x 13
generation y 13-14
Ghana 89
global terrorism 24
globalisation 5, 7, 21, 24,
    65, 80, 87, 106, 137, 139
'glocalisation' 82
goals of education 144
GPS 24
Gramsci 138

Haiti 89
hegemony 138-9
Hegel 139
'high modernity' 5, 24
historic trends 134*ff*

Iceland 142
imagination 31, 32, 52, 59,
    73, 76, 77, 88*ff*, 93, 103,
    106, 115
immigration 139
India 89
individualism 20, 76, 80,
    81*ff*, 105-6, 111, 120-1,
    127
indoctrination 30, 144
innovation 5, 49, 52, 54, 80,
    103, 111-2, 133-4, 140*ff*
Institute for Public Policy
    Research 68, 98, 101
internet use 90, 102
intrinsic motivation 79
iPhone 66, 143
Ireland 60

Kyrgyzstan 89

league tables 25
literacy 12-13, 30, 48*ff*,
    108*ff*, 123*ff*
locus of control 78

Massachusetts Institute of
    Technology 65*ff*
Mexico 89
Microsoft 61, 81
Middle East 24
mobile phones 1-3, 9, 12,
    39, 44, 71, 79, 90, 102-
    3, 121, 143, 144
Montaigne 30
Mozambique 89
Mozart 20

National Advisory
    Committee on Creative
    and Cultural Education
    135
neuroscience 77, 79*ff*
Nigeria 89

Ps *see* four Ps
Pacific Rim 24
parental roles 4
pedagogy 25, 27, 32, 52-3,
    67, 68, 74, 124, 125*ff*
performativity 21, 25, 28,
    126-8, 135
Pestalozzi 73
Piaget 27, 73, 74, 135
Plato 30
play 8*ff*, 23, 37, 33, 37*ff*,
    42*ff*, 47*ff*, 54, 56*ff*, 63*ff*,
    68-69, 71*ff*, 87*ff*, 90*ff*,
    95, 97*ff*, 126*ff*, 131*ff*,
    148
playful learning 2, 68
possibility thinking 21, 22,
    26, 31, 35*ff*, 61*ff*, 107,
    113, 114-5, 121, 129,
    130
possible education futures
    127, 133*ff*
possible worlds 76
privacy 11, 50, 68, 95, 97-8,
    101, 118, 124-5, 148
protection, 11
psychology 19, 20
relativism 140

robotics 23
Rousseau 30
Royal Society of Arts 147

satellite navigation systems
    143
school dropout 132
school ethos 132
science 19, 20, 26, 74
'self-actualisation' 6

self-efficacy 78
social capital 131*ff*, 138, 144
social change 5*ff*, 125
social class 62, 137
social disadvantage 132
socialisation 30, 100, 144
social networking 9, 10, 14, 37, 38, 41*ff*, 60, 64, 66, 69, 72, 75, 77, 78*ff*, 88*ff*, 91, 97, 123, 141
social responsibility 39
Somalia 89
social mobility 137, 139
South Africa 60
spiritual meaning 25

Taiwan 30, 60, 85
teacher-centred pedagogy 74
teachers and technology 116
teaching style 118-9
technology *see* digital revolution
tripartite school system 138
Twitter 45, 83, 97

UK Literacy Association 13
uncertainty 21, 29, 116, 122*ff*, 137, 141
UNESCO 89
UNICEF 95
United States 9, 60, 74, 80, 82, 115, 120, 132, 145

Vietnam 89
visual literacy 86, 108, 109*ff*, 149
voice 14, 17, 33, 45, 56, 61, 64, 83, 88, 92*ff*, 108-9, 123, 136, 139, 148-9
Vygotsky 27, 73, 74, 76, 125

wealth creation 32
Welfare State 3
Wikipedia 120

Yeats, W B 141, 148
YouTube 46, 82
Youth Culture Trust 26

Zambia 89

Also from Trentham

CREATIVE LEARNING 3–11
and how we document it
edited by Anna Craft, Teresa Cremin
and Pamela Burnard

The desirability of creativity in learning is being emphasised more and more in Europe, the West and the East. Creative learning derives its uniqueness from certain enabling conditions. Defining and documenting it is slippery and problematic, but has to be done if we are to develop creativity meaningfully in schools.

This book focuses on the how, what and why of creative learning. It seeks to explore new theoretical, practical and methodological directions for engaging with it. It offers:

- evidence-based research by researchers and practitioners in the UK, USA, China, SE Asia, India and Europe

- case study accounts of practitioner research work with children in a variety of settings

- theoretical chapters reviewing research methods, theorising about these processes, synthesising findings and insights, and drawing on themes arising from the case studies.

Creative Learning 3–11 is for everyone with an active interest in creativity in education – teachers, students, educational politicians, researchers, inspectors and advisors, trainers, policy developers, an educationally interested public, opinion formers and parents. It will be an essential reader on teacher education courses at all levels, and will provide critical support material for schools seeking to develop creative ways of learning and teaching.

Anna Craft is Professor of Education at the University of Exeter and at the Open University, and is founding co-editor of the international journal, *Thinking Skills and Creativity*. **Teresa Cremin** is Professor of Education (Literacy) at the Open University. **Pamela Burnard** is Senior Lecturer in the Faculty of Education at the University of Cambridge. Together the editors coordinate the British Educational Research Association Special Interest Group on Creativity in Education.

2008, ISBN: 978-1-85856-410-4
186 pages, 244 x 170mm, Price £17.99

www.trentham-books.co.uk

Some reader's comments on *Creativity and Education Futures*

A book for our times. An elegant and engaging account of the changing nature of childhood in the 21st century. With clarity, conviction and immense expertise, Anna Craft points to the practical possibility of reclaiming the restless quest of education from the dismal treadmill of so much of contemporary schooling. **Professor Michael Fielding, Institute of Education, University of London, UK**

Packed with relevant information and rich in ideas – with welcome clarity in an engaging style. Theoretically sophisticated and grounded in practice, this book should be read by anyone interested in how digital technologies are impacting children and youth today, and how we can use these new resources to enhance education. **Professor Kieran Egan, Simon Fraser University, Canada, author of The Future of Education**

In this thoughtful, carefully researched and insightful book, Professor Craft addresses the urgent question of how we can negotiate the complex challenge of balancing the risks and opportunities that face children in contemporary society. By seeing the future as something that can be co-created by children and teachers, it helps educators to reclaim socio-technical change as an arena for creativity, rather than a force beyond our control. **Professor Keri Facer, Education and Social Research Institute, Manchester Metropolitan University, UK**

A timely and important book that brings together contemporary views of young people, digital technologies and creativity – with a bang! Full of insight and interesting implications. **Professor Guy Claxton, University of Winchester, England, author of What's the Point of School?**

Of all the books about computers and classrooms, this one is unique in its emphasis on creativity. It is a valuable contribution to our still-unfolding understanding of how computers might transform schools. **Professor Keith Sawyer, Washington University in St. Louis, USA**

If you are sceptical (or just unsure) about the role of ICT in education then you should read this book. **Dr Peter Twining, The Open University**